Road Biking™ Colorado's Front Range

Help Us Keep This Guide Up to Date

Every effort has been made by the author and editors to make this guide as accurate and useful as possible. However, many things can change after a guide is published—trails are rerouted, regulations change, techniques evolve, facilities come under new management, etc.

We would love to hear from you concerning your experiences with this guide and how you feel it could be improved and kept up to date. While we may not be able to respond to all comments and suggestions, we'll take them to heart, and we'll also make certain to share them with the author. Please send your comments and suggestions to the following address:

The Globe Pequot Press
Reader Response/Editorial Department
P.O. Box 480
Guilford, CT 06437

Or you may e-mail us at:

editorial@GlobePequot.com

Thanks for your input, and happy trails!

A **FALCON** GUIDE®

Road Biking™ Series

Road Biking™
Colorado's Front Range

Robert Hurst

FALCON GUIDE®

GUILFORD, CONNECTICUT
HELENA, MONTANA
AN IMPRINT OF THE GLOBE PEQUOT PRESS

A FALCON GUIDE ®

To buy books in quantity for corporate use
or incentives, call **(800) 962–0973, ext. 4551,**
or e-mail **premiums@GlobePequot.com.**

Contents

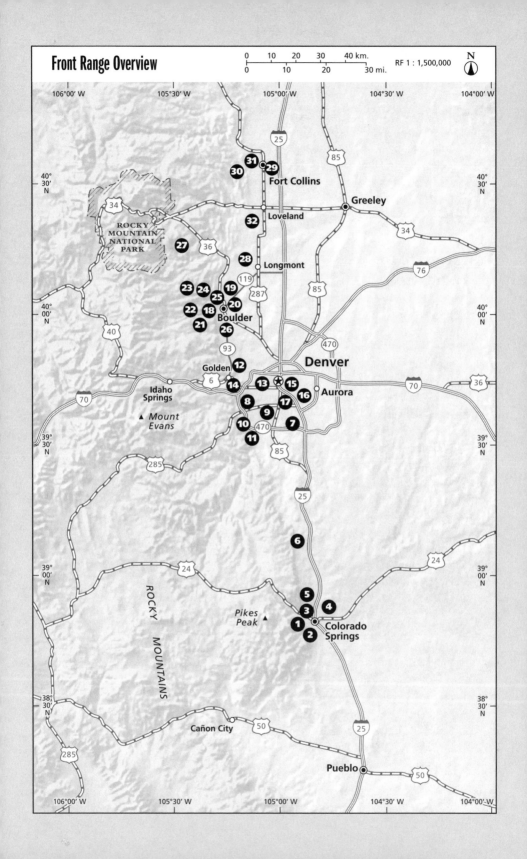

Front Range Overview

0 10 20 30 40 km.

0   10   20

30 mi.

RF 1 : 1,500,000

N

106°00' W   105°30' W   105°00' W   104°30' W   104°00' W

40°
30'
N

ROCKY
MOUNTAIN
NATIONAL
PARK

31 29
30
Fort Collins

Greeley

Loveland

32

27

28 Longmont

23 24
25 19
20
22 18
21
26

Boulder

Denver

Golden 12
14 13 15
8   17 16   Aurora
9
10
11

Idaho
Springs

▲ Mount
Evans

40°
30'
N

40°
00'
N

39°
30'
N

6

ROCKY

MOUNTAINS

5
3   4
1   Colorado
2   Springs

Pikes
Peak ▲

Cañon City

Pueblo

39°
00'
N

39°
30'
N

38°
30'
N

106°00' W   105°30' W   105°00' W   104°30' W   104°00' W

Acknowledgments

Whoever or whatever is responsible for shaping this earth, for making it colossally bumpy with mountain ranges, for placing upon it smooth roads and twisting trails, and for giving us the strength to ride it all, I thank you.

Thanks to Scott Adams, who gave me the opportunity to write this and other books, and who continues to exhibit biblical amounts of patience with my slow progress. Thanks as well to the others at Globe Pequot, from the production department to the sales guys, especially those whose jobs I made more difficult by being late with the manuscript.

Thanks to Michelle and Lani for filling in when I needed it.

To my family, I would never be able to finish any project like this without your support. Thank you.

Introduction

The population of Colorado, now rivaling that of small countries like Ireland, is expected to continue growing at a rate of about one million persons per decade. As usual, the vast majority of these new residents will plant themselves on the narrow swath of land known as the Front Range.[1] This growth has startling physical manifestations. The Front Range looks and feels nothing like it did twenty years ago. Twenty years from now it will be a completely different place than it is today.

On the Front Range entire neighborhoods sprout up almost overnight, spreading over hill and plain. For someone concerned with maps and routes and such—guidebook readers and authors, for instance—this creates interesting problems. Everything seems to be under construction. There are new roads, new eight-lane highways laid out across empty farmland in ghostly anticipation of things to come. Old roads are rerouted, removed, and resurfaced. At least one portion of every path is getting a face-lift, getting torn out, being extended for miles, whatever. It's impossible to keep up. The whole place is in a state of flux. So, quite often in this book you will run across phrases like "At the time of this writing . . ." That's a favorite. Also, watch for this bad boy: "By the time you read this . . ." Such phrases are necessary when you're trying to capture a fleeting moment in time with the printed word. Using this book and riding these loops—just being here against the mountains where the weather changes every five minutes—will certainly require some ability to go with the flow. That's good practice for life in general.

One of the specific changes that has been of great concern to cyclists here is the very noticeable increase in traffic volume on just about every Front Range road. This area has never been known for calm, quiet traffic, but now it's getting crazy. Lots of the old favorite roads, quiet country roads for a Sunday jaunt, are now overrun by suburban traffic. This change affects every road on some level, but is most evident in East Colorado Springs, in Douglas County, and on the plains east of Boulder.

The overpopulated Front Range is still a good place to ride a bike on the roads. There are lots of cyclists here, so motorists get some practice sharing the road with bikes. Bicycles are a big, generally positive part of the culture here. Cyclists aren't the alien beings here that they are in some other regions of the country. Exercise some thoughtful route finding, and ride in a cooperative, commonsense fashion, and you'll be fine on Front Range roads.

---

[1] According to United States Census figures, Douglas County south of Denver, one of the nation's fastest-growing counties in the 1980s, added another 115,000 people between 1990 and 2000, an increase of 191 percent. Colorado Springs and Fort Collins each grew by about 30 percent in that decade, and the population of Denver increased almost 20 percent. In raw numbers Colorado Springs added 120,000 residents and the Denver metro area added about 500,000 residents. Growth rates have slowed dramatically in recent years due to a recession and job losses. The population of Colorado is expected to continue increasing at a rate of about one million per decade, and currently stands at around 4.5 million.

The Platte River Trail at Confluence Park

But Front Range cycling isn't all about roads anymore. Things have *really* changed in that regard. Over the past few decades, extensive networks of bike paths have been constructed in every Front Range city. This area is a laboratory of sorts, testing various types of off-street MUPs (multiuse paths). Some of these paths have evolved into rather useful tools for bicycle transportation. They are not perfect, of course, and there is much controversy surrounding them, but here they are.

At present, riding the Front Range is a lucky amalgam of road riding and MUP riding, so this book will represent that same mix. To those who are aghast that a road bike guide would include rides on multiuse paths, I suggest these purists open their minds to the new possibilities that are before them. While introducing new types of problems, these facilities have enhanced the Front Range riding experience in many ways. Even the most confident and experienced road riders, unflappable in heavy traffic, have learned to use the MUPs to their advantage. To those who *only* ride the paths, I encourage you to get out and try some of these great canyon climbs and tours through the farmland. No path will take you there.

Even if we could somehow throw a force field up around California and Texas and hold Colorado's population growth to zero, Front Range cyclists would still have to deal with dizzying doses of change, just by rolling from one area to another.

If variety is the spice of life, then the Front Range is one spicy place. This guide celebrates that diversity with rides on the flattest flats and the highest hills, from the forests to the farmlands, and on everything in between. That means there will be a wide range of difficulty as well—rides for every level of fitness and ability. There are easy rides, middlin' rides, tough rides, and a few very tough rides. In this book these are known as rambles, cruises, challenges, and classics, respectively. Perhaps I have skewed the scale just a little. I suspect there are some rambles that could be considered cruises and some cruises that could be considered challenges. But don't be alarmed, y'all; that's the way we do it here. Keep riding the Front Range, and the climbs get flatter as your legs get thicker and your lungs get wider.

It doesn't take a supersleuth to detect the bias in this guide. It's a fairly typical Front Range bias. I like climbs. Long, steady climbs and short, steep climbs. Long, steep climbs. When I started out on this project, I may have had an inclination to include every great climb from Fort Collins to Colorado Springs. Well, there are so many that I didn't get them all. The final ride list, however, certainly includes a proud lineup of awesome hills. There are some hills missing, but I think I got the most difficult of them—Golden Gate, Magnolia, Gold Hill, Rattlesnake. If you ride them all, you will find out a thing or two about yourself along the way. Some readers may have been hoping to see some more very long rides included, but the intensity is definitely there.

To me, having grown up here on this giant geographic ramp, battling gravity at every turn, climbing is what it's all about. Of course, I realize that not everybody will feel that way. Those who don't share this love for climbs will find plenty of easy, flat (but still rewarding) rides in here. And if these less gung-ho riders should happen to attempt one of these hilly challenges someday—I hope they will—and they decide enough is enough, they can just point their bikes back down whatever hill they're on and coast all the way home. It's another convenient feature of living on the world's biggest half-pipe.

That is the beauty of the Front Range. It's all these places at once. Mountain and plain. Urban and desolate. Yuppie and gritty. Dirt and pavement. Road and path. Up and down. Take your pick.

Such was my summer, riding all the great canyons, gliding along the Peak-to-Peak, spinning across the flatlands. Trying to sneak in a mountain bike ride here and there. As you might imagine, it's been a pretty fine year.

Riding in Traffic

Riding a bicycle in Front Range traffic is relatively easy compared to riding in many metropolitan areas of similar size. It's not that Front Range traffic is any less heinous than the traffic in other cities, it's just that cycling is quite popular here, entwined in this region's cultural fabric across all economic classes. This means that area drivers are used to seeing candy-colored racers and racer wannabes on the roads, as well as

Highway 6 from a curve on Lookout Mountain

working class heroes on WalMart bikes, and even bike messengers carving up downtown traffic. The drivers may not like bicyclists, but at least they aren't freaked out
by us any more. Through familiarity over the decades, Front Range drivers and
cyclists have achieved a tenuous balance on area streets, allowing experienced riders
to slide through the population centers with great ease.

   If you're new to riding in traffic here or elsewhere, follow a few basic guidelines
and build on them:

   1) Ride in the same direction as motor traffic. 2) Don't ride in the area within
about 3.5 feet from the sides of motor vehicles—this is known as the "Door Zone"
and you are to avoid it like the plague unless your are riding extremely slow, for reasons which should be obvious. Ride far away from any parked cars, in fact, out
toward the center of the lane, or even farther to the left, to maintain a fat *buffer zone*
between yourself and all the ridiculous action that will come flying at you from stage
right. (Trust me, it will. When it comes, you want to see it early and be as far away
as reasonably possible.) When a car approaches behind you, relinquish this central
position momentarily and slide gently to the right to allow an easy pass, if possible.
This is the dance of urban cycling, constant give and take. This *cooperative cycling* is
ultimately more effective than maintaining grim possession of an entire lane in most

situations. 3) When you approach intersections, try to ease into the appropriate lane, depending on whether you want to turn right, go straight, or turn left. This is called *destination positioning.* 4) Perhaps most importantly, *stop doing really stupid stuff.* Seriously. Most of beginning cyclists' worst accidents are caused by the beginners themselves, when they ride out of driveways, off the sidewalk and into the street, or right through stop signs and red lights—without looking. There is a correct way to bend the rules in traffic, and that ain't it. Stop it, stop it now. There will be plenty of idiot behavior coming from the rest of 'em, don't add your own.

Of course it's not always so simple as even that mangled paragraph. For instance, how can we always stay out of the Door Zone but also give drivers enough space to pass? On many streets it just won't be possible, and cyclists will have to "take the lane" and may even have to bottle up motor traffic a bit to ride safely. But this should not be a persistent concern, as the Front Range still offers multiple route options, in almost all areas, that allow for safe and easy riding on relatively wide streets. Route choice is key. Don't just ride the same route you would use in a car. There is a network of quiet streets and wide curb lanes out there—use them when possible and you will be able to eliminate almost every vestige of conflict from your rides.

When choosing a street, traffic volume is just one consideration, and maybe not a very important one. Look for streets with plenty of space on the right to allow a brand of lane-sharing with faster vehicles that will be minimally disruptive to you. The ideal cycling street would also have few intersections, few reasons for drivers to crank hard turns across your line. Traffic would move much slower than highway speed.

The presence of a bike lane painted on the street is helpful, though it will be limited in its actual usefulness, let's put it that way. Bike lanes show up on streets that are already wide enough for lane-sharing. In practice I ignore the painted lines. Quite often I happen to be riding within a bike lane, but that's just where I would be riding anyway, even if there were no painted lines. Some bike lanes are partially within the Door Zone, requiring riders to stay on the far left side of the bike lane. On some narrow streets riders may be better off positioning themselves closer to the center of the street, or at least the center of the lane, rather than remaining inside the bike lane—sometimes the bike lane just doesn't give you enough buffer from typical right-side hazards. Remember that Colorado's legal requirement to ride as far to the right "as practicable" only applies if there is faster traffic approaching from the rear. Otherwise, use all the space available to you.

If you're searching for ideal cycling streets, with all your favorite ingredients in perfect harmony, you won't find much. But there are plenty of adequate routes out there for our needs. If we can find them and use them, riding through Front Range cities is a fairly easy task.

The Risk of Riding in Traffic and How to Deal with It

While riding a bicycle in American traffic, the average cyclist is subject to a risk of serious injury that is similar in magnitude to the risk faced by average drivers and

pedestrians in traffic. Clearly, there is no shortage of traffic accidents and injuries, and the range of potential injury is ugly. Insofar as just being in traffic is dangerous, riding a bike in traffic is dangerous. That's reality. Don't turn away from it or pretend the risk doesn't exist. The way to beat the danger of riding in traffic is to understand it, to focus on it, to face it head on. The danger of traffic is a sneaky and cowardly one—it waits until you drift off, look away, or start daydreaming. It waits until you get too comfortable or tired and let your guard down. It won't beat you mano a mano. This is mighty good news. It means that cyclists have the power to steer their own fate. It means that cyclists can avoid the vast majority of collisions, even those that are caused by random motorists' idiot mistakes, just by paying close attention to the danger. *Vigilance,* they call it.

Unfortunately, few road users, whether they be cyclists or drivers or whatever, appreciate the degree of awareness that is necessary to stay safe—truly safe—in crowded traffic. Those who do usually have been out there a long time, and have had a collision or two to kick them down the learning curve. Novice bicyclists are far more likely to get into trouble in traffic than their highly experienced, scarred-up counterparts.[2] It's not about skill level—it's that the beginners don't have the right attitude. At first, they tend to be too fearful and tentative, misunderstanding the danger of riding in traffic. Then they become overly confident, still misunderstanding the danger, but harboring a more perilous version of misunderstanding this time. This is the road to disaster. One hopes that at least a few beginners out there will heed the wisdom of their far more experienced comrades-on-wheels and employ an advanced mindset preemptively, without having to learn the lesson in the traditional, painful fashion. I honestly don't have much hope for that, though. People are pretty predictable when it comes to these things. They need to find out for themselves.

So—what is it that very experienced riders learn after years in traffic? They learn that they can eliminate all of their own stupid, illegal maneuvers and still be vulnerable to the stupid, illegal maneuvers of those around them. They learn that, when it comes right down to it, *anticipating* the idiot moves of drivers and pedestrians is the name of the game. It takes most cyclists many years and a bloody injury or two to really absorb that lesson, so I hope you consider my words carefully.

At the top of the list of drivers' most popular idiot moves is simply failing to notice the cyclist. They pull away from a stop sign or they crank a left into a seemingly defenseless rider. Never saw ya, pal, sorry. The left turns are especially damaging, as left turners tend to carry a good deal of speed and cause head-on collisions

◀ *A bike commuter pedaling past the Brown Palace Hotel in Denver*

---

[2] John Forester, *Bicycle Transportation: A Handbook for Cycling Transportation Engineers* (Cambridge, Mass.: MIT Press, 1994), p. 41. Forester compiled statistics from multiple studies of bicycle accidents and estimated that just ten years of experience reduces a cyclist's accident rate (per hour or mile of riding) by about 80 percent.

and heavy impacts with cyclists they failed to see. The vast majority of car-bike collisions involving experienced adult riders are of this general sort—an unseen cyclist victimized by an inattentive driver.[3] Blowers of stop signs and red lights, crankers of ill-advised left turns, nonlooking pullers out from driveways and parking spots: Experienced riders learn to anticipate these mistakes and avoid violent contact by keeping a vigilant eye on the disposition of every other vehicle and pedestrian around, and by subtly adjusting speed and position to neutralize an ever-changing worst-case scenario. Refusing to resign themselves to fate or depend on continued good luck, these riders are rarely—almost never—caught off guard by a bad driver. Cyclists who think this riding style is overly paranoid simply don't understand the stakes involved, and I worry about them.

As unforgiving as traffic can be, riding a bicycle through it is incredibly rewarding. That's the kicker. The other popular forms of personal transportation, driving and walking, aren't fit to carry cycling's jock. Not only does cycling provide incredible health benefits that the other forms of transportation can't, it is also profoundly fun and fulfilling besides. The benefits of cycling dwarf the risks, as long as we understand and respect those risks.

In Defense of Dirt

Thumb through this book and you'll see that more than a few rides incorporate sections of dirt roads into the routes. This being a road bike guide, some riders may be put off by my apparent fondness for dirt, while some others may be pleasantly surprised.

While pavement has become a major theme here, dirt roads are still a fact of life on the Colorado Front Range. Especially in the mountains, it is often difficult to string together a cool loop without riding any dirt. Those who refuse to take their road bikes off the pavement will cheat themselves out of some of the area's best rides. If you want to complete a loop using a classic climb like Flagstaff, Sugarloaf, Magnolia, Gold Hill, or North Cheyenne Canyon, it's easily done, but you have to kick up a little dirt to do it. Otherwise you're stuck with an out-and-back situation.

This dirt riding is a good thing on many levels. Not only does it allow us to connect myriad awesome, otherwise unconnectable loops in the Front Range mountains, it's an end in itself. Some riders consider the sensation of riding a road bike on dirt to be among the most delicious physical sensations available to them. Whether you love the floating, slightly out-of-control sensation or not, it is undeniably helpful for improving handling skills.

---

[3]Most often, experienced adult riders are not legally at fault for their car-bike collisions. The most common motorist-caused car-bike collisions involve a driver failing to yield at a stop sign or turning left into the cyclist. See Forester's general discussion of traffic accident patterns in *Bicycle Transportation,* pp. 41–61.

A dirt road up Left Hand Canyon

If a rider avoids dirt roads because he or she thinks they will be too rough, may I humbly suggest that this line of thinking might be a bit irrational. Have you noticed the condition of the pavement in these parts? Some of our favorite paved roads are so hacked up, they give a stuttering, jarring ride that would make any dirt road proud. The streets in central Denver are as bad as any city streets this side of Port-au-Prince. The mountain highways are brutalized and torn apart by a relentless freeze-thaw cycle. Honestly, sometimes rolling onto the dirt is a relief.

To deal with road damage, on pavement or on dirt, it is probably better to ride with a relatively sturdy wheelset. A slightly wider tire is also very helpful—say, 25c or wider. Cheap tires may also help psychologically, although many cyclists ride dirt roads on top-shelf racing tires. These tires wear very quickly on pavement or dirt, but they have a nice "feel." Keep your tires pumped up to avoid pinch flats.

Sometimes the aversion to dirt can be attributed to poor technique—generally speaking, the rider is not relaxed enough. A vicious cycle ensues: The rider tenses up, grips the brakes, rides poorly, and grows less confident, and thus more tense. The trick on dirt is to reverse the cycle. Confidence and relaxation breed good riding, which leads to further confidence and relaxation, and so on.

Still, there will be folks who hate riding dirt roads, and some of these haters will never be persuaded. Even these abstainers from dirt will find plenty of pavement in this guide. And all the loops with dirt sections are mostly pavement—just cut out the dirt part and ride the rest.

Those who continue to boycott the dirt are missing out on one of the best aspects of riding the Front Range, skinny tires or not. Dirt is good.

Notes on Mileage Cues and Bicycle Computers

The mileage numbers in this guide look awfully official, and we like to think they are, but I'm going to take a second here and urge you all not to get overly excited about these numbers. That's not to say I don't have confidence in the numbers. But there are many factors that must coincide if you, the rider/reader, are going to be able to follow along with the mileage cues and match up perfectly at every turn throughout the ride. In fact, it is quite unlikely that this will happen.

The numbers, you might notice, are to the nearest tenth of a mile. Well, that's a city block right there. I've had to round up or down to the nearest tenth—if your reading differs from mine by just a little bit, and you round down where I round up, for instance, suddenly you're wondering if you're on the same ride. And there is much potential for the readings to vary. You might not realize how important it is to program your odometer with the *exact* circumference of your front wheel and tire. If you are just a few centimeters off, and plug in, say, 215 instead of 220, your mileage readings will be off by 2.5 percent. Just changing the brand of tire can throw off the calculation. By the end of a long ride, with your computer compounding the very small variation with every revolution of your wheel, you could be off by a mile or more. The moral of the story is this: Unless you have calibrated your odometer with a precise rollout, don't even think about getting good numbers.

Consider other likely scenarios: You're out doing one of these rides and your hat flies off, so you turn around to go pick it up. Or you ride a little ways up a dirt road to check out the view. Even if your computer is calibrated exactly, you will throw your reading off enough to put doubts in your mind at the next intersection.

The remedy for all this odometer trouble is to simply use the numbers as a general guide and realize that what you see on your computer might differ a little bit from what's in the book, and that's okay. It's not an exact science. The numbers are still quite useful if you realize the shortcomings and use them wisely. Most of the routes in here are straightforward and easy to follow on the map. My advice, then, is to not rely on the mileage cues as your only guide, but to use them in conjunction with the map, the ride description, and, most important, your own powers of observation.

How to Use This Guide

The thirty-two rides in this book range from a 4.8-mile ramble to a 75.4-mile classic. To help you match the ride level with your ability, experience, and attitude, we've classified them into four groups based on their length and terrain. But don't get hung up on the definitions. What we call a "ramble" may seem more like a "classic" to a beginner, but the more accomplished among us may laugh at some of the rides we call "challenges." No matter what, some rides will be borderline, so it's always best to pull out a good map to make your own assessment.

Rambles are the most basic of rides, accessible to almost all riders. They can be easily completed in one day and follow flat to slightly rolling terrain and cover less than 35 miles.

Cruises are intermediate in difficulty and distance. They are generally 25 to 50 miles long and may include some moderate climbs and descents. An experienced rider can easily complete a cruise in one day, but inexperienced or less fit riders may want to take two days, with an overnight stop.

Challenges are difficult and suited to experienced riders in good condition. Beginning riders who take on a challenge may find themselves cursing the road, this book, and life in general halfway through a ride. These routes are tough. They are usually 40 to 60 miles long and include steep climbs and descents. Water and food may not be available, requiring you to bring adequate supplies along.

Classics are the most difficult rides in this book. Typically they are at least 60 miles in length and include tough climbs and descents. They may take you far away from such civilized needs as water or food and thus require you to carefully plan ahead. Tackle them only if you are fit and comfortable in the hinterlands on a lonely road.

So which ride or rides are for you? It depends. Feel like trying to initiate a friend into the sport? Go for an ultrascenic ramble. Experiencing the need to hammer your brains out and proclaim your virility? There are a few classics in here that will give your body the thrashing it desires—just be sensible about it and don't exceed your own limits. Of course, most of the rides are somewhere inbetween these two extremes.

How to Use the Maps

The maps in this book use shaded, or shadow, relief. Shadow relief does not represent elevation; it demonstrates slope or relative steepness. This gives an almost 3-D perspective of the physiography of a region and will help you see where ranges and valleys are.

Map Legend

Transportation

Limited Access Freeway	▭▭▭▭
U.S. Highway	▭▭▭▭
Featured U.S. Highway	●▭●▭●
State Highway	────────
Featured State Highway	────────
Local Road	────────
Featured Local Road	────────
Interstate Highway	(25)
U.S. Highway	(85)
State Highway	(14)
Trail	----------
Featured Trail	▪▪▪▪▪▪▪▪
Bike Dismount Area	••••••••••
Starting Point	START 🚲 ▪▪▪▪▪▪
Mileage Marker	10.0 ▪▪▪▪▪▪
Directional Arrow	→ ▪▪▪▪▪▪

Boundaries

National Park,
Large State or
Local Park

Population

Large City	**DENVER**
City	**Greeley** ◉
Town	**Orodell** ○

Hydrology

Reservoir or Lake	*Lake*
River or Creek	*Creek*

Physiography

Terrain (Shaded Relief)

Mountain,
Peak, or Butte ▲ *Peak*

Valley

Symbols

Building or Structure	■
Museum	🏛
Point of Interest	▫
Ride Number	㉗
Small Park	🌲
Ski Area	⛷
University	⚑
Visitor Center	❓
Zoo	🦭

Grids

Latitude / Longitude	38°
Number and Ticks	53' — N

Colorado Springs

The city of Colorado Springs is delightful eye candy for mountain lovers. A sharp line of tall foothills, deep green with ponderosa pine, spruce, and fir, towers over the city. Beyond and above those mountains lies another line of taller mountains, jagged with black shadows and huge outcroppings like Sentinel Rock. And lording over it all is the massive east face of Pikes Peak, looking like it might topple over at any second and bury half a million people under a pile of granite boulders the size of houses.

Even more so than Boulder, Colorado Springs is one with the mountains. Unfortunately, unlike Boulder, the Springs only has a few paved roads reaching from town into the hills. What the Springs does offer to road cyclists, in great abundance, are fun roads within the city or just outside of it. From the otherworldly Garden of the Gods to quirky Manitou Springs, from narrow North Cheyenne Canyon to the oasis of Palmer Park, the top-quality riding here should not be underestimated and should not be missed. Combined with some of the widest city streets in the world—streets originally designed to impress upon visitors and residents a sense of overt luxury and quality of life—the little foothill rides around the edges of Colorado Springs become the ingredients for uncommon epics or stand alone as perfect afternoon adventures.

It is good policy to bring two types of bicycles, road and mountain, to Colorado Springs, as the Pikes Peak region is also home to some of the finest single-track anywhere. But those who only ride road bikes will find plenty of great pavement to explore around these parts, and some road bike–friendly dirt as well. Before mountain bikes became popular, my friends and I had a great time riding our road bikes on the trails.

Colorado Springs catches a lot of hell for being home to legions of religious fundamentalists and ultraconservative folk. It's been called backwards and boring. From a cyclist's point of view, all is forgiven.

1 North Cheyenne Canyon Challenge

This ride dishes out a great deal of action in a short time and small space. Starting with a classic 3.2-mile climb up North Cheyenne Canyon[1] between walls of crumbling granite, this route takes you up to Gold Camp Road, a dirt shelf road perched high in the foothills over Colorado Springs. A lung-buster climb, phenomenal views, and interesting technical challenges await. This loop is quite short, but can be easily linked with other routes on the west side of Colorado Springs.

Start: At the mouth of North Cheyenne Canyon, just west of Colorado Springs.
Length: 13.1-mile loop.
Terrain: Tight, twisty canyon climb that gets rather steep; slight descent on dirt road with associated technical challenges; hilly residential zone.
Traffic and hazards: Weekends and warm weather add up to lots of sightseeing traffic on the road up North Cheyenne Canyon, which is undeniably narrow. There is rarely space to ride to the right of the white line. But traffic tends to ascend the canyon rather slowly, tourist-style, and cyclists should have little trouble with traffic conflicts on the way up. There are a few tight right-hand turns—blind turns—where drivers might have to wait a bit behind a bicyclist in the turn, but nothing too serious. In general, the passes come fairly easily even to the flatlander tourists, but help them out by moving far to the right when it is safe for them to pass, and by moving to the left to keep them corralled when passing would be inadvisable. It is quite probable that the air will smell intermittently like burning brakes. Other hazards include the unpaved surface of Gold Camp Road and gravel and road damage on the paved portions of the loop. In general, surface hazards will be more intense here than they would be on your typical road ride.

Getting there: From north or south of Colorado Springs, take Interstate 25 to the Tejon Street exit and go south a few blocks on Tejon to Cheyenne Boulevard. Take a right on Cheyenne Boulevard and head west approximately 2.5 miles to the fork in the road. Here Cheyenne Canyon splits into north and south components, and here the ride begins. From downtown Colorado Springs go south on Tejon Street approximately 2 miles to Cheyenne Boulevard, then go right approximately 2.5 miles to the start. Parking is available in a small lot just west of the fork, another somewhat larger lot a few tenths of a mile farther up the canyon, and in various other spots around this intersection and the Starsmore Discovery Center. Better yet, ride a bike to this short loop from anywhere in town.

Gold Camp Road

---

[1] For some reason that I have never been able to fully grasp, this canyon is quite often written down as "North Cheyenne Cañon," using the original Spanish spelling instead of the Americanized *Canyon*. In my opinion those using the Spanish spelling should go all out and use the Spanish pronunciation as well (con-YONE).

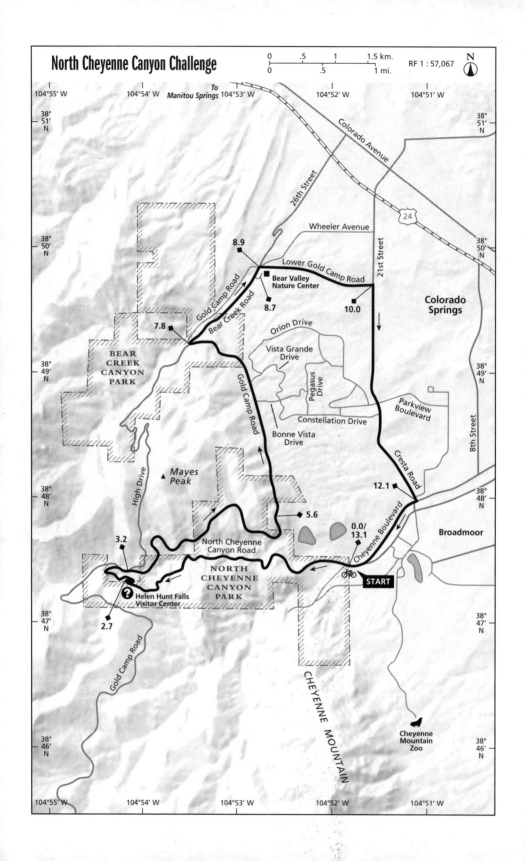

The Ride

At only 13.1 miles this ride would seem to be an unlikely candidate for the "challenge" category. Knowing this loop as I do, I just couldn't label it as a "cruise" in good conscience. This is a tough little ride, made for those who want to get right down to brass tacks and find out what their legs can do. "Challenge" is a good word for it.

The climbing begins right off the bat, and what a great little climb this is. The road nestled in the canyon next to Cheyenne Creek rises in a gentle but noticeable way at first, winding past groups of picnickers/partiers, rock climbers getting ready to do their thing on the crumbling granite walls, and hikers swarming the trailheads of the Mount Cutler Trail (no bikes) and the Columbine Trail (yes bikes). The climb progresses in steepness and general difficulty until a tough sun-baked and gravel-strewn grade at around mile 2 (MINE HILL—14% GRADE a sign proclaimed back in the old days). Passing the water station on your left is your warning that things are about to get serious. The Mine Hill section is difficult to master. If you are climbing it on a very hot day, look out.

After Mine Hill the road settles down again on approach to the turn at Helen Hunt Falls. This beautiful waterfall is a favorite tourist destination, with the associated hassles of a busy parking lot. The waterfall is not named for the costar of *Twister*, but for Helen Hunt Jackson, wife of Colorado Springs cofounder William Jackson. On a side note: One of the daughters of William Jackson (with Helen Hunt's niece—long story) was Helen Jackson, a teacher and promoter of environmental causes. She rode a bicycle all over the Springs back when adults simply did not ride bicycles and was given the nickname "Bicycle Lady."[2]

The road builds again past Helen Hunt Falls, winds up a few switchbacks—the last of which is suitably steep for the climb's final turn—and finds the top after 3.2 miles, where it spills out into the dirt parking lot of the local multiuse single-track trail system. The elevation gain here at the high point of the ride is a healthy 1,250 feet.

Here it is proper to utter an exclamation like "Yow!" The sight of so many cars packed into this parking area on the weekends has been consistently shocking to this author, a native Springsoid. Not very long ago it was unusual to see more than four or five cars in the lot at the same time. In the mid-1980s mountain bikers were still seldom seen around here, and the only people using the trails were motorcyclists, hard-core day hikers, and dudes looking for an out-of-the-way place to get high or dump a body. The explosion in the number of people flocking to the North Cheyenne Canyon trail system is a function of the growing population at large and the growing popularity of hiking and mountain biking within that population. The population of trail users is growing faster than the population of the city as a whole.

---

[2]Lani Carroll Hinkle, "The Jackson Family," *The Colorado College Bulletin* (April 2001), www.colorado college.edu/Publications/TheBulletin/April2001/family.htm.

Three dirt roads sprout from this parking area. One, to the west, is blocked to motor traffic.[3] Of the two dirt roads that begin right in front of you, one climbs steeply away from the parking area (the High Drive, which is gated in the off-season), left, and the other takes the low route, right. Take the low road. This is Gold Camp Road.

You might notice, at this point, that the pavement has run out. Oh, yeah. I was gonna tell you about that. I know this is a road bike guide, but it ain't gonna kill anybody to ride their road bike on the dirt. It might actually become one of your favorite things to do, as it is one of mine. Those who wish to keep their bicycles sparkly clean, or who are using ultralight equipment that is just barely supporting their girth as it is, should not attempt such a ride; those bike handlers who are less than confident might also shy away from this route, although they would benefit from trying it. Riding dirt on a road bike is a great way to sharpen handling skills for mountain biking as well as road riding.

The all-pavement option—by far the most common option among area road cyclists—is to turn around at the first sight of dirt and head back down the canyon (an adventure in itself, with the typical gravel patches on the road and the inattentive drivers). It is likely the section of Gold Camp Road ahead will be notably harsh in places, with washboard, potholes, and sizable chunks of granite—rolling it on a road bike can be a bit tricky. A little adventurous, but definitely doable.[4]

There are also two short tunnels along this dirt road section. Be prepared for potholes and deep gravel in the tunnels.

The road contours around the east face of the mountain, continuing a gradual but speedy descent and giving a great view of the town at a spot called Point Sublime. Point Sublime has also been the scene of multiple unfortunate incidents involving cars and gravity. A peek over the edge reveals the shells of wrecked vehicles, some many decades old.

You'll transition to pavement again after mile 5.6, at the top of a straight and very long descent. Road damage has been an issue on this paved section, as it is on the dirt. Off to the right several residential streets reach up to the Gold Camp shelf. You can use one of these roads—Bonne Vista Drive, say—to drop off the side of the hill

---

[3] For the time being at least. There is a group trying to open this section of Gold Camp Road to motor traffic to open up another route between Colorado Springs and the now bustling gambling town of Cripple Creek.

[4] Those who want to enjoy even more dirt have plenty of options from the parking area. Try the traditional mountain bike route from here: Go west past the gate and toward the turn of the canyon on the section of Gold Camp Road that is closed to motor traffic, and find the singletrack on the right side. Singletrack can also be accessed at the top of the High Drive, at the first switchback above Helen Hunt Falls, from the parking area below the lower tunnel, and from more than a few other spots. Generally, the trails are smooth but have steep sections that are usually traction-poor with loose gravel. Cyclo-cross bikes with triples are fun to ride here, lots of sliding in the turns. You wouldn't be the first person to ride a road bike on these trails.

and begin filtering through the neighborhood streets down to 21st Street/Cresta Road. This loop, however, continues on Gold Camp all the way around the north side of the long mountain, then turns and descends Bear Creek Canyon.

Gold Camp Road has brought you all the way out of the mountains and into the residential neighborhoods of southwest Colorado Springs. After traversing the foothills on hilly, suburban 21st Street (turning into Cresta Road), make the right turn back up the canyon at mile 12.1.

As short as it is, this loop lends itself to being attached to other local rides. For instance you can add excellent mileage by side-tripping up South Cheyenne Canyon, heading up toward the Cheyenne Mountain Zoo and Old Stage Road, or simply cruising aimlessly around the Broadmoor mesa.

Miles and Directions

0.0 Start riding up North Cheyenne Canyon from its intersection with South Cheyenne Canyon Road, near the Starsmore Discovery Center.

2.7 Pass Helen Hunt Falls and the Helen Hunt Falls visitor center. The road begins climbing some switchbacks.

3.2 Reach the top of the hill. At the dirt parking lot, turn right onto Gold Camp Road.

5.6 You're back on pavement, but still Gold Camp Road.

7.8 At a stop-signed three-point intersection, take a hard right onto Bear Creek Road.

8.7 Pass the Bear Creek Nature Center.

8.9 Take a right on Lower Gold Camp Road, headed east.

10.0 Turn right on 21st Street. This is a fast downhill, but traffic is sketchy.

12.1 Turn right on Cheyenne Boulevard, heading west again up the canyon.

13.1 Arrive back at the mouth of North Cheyenne Canyon.

Ride Information

Information

Colorado Springs and Pikes Peak Convention and Visitors Bureau, 515 South Cascade Avenue, Colorado Springs; (877) 745-3773 or (719) 635-7506; www .coloradosprings-travel.com.

Manitou Springs Chamber of Commerce & Visitors Bureau, 354 Manitou Avenue, Manitou Springs; (800) 642-2567 or (719) 685-5089; www.manitousprings.org.

Events/Attractions

The Starsmore Discovery Center, 2120 South Cheyenne Canyon Road, Colorado Springs;

(719) 587-6146; tfocc.org/visitorcenter.html. Features visitor information, a stuffed lion, guided nature hikes, these sorts of things. Located at the entrance to North Cheyenne Canyon, very near the start/finish of this loop.

The Helen Hunt Falls Visitor Center, 4075 North Cheyenne Canyon Road, Colorado Springs; (719) 633-5701; www.springsgov .com/Page.asp?NavID=781. Guided hikes, exhibits, books and maps for sale, and, most importantly, water and soda. Open from Memorial Day through Labor Day—in other words, closed for Colorado's prime cycling months of September and October.

Restaurants

Edelweiss Restaurant, 34 East Ramona Avenue, Colorado Springs; (719) 633-2220. German and Continental fare: schnitzel, cucumber salad, and Paulaner beer. Reservations probably a good idea but not required. Near the eastern terminus of Cheyenne Boulevard.

La Casita Patio Cafe, 306 South 8th Street, Colorado Springs; (719) 633-9616. Quality fast-food Mexican, well-situated at the corner of Highway 24 and 8th Street in west Colorado Springs. Drive through, or go inside to fully experience the salsa bar and loud ranchero music. Freshly made tortillas make the meal.

Adam's Mountain Cafe, 110 Canon Avenue, Manitou Springs; (719) 227-0839. A good selection of healthy, reasonably priced food in Manitou Springs. Highly recommended for breakfast before the ride or a big meal after.

Montague's Coffee Shop, 1019 South Tejon Street, Colorado Springs; (719) 520-0672; or 118 West Colorado Avenue, Colorado Springs; (719) 447-1004. Laid-back coffee shop and light lunch fare in big comfortable chairs. The Tejon location is right next door to the thrift shop. Go visit the nice ladies in the thrift shop if you happen to go, and buy a thing or two—all the money goes to homeless shelters and such.

Conway's Red Top, 1520 South Nevada Avenue, Colorado Springs; (719) 633-2444. "Best hamburger in town." Well, that's up for debate, but it's a big burger. Also, malts and shakes.

Accommodation

Hearthstone Inn, 506 North Cascade Avenue, Colorado Springs; (719) 473-4413. Bed and breakfast just north of downtown Colorado Springs.

Maps

Delorme: Colorado Atlas & Gazetteer: Page 62 D-3.

2 Broadmoor Cruise

This is a fun, convoluted route reaching into the shady corners of southwestern Colorado Springs, on and around the Broadmoor mesa. The centerpiece of this short ride is a moderately difficult climb to the Cheyenne Mountain Zoo.

Start: The intersection of North and South Cheyenne Canyons.
Length: 7.8-mile figure eight.

Terrain: Hilly, but not mountainous.
Traffic and hazards: Traffic is moderate on these tourist and residential roads.

Getting there: From north or south of Colorado Springs, take Interstate 25 to the Tejon Street exit and go south a few blocks on Tejon to Cheyenne Boulevard. Take a right on Cheyenne Boulevard and head west approximately 2.5 miles to the fork in the road. Here Cheyenne Canyon splits into north and south components, and here the ride begins. From downtown Colorado Springs go south on Tejon Street approximately 2 miles to Cheyenne Boulevard, then go right approximately 2.5 miles to the start. Parking is available in small lots just west of the fork, on both South Cheyenne Canyon Road and North Cheyenne Canyon Road, and in various other spots around this intersection and the Starsmore Discovery Center. Better yet, ride a bike to this short loop from anywhere in town.

Colorado Springs ▶

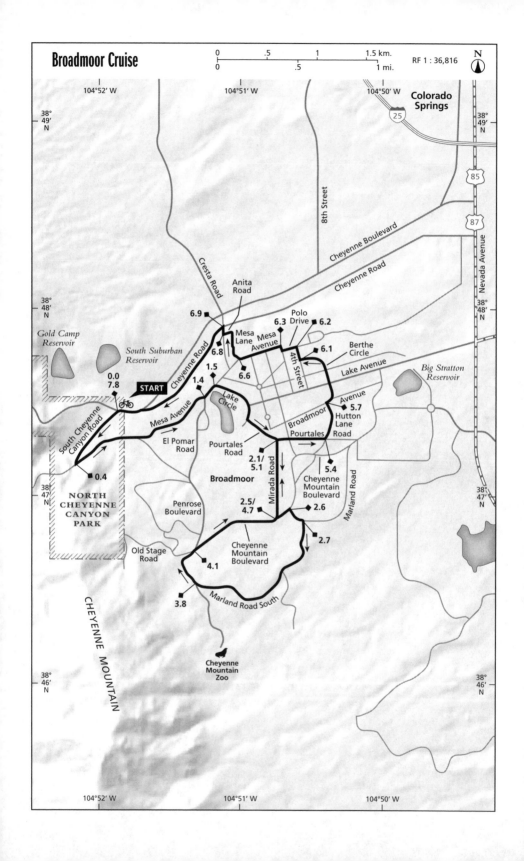

Broadmoor Cruise

0   .5   1   1.5 km.
0   .5   1 mi.

RF 1 : 36,816

N

104°52′ W
104°51′ W
104°50′ W

Colorado Springs

25

85

87

38°49′ N
38°49′ N

Cresta Road

8th Street

Cheyenne Boulevard

Cheyenne Road

Nevada Avenue

Anita Road

38°48′ N
38°48′ N

6.9

Mesa Lane

Mesa Avenue

Polo Drive

6.3   6.2

6.8

6.1

Berthe Circle

Big Stratton Reservoir

Gold Camp Reservoir

South Suburban Reservoir

Cheyenne Road

1.5

6.6

4th Street

Lake Avenue

0.0
7.8

START

1.4

Lake Circle

Avenue

5.7

Hutton Lane Road

Mesa Avenue

El Pomar Road

Pourtales Road

Broadmoor Pourtales

South Cheyenne Canyon Road

0.4

2.1/
5.1

Broadmoor

Mirada Road

Cheyenne Mountain Boulevard

5.4

Marland Road

38°47′ N
38°47′ N

NORTH CHEYENNE CANYON PARK

Penrose Boulevard

2.5/
4.7

2.6

Old Stage Road

4.1

Cheyenne Mountain Boulevard

2.7

3.8

Marland Road South

CHEYENNE MOUNTAIN

Cheyenne Mountain Zoo

38°46′ N
38°46′ N

104°52′ W
104°51′ W
104°50′ W

The Ride

Of all the Front Range towns, the site of the city of Colorado Springs is the most beautiful. While Denver is out on the plains, the Springs is scrunched right up against the mountains. These aren't the drab-looking, deforested foothills seen up north. The mountains looming over the Springs come with a thick coat of dark green pine. The easterners who first came out to the shadow of Pikes Peak took one look around and knew they were sitting on a gold mine. They knew people would come here and empty their pockets just to be in a place like this.

Southwest Colorado Springs is a paradise for road bikers who are willing to poke around a little bit and explore. There is much to be discovered. This ride follows a funky but fun route that links some of the points of interest in the Broadmoor area. More importantly, this ride features some of the best road sections in town.

Start in Cheyenne Canyon and head up South Cheyenne Canyon, the lesser-known cousin of North Cheyenne Canyon, to the Seven Falls entrance arch. (Seven Falls is a tourist trap, one of many in western Colorado Springs, and its access road is off-limits to bikes.) Turn a sharp left here and roll fast along Mesa Avenue. Mesa takes you right up to the back door of the Broadmoor Hotel, then around the front for a good look. In an attempt to attract the richest tourists, the Broadmoor was built to be as flashy as anything offered in Europe.

Continuing south of the hotel, pedal along between the fabled Broadmoor golf course and some truly ridiculous mansions, one of which is owned by the notorious Reverend Moon. At this point you are headed to the base of a great little climb to the Cheyenne Mountain Zoo. Instead of heading west straight up Cheyenne Mountain Boulevard, take the scenic route, using forgotten Marland Road South to make the climb. This is one of the best little road climbs around, winding along the southern boundary of the golf course. Traffic is almost nonexistent on this road, unless you count the deer.

At the zoo road it's a short jaunt to the lower entrance if you want to look at caged beasts. (If you get there by four o'clock, you can get in, but you can't take your bike into the zoo itself.) The descent on the zoo road puts you at a respectable high speed through the intersection with Penrose Boulevard—be careful, please. Below the intersection obnoxious speed can be achieved on a road with good sight lines.

The fast descent brings you back to the base of the climb, where you can choose to cowboy up and repeat. If not, shoot into the neighborhood of giant houses on expansive lots, the nicest neighborhood in town. Use tree-covered Hutton Lane to slide through the grounds of the Colorado Springs School (a private K–12), and drop back over the side of the mesa and into Cheyenne Canyon for the final stretch.

Miles and Directions

0.0 Start riding west up South Cheyenne Canyon Road from its intersection with North Cheyenne Canyon Road.

0.4   Turn left onto Mesa Avenue.

1.4   Take a left. (The sign makes it look like you are turning onto Park Avenue, but I believe, technically, that this is still Mesa Avenue, and Park Avenue is to the right.)

1.5   Veer right onto Lake Circle. This takes you past the Broadmoor Hotel and becomes Pourtales Road.

2.1   Veer right off of Pourtales Road onto Mirada Road.

2.5   Take a sharp left onto Cheyenne Mountain Boulevard briefly.

2.6   Take a right on Marland Road.

2.7   Take a right on Marland Road South.

3.8   Take a right onto Cheyenne Mountain Zoo Road. Begin a mad descent. **Option:** Take a left here and ride 0.3 mile to the zoo.

4.1   Take a high-speed right onto Cheyenne Mountain Boulevard.

4.7   Curve around to the left, now on Mirada Road again. (You have just completed a little side loop to the zoo.)

5.1   Hang a right onto Pourtales Road.

5.4   Turn left onto Hutton Lane. Pass the Colorado Springs School.

5.7   Take a right onto Broadmoor Avenue.

5.8   Stay the course as Broadmoor Avenue become Berthe Circle.

6.1   Now facing west, take a right onto Fourth Street.

6.2   Take a left on Polo Drive.

6.3   Take a right on Third Street, then a quick left on Mesa Avenue.

6.6   Take a right on Mesa Lane, just for fun.

6.8   Turn left on Anita Road, then a quick right on Cresta Road.

6.9   Turn left on Cheyenne Road.

7.8   Return to the fork where you started.

Ride Information

Information

Colorado Springs and Pikes Peak Convention and Visitors Bureau, 515 South Cascade Avenue, Colorado Springs; (877) 745-3773 or (719) 635-7506; www.coloradosprings-travel.com.

Manitou Springs Chamber of Commerce & Visitors Bureau, 354 Manitou Avenue, Manitou Springs; (800) 642-2567 or (719) 685-5089; www.manitousprings.org.

Events/Attractions

Cheyenne Mountain Zoo, 4250 Cheyenne Mountain Zoo Road, Colorado Springs; (719) 633-9925, ext. 111; www.cmzoo.org. Hours are seasonal: Memorial Day to Labor Day,

9:00 A.M. to 6:00 P.M. with last admission at 4:00 P.M.; Labor Day to Memorial Day, 9:00 A.M. to 5:00 P.M. with last admission at 4:00 P.M. Adult admission $12.

Restaurants

Edelweiss Restaurant, 34 East Ramona Avenue, Colorado Springs; (719) 633-2220. German and Continental fare: schnitzel, cucumber salad, and Paulaner beer. Reservations probably a good idea but not required. Near the eastern terminus of Cheyenne Boulevard.

La Casita Patio Cafe, 306 South 8th Street, Colorado Springs; (719) 633-9616. Quality fast-food Mexican, well-situated at the corner of Highway 24 and 8th Street in west Colorado

Springs. Drive through, or go inside to fully experience the salsa bar and loud ranchero music. Freshly made tortillas make the meal. **Adam's Mountain Cafe,** 110 Canon Avenue, Manitou Springs; (719) 227-0839. A good selection of healthy, reasonably priced food in Manitou Springs. Highly recommended for breakfast before the ride or a big meal after. **Montague's Coffee Shop,** 1019 South Tejon Street, Colorado Springs; (719) 520-0672; or 118 West Colorado Avenue, Colorado Springs; (719) 447-1004. Laid-back coffee shop and light lunch fare in big comfortable chairs. The Tejon location is right next door to the thrift shop. Go visit the nice ladies in the thrift shop

if you happen to go, and buy a thing or two—all the money goes to homeless shelters and such. **Conway's Red Top,** 1520 South Nevada Avenue, Colorado Springs; (719) 633-2444. "Best hamburger in town." Well, that's up for debate, but it's a big burger. Also, malts and shakes.

Accommodation

Hearthstone Inn, 506 North Cascade Avenue, Colorado Springs; (719) 473-4413. Bed and breakfast just north of downtown Colorado Springs.

Maps

The Map of Greater Colorado Springs (Macvan Productions).

3 West Colorado Springs Cruise

This economy-sized loop tours some prime terrain in the western half of Colorado Springs, where great road cycling abounds. Starting from downtown, you will head west to the Garden of the Gods, cruise through Manitou Springs, and pass through the hilly southwest suburbs before looping back to the start.

Start: Downtown Colorado Springs. The mileage cues start at the corner of Cascade Avenue and Bijou Street. (There are several alternate starting points available around this loop—Garden of the Gods, for example.)
Length: 22.4-mile loop.
Terrain: Rarely flat, yet no very long hills. The back side of the loop involves winding sightseeing roads through the gorgeous rock formations of the Garden of the Gods and a little dip into the village of Manitou Springs on tight streets. A bit of everything here.
Traffic and hazards: There are a few high-traffic sections, but primarily this is pleasant cruising on relatively bicycle-friendly streets in

an urban/suburban setting. The section of Manitou Avenue/Colorado Boulevard from the congested village of Manitou to 26th Street can be nasty. Some riders may prefer using Pikes Peak Avenue, 1 block north. In general, streets along this route are wide and sharing the road with horseless carriages is no problem. There is now a helpful bike lane on Uintah Street, on what used to be a quite dicey section under the highway. The short section from the highway up to the Mesa turnoff is still a little skinny for comfort. Watch for the usual Door Zone[1] hazards in various places around the loop. Garden of the Gods is a tourist spot, so there are tourists there. Crazy

---

[1]The Door Zone is the space within about 4 feet from the side of any parked car. A cyclist traveling within the DZ is in grave danger of colliding with a suddenly open door. The cure for this is to avoid the DZ like the plague it is.

how that works. Tourists drive funny—see if you don't agree. The road surfaces in the Garden are generally fantastic, and there is a wide bike lane set aside on the curvy blacktop. (Actually, it is a lane for bicyclists and pedestrians, but there aren't many of either.) Cresta Road/21st Street is not my favorite road to ride upon, but that didn't stop me from riding it about a half-million times when I was a kid. There was a lot less traffic back then.

Getting there: This ride begins right in downtown Colorado Springs. Just find Cascade Avenue and head north. Cascade is 2 blocks west of Nevada Avenue, which could perhaps be considered the main north-south avenue, and 1 block west of Tejon Street. The mileage cues begin at the intersection of Bijou Street and Cascade.

The Ride

The west side of the Springs is packed with memorable features: strange tourist traps, excellent scenery, and fantastic cycling opportunities. Starting right from the heart of downtown Colorado Springs, this loop manages to visit many of these interesting destinations in a relatively short tour.

Barely out of the downtown area, this route cuts right through the Colorado College[2] campus on Cascade Avenue. Cascade is a truly awesome street, for cycling and otherwise. The street is lined with huge trees and nineteenth-century millionaires' mansions that were built soon after the fledgling city sprouted as a resort, a real estate get-rich-quick scheme, and a sanitarium for tuberculosis patients. This loop uses just a smidge of Cascade, unfortunately. Come back sometime and ride the rest of it. In the meantime a left turn after just 1 mile puts you on Uintah Street headed west, straight at monstrous Pikes Peak, looking much closer than it really is. Uintah goes under Interstate 25; the interchange is frantic and crowded with traffic, but a recently established bike lane is a huge improvement over the Uintah of old. West of I–25 comes the first climbing of the ride and a quick turn onto Mesa Road.

Mesa Road has been a traditional, well-loved route for local riders—the back door to the Garden of the Gods. The climb is slight, starting as a moderate faux canyon, then softening to a false flat on the mesa, where it passes Holmes Middle School, Coronado High School, and the exclusive Garden of the Gods Country Club, a favorite of Texas oil barons. The climb is gentle, but relentless.

Taking a sharp left onto 30th Street, you have a choice of getting onto a bike path or staying on the road, somewhat skinny for the high motorcar speeds at this point. Before too long comes the right turn into the Garden of the Gods, the collection of towering red-and-white sandstone formations that can be seen from most places around town.

If not for the heavy volume of tourist traffic, you could almost say that the collection of roads through and around the Garden of the Gods is perfect for cycling.

---

[2]Many of those associated with Colorado College will be quick to point out that the name of the school is actually *The* Colorado College. Whatever . . .

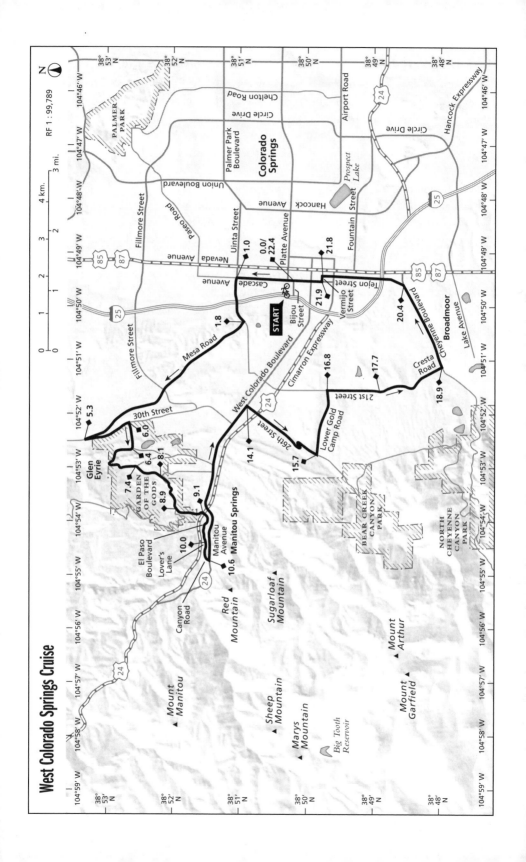

West Colorado Springs Cruise

RF 1 : 99,789

The road surface itself is as smooth as you'll find anywhere in Colorado (because tourists get the good stuff; for the same reason the Peak-to-Peak Highway is emphatically well groomed). The roads in the Garden dip and climb pleasantly, never straight for very long. There is even a segregated bicycle-pedestrian lane on these roads. Bike lanes are always the source of mixed feelings, but this baby is very wide and doesn't seem to cause any problems. The Garden is *the* perfect spot to pull off the road, push your bike up a trail a bit, sit on a rock, and eat that sandwich that's been fermenting in your backpack. There is no better place to eat a sandwich than the Garden of the Gods, with the Peak over your shoulder.

Note that the route described here leaves out some of the prime Garden roads in the interest of practicality. If you've got the time and the legs, do an extra loop, using the classic Ridge Road climb to reenter the park.

Exiting the Garden, turn right and roll toward Manitou Springs. Find an unorthodox little street that rolls behind the shops. Note how the buildings have been built over the flowing creek. There's a very Old World feel through here. This street is actually called Lover's Lane, but you wouldn't know it because the street signs are claimed for souvenirs. Loop back down through Manitou on the main drag. Consider stopping for candy and trinkets, a quick game of Skee-Ball at the Penny Arcade, or a dulcimer. Also consider a very short side trip up Ruxton Avenue, or onto the steep slopes of the quaint neighborhood overhead, where some of the houses seem to defy gravity. Historically, Manitou has been famous for its witches and prostitutes, and prostitute-witches. Oh, and for its several springs, of course, which were used by the Indians long before there was a town here. Now Manitou is known for souvenir shops, New Agey–ness of all stripes, mediocre Mexican food, and bikers. The other kind of bikers. And I'm not talking dentists with Harleys, but real bikers, who make their livings from, you know, biker things. It turns out that these are some of the sanest individuals in town.

Out of Manitou and Old Colorado City, the route heads south up 26th Street, past a cemetery and a neighborhood tucked away against the foothills, and climbs a substantial hill. It becomes apparent that this southwestern sector of the Springs is quite hilly. From the intersection of 26th and Gold Camp Road, a rider can climb Gold Camp or Bear Creek Canyon or take a left (east) and cruise down to 21st Street. Do the latter and head east for this loop, but consider a foray into Bear Creek Canyon, and around the entire perimeter of Gold Camp Road, at a later date. Lower Gold Camp Road sits atop what appears to be a garden-variety hill, but the hill in fact is a huge tailings pile left over from the boom days of the Colorado mining industry, when an ore smelter was in constant operation near here. The smelter's smokestack survives and can still be seen peeking up from behind the hill.

At mile 16.8 take a right onto 21st, descend north off the tailings pile, across the flats by Bear Creek Park, and climb another short, sharp one. 21st Street is hilly like a camel's back or a sine curve. This is pretty much the last climb of the loop, even though you're still on the back side. Busy 21st Street bisects the Skyway suburb, with all the streets named for constellations, planets, and such, and descends past Cheyenne Mountain High School into the valley of Cheyenne Creek. Take a left and roll east on a slight downhill to Tejon Street. Tejon is a busy—but recently refurbished and partially bike-laned—street that takes you straight into downtown and back to the start/finish. Those last 4 miles fly right by.

Miles and Directions

0.0 From downtown Colorado Springs head north on Cascade Avenue from the intersection of Cascade and Bijou Street.

1.0 Take a left on Uintah Street.

1.8 Turn right onto Mesa Road.

5.3 Take a sharp left onto 30th Street. (Or use the bike path west of the road.)

6.0 Take a right and enter the Garden of the Gods.

6.4 Take a right here (you don't have a choice) and start a modest climb.

7.4 Stay right here, and through the next few intersections, as you trace the western edge of the Garden of the Gods Park.

8.1 Stay right.

8.6 Stay right.

8.9 Don't turn right onto the dirt Rampart Range Road.

9.1 Pass the turn to Cedar Heights subdivision, then take a right onto El Paso Boulevard. Stay on El Paso, passing all side streets, until . . .

10.0 Across from a park and playground, take a right onto Lover's Lane. It is quite possible that the street sign has been ripped off. (Don't turn onto Washington Boulevard, but the other street.)

10.2 Roll through the stop sign.

10.3 Turn right onto Canyon Road.

10.4 Turn left at the post office.

10.6 Turn left on the main boulevard, Manitou Avenue. Traffic can be tight but speed limits are low until the road leaves Manitou; all vehicles are expected to stop for pedestrians in crosswalks.

14.1 Take a right onto 26th Street southbound. (Note: The loop can be shortened here by staying the course and taking Manitou Avenue/Colorado Boulevard straight into downtown. Traffic gets more ridiculous as you approach downtown from this direction.)

14.2 Cross the Cimarron Expressway at a light.

15.7 After one and a half miles of moderate climbing, take a left onto Lower Gold Camp Road, heading east and down.

16.8 Turn right onto 21st Street. Swoop down past Bear Creek Park and up another hill.

17.7 Reach the top of this loop's last notable climb.

18.9 Take a left on Cheyenne Road. (Note: To further enhance this loop, turn right here and peruse Cheyenne Canyon, or head straight up into the Broadmoor neighborhood to check out the hotel, the zoo, and some of the nicest homes you'll ever see.)

20.4 Angle left onto Tejon Street. (There is actually one itty-bitty climb along this stretch.)

21.7 Pass the Olde Town Bike Shop on the left.

21.8 Turn left on Vermijo Street for 1 block, as Tejon turns into a one-way street going the other way.

21.9 Take a right on Cascade Avenue.

22.4 Arrive back at the intersection of Cascade and Bijou Street.

Ride Information

Information

Colorado Springs and Pikes Peak Convention and Visitors Bureau, 515 South Cascade Avenue, Colorado Springs; (877) 745-3773 or (719) 635-7506; www.coloradosprings -travel.com.

Restaurants

Little Bangkok, 109 East Pikes Peak Avenue, Colorado Springs; (719) 442-6546. Small, casual, family-run Thai restaurant in downtown Colorado Springs, across from Acacia Park near the Peak Theater. The food is very, very good.

Everest Nepal Restaurant, 28 East Bijou Street, Colorado Springs; (719) 473-3890. Friendly place downtown with exotic, incredibly tasty food.

Luigi's, 947 South Tejon Street, Colorado Springs; (719) 632-7339. Very popular little Italian place. The food is good, not spectacular, but the atmosphere is cozy, occasionally energetic.

Gertrude's, 2625 West Colorado Avenue, Colorado Springs; (719) 471-0887. Perhaps the best filet mignon in all the land. Small, intimate setting. Reservations please.

Poor Richard's Feed and Read, 324½ North Tejon Street, Colorado Springs; (719) 632-7721. Bookstore and food combined, just north of downtown on Tejon. A Springs tradition.

José Muldoon's, 222 North Tejon Street, Colorado Springs; (719) 636-2311. Casual Mexi-merican in a dark cavern of a space, downtown across Tejon from Acacia Park. Beeg, beeg margaritas.

La Casita Patio Cafe, 306 South 8th Street, Colorado Springs; (719) 633-9616. Quality fast-food Mexican, well-situated at the corner of Highway 24 and 8th Street in west Colorado Springs. Drive through, or go inside to fully experience the salsa bar and loud ranchero music. Freshly made tortillas make the meal.

Edelweiss Restaurant, 34 East Ramona Avenue, Colorado Springs; (719) 633-2220. German and Continental fare: schnitzel, cucumber salad, and Paulaner beer. Reservations probably a good idea but not required. Near the eastern terminus of Cheyenne Boulevard.

Accommodation

Hearthstone Inn, 506 North Cascade Avenue, Colorado Springs; (719) 473-4413. Bed and breakfast just north of downtown Colorado Springs.

Maps

Delorme: Colorado Atlas & Gazetteer: Pages 62-63 B-3, B-4.

4 Palmer Park Ramble

Starting from downtown Colorado Springs, head northeast using residential streets and a section of bike path. Loop back to the central business district after a short but memorable climb to the high point of scenic Palmer Park.

Start: The intersection of Cascade Avenue and Bijou Street in downtown Colorado Springs.
Length: 14.9-mile loop.
Terrain: Flat until the vicinity of Palmer Park. In the park there is a climb that is fairly steep, but still moderate overall due to its lack of significant length.

Traffic and hazards: Traffic is moderate overall. The Rock Island path crosses several major streets—as long as you don't just bolt out into the street without looking, you should be all right.

Getting there: Take Interstate 25 to the Bijou Street exit (exit 142). Go east on Bijou—Bijou will actually curve to the south and funnel you onto Kiowa Street, as Bijou is a one-way street going west—into downtown Colorado Springs and park. The mileage cues begin at the intersection of Bijou and Cascade.

The Ride

Palmer Park is a large undeveloped tract of rugged land buried in the midst of the northern suburbs of Colorado Springs. To call it a park hardly does it justice. The roads cutting through this forested and rocky oasis are like actual mountain roads, fighting up inclines, twisting around tight curves. In short, it's awesome.

To pedal over to Palmer Park from downtown, many routes will work. This one heads due north on the grand avenues, past Colorado College, and turns east onto the Rock Island Trail, an MUP (multiuse path) that follows the old Rock Island railroad line through town.

The Rock Island bicycle-pedestrian path is surfaced with asphalt, which is fine when it's brand-new but tends to deteriorate precipitously. The vast majority of MUP mileage in Colorado Springs is asphalt- or gravel-surfaced. At the time of this writing, much of it was unsuitable or just barely suitable for road bikes.[1] There is not much of the wide, smooth concrete-type stuff that Denverites take for granted. As for the Rock Island Trail, the surface is fine for the time being.

After 2.6 miles of road travel, and a similar length of MUP, turn left off of the Rock Island onto Chelton Road, which has a small bike lane, and a short hill. Drop down on Maizeland Road and enter Palmer Park. Passing through the gates, the

---

[1]The Fountain Creek Trail south along the Pikes Peak Greenway, for instance, looks great on the map, but in person is a choppy mess of deteriorating asphalt. So is the section of Monument Creek trail on the north side of town. The Shooks Run Trail wrestles with the street grid at almost every block and is therefore almost unusable for anything but the most low-key recreational pursuits.

Great riding in the middle of the city, Palmer Park

climbing begins almost immediately and is sustained for an impressive mile, just long enough to get the blood pumpin'. At the top there's an intersection and a choice: Go right and drop out of the park immediately, or go left and cruise along the high ridge to an overlook with picnic benches and such. The overlook road is recommended, especially in the early-morning or late-afternoon sun. This side trip adds less than 2 miles to your ramble through the park.

Drop out the back of Palmer Park on the only road available for that purpose. This road is Paseo Road, and it ushers you gently through the residential area on a diagonal and back to the Rock Island Trail. Apart from the big arterials like Academy Boulevard and Circle Drive, traffic is quiet in these neighborhoods.

At 14.9 miles in length, this ride is short, but it could certainly be shorter. There are parking areas in Palmer Park itself, enabling riders to put together a very short loop using just the park's roads and Chelton Road if they wish.

Colorado's urban-dwelling cyclists spend much of their remaining time on this earth trucking off to the middle of nowhere just to smell some pine trees and ride on curvy, hilly roads. Here we have bite-sized sections of real mountain road right in the suburbs. Palmer Park is kind of like a mini-Snickers—it may be mini but it's still damn good.

Palmer Park Ramble

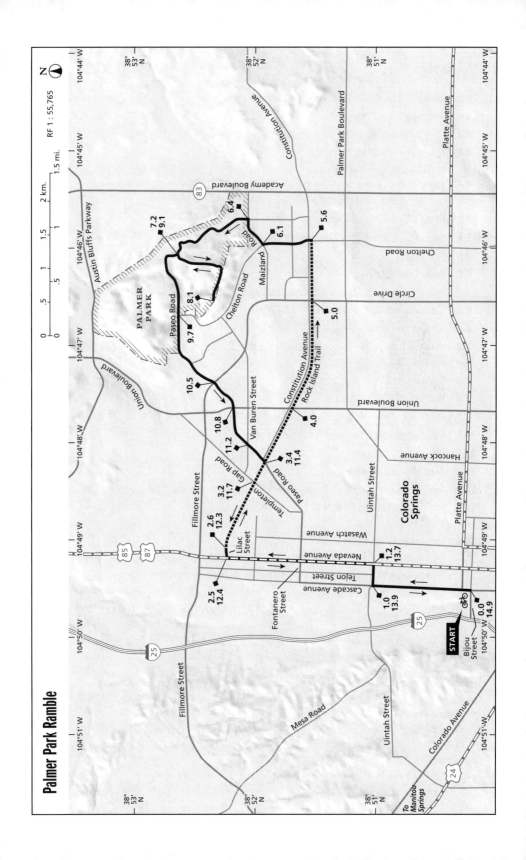

RF 1 : 55,765

N

1.5 mi.

2 km.

PALMER PARK

Colorado Springs

START

Miles and Directions

0.0 Start riding north up Cascade Avenue from Bijou Street.

1.0 Take a right on Uintah Street.

1.2 After 2 blocks take a left onto Nevada Avenue.

2.5 Take a right on Lilac Street.

2.6 At the end of the street, continue straight on the Rock Island Trail, a bicycle-pedestrian path that follows the tracks of the old Rock Island line. (This is also the northernmost end of the Shooks Runs Trail.)

3.2 Cross Templeton Gap Road.

3.4 Cross Paseo Road. (You'll be coming back down Paseo later on.)

4.0 Cross Union Boulevard.

5.0 Cross Circle Drive.

5.6 Take a left onto Chelton Road. A bit o' climbin' follows.

6.1 Turn right on Maizeland Road.

6.4 Turn left and enter Palmer Park.

7.2 Near the high point of the park, take a left here to ride the pleasant ridgetop road to an overlook.

8.1 Enjoy the overlook, then turn around.

9.1 Turn left here to resume the loop.

9.7 Exit Palmer Park. (You are on Paseo Road.)

10.5 Cross Circle Drive; continue on Paseo Road.

10.8 Cross Union Boulevard.

11.2 Cross Van Buren Street.

11.4 Take a right onto the Rock Island path, now headed in the opposite direction as before.

12.3 The path ends at the corner of Lilac Street and Weber Street. Continue straight on Lilac for a block.

12.4 Turn left onto Nevada Avenue.

13.7 Take a right onto Uintah Street. (This is just to make it a little easier on yourself—if Nevada feels right, by all means keep riding it all the way into downtown.)

13.9 Turn left on Cascade Avenue.

14.9 Arrive back downtown at the intersection of Bijou Street and Cascade Avenue.

Ride Information

Information

Colorado Springs and Pikes Peak Convention and Visitors Bureau, 515 South Cascade Avenue, Colorado Springs; (877) 745-3773 or (719) 635-7506; www.coloradosprings-travel.com.

Restaurants

Poor Richard's Feed and Read, 324½ North Tejon Street, Colorado Springs; (719) 632-7721. Bookstore and food combined, just north of downtown on Tejon. A Springs tradition.

Little Bangkok, 109 East Pikes Peak Avenue, Colorado Springs; (719) 442-6546. Small, casual, family-run Thai restaurant in downtown Colorado Springs, across from Acacia Park near the Peak Theater. The food is very, very good.

Everest Nepal Restaurant, 28 East Bijou Street, Colorado Springs; (719) 473-3890. A friendly place downtown with exotic, incredibly tasty food.

José Muldoon's, 222 North Tejon Street, Colorado Springs; (719) 636-2311. Casual Mexi-merican in a dark cavern of a space, downtown across from Acacia Park on Tejon Street. Beeg, beeg margaritas.

Luigi's, 947 South Tejon Street, Colorado Springs; (719) 632-7339. Very popular little Italian place. The food is good, not spectacular, but the atmosphere is energetic.

Accommodation

Hearthstone Inn, 506 North Cascade Avenue, Colorado Springs; (719) 473-4413. Bed and breakfast just north of downtown Colorado Springs.

Maps

The Map of Greater Colorado Springs (Macvan Productions).

5 Woodmen Cruise

Woodmen Road is the star of this quick loop around the hilly northwest suburbs of Colorado Springs. Even though this area has been filled in with houses, the terrain is still perfect for a moderate yet bracing workout.

Start: Near Woodmen Road and Interstate 25. More specifically, the parking area located just south of Woodmen Road on the west side of Corporate Drive.

Length: 11.7-mile loop.

Terrain: The area is hilly, but the road climb is fairly gentle until around mile 4.0, where there is a sustained pitch of about 10 percent grade.

Traffic and hazards: Traffic is the downside of this loop. These roads are well used but also fairly wide and accommodating. The very start of this loop requires negotiating a short section of road with very high traffic, but a stunted sidewalk is available for those who want it.

Getting there: Take I-25 to the Woodmen Road exit (exit 149) and go west on Woodmen Road 1 block. Turn left (south) on Corporate Drive and turn right into the big parking area.

The Ride

The beginning of this short but moderately strenuous loop is problematic. The parking area south of Woodmen Road on Corporate Drive is the natural start/finish for this one, but unfortunately its location leaves you to deal with about a quarter mile of high-traffic multilane road right off the bat. It is certainly possible to negotiate this section (of Woodmen Road between Corporate Drive and Rockrimmon Boulevard) by using the right side of the right lane. There is room on the roadway,

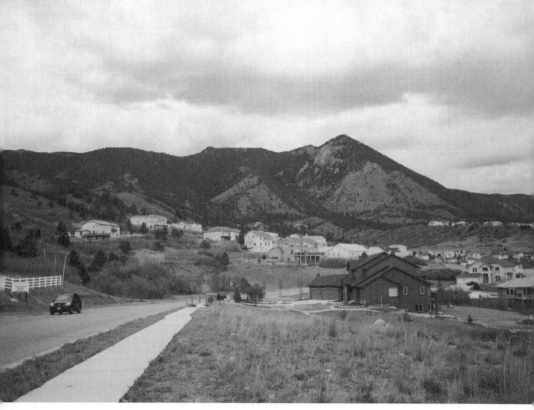

Cruising in the hilly suburbs

but many cyclists will probably feel more comfortable using the skinny sidewalk for this brief section. There will be some relief from the traffic as soon as Woodmen breaks away from Rockrimmon Boulevard, just 0.3 mile up the road.

Woodmen Road, when you consider just the lay of the road, the way it flows across the rugged landscape, is a joy to ride. It keeps you on your toes, with something different around every turn. The traffic is a little much sometimes, especially if you know what it was like, say, fifteen or twenty years ago.

Woodmen rolls right up to the front gate of the Mount Saint Francis convent (home of the Sisters of Saint Francis of Perpetual Adoration), then, as if it has realized where it was going at the last moment, goes around in a wide circle. As it goes around the north side, it climbs in a rather serious fashion—for most riders this will likely be an out-of-saddle experience. At the west end of the arc, and near the high point, is the Blodgett Peak trailhead.

Unfortunately, at this far side of the loop, the interesting climbing on Woodmen Road is a mere memory unless you want to go back and do it again. It's pretty much one long descent from here back to Monument Creek. Bittersweet. To get back down to creek level, you'll cut through the heart of the subdivision below on

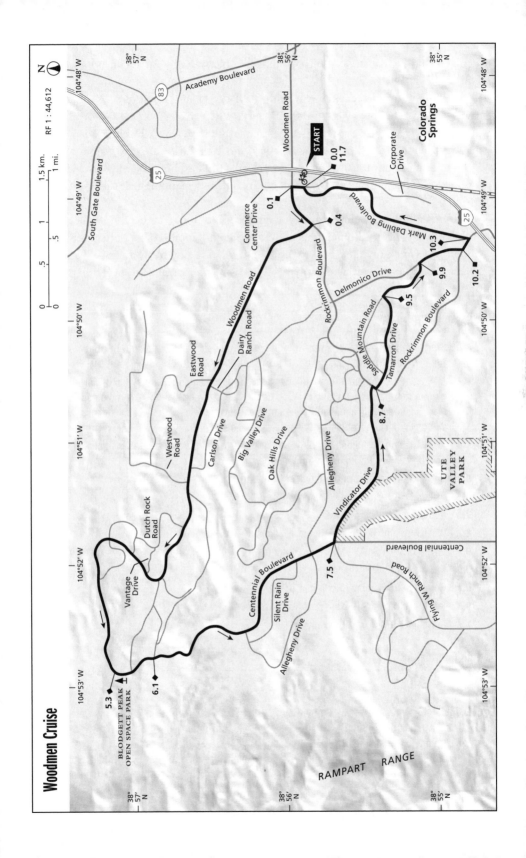

Woodmen Cruise

RF 1 : 44,612

N

1.5 km.
1 mi.

Academy Boulevard

83

South Gate Boulevard

Woodmen Road

25

START
0.0
11.7

Colorado Springs

Corporate Drive

Commerce Center Drive

0.1

0.4

Mark Dabling Boulevard

Rockrimmon Boulevard

Delmonico Drive

10.3

9.9

9.5

10.2

Woodmen Road

Eastwood Road

Dairy Ranch Road

Saddle Mountain Road

Tamarron Drive

Rockrimmon Boulevard

Westwood Road

Carlson Drive

Big Valley Drive

Oak Hills Drive

Allegheny Drive

8.7

Dutch Rock Road

Vantage Drive

Centennial Boulevard

Vindicator Drive

UTE VALLEY PARK

Silent Rain Drive

Allegheny Drive

Centennial Boulevard

7.5

Flying W Ranch Road

5.3

6.1

BLODGETT PEAK OPEN SPACE PARK

RAMPART   RANGE

38° 57' N

38° 56' N

38° 55' N

104°48' W

104°49' W

104°50' W

104°51' W

104°52' W

104°53' W

secondary residential streets, thus avoiding the heavy traffic on Rockrimmon and other big boulevards.

At the bottom of the loop, you can use Mark Dabling Boulevard (as described in the mileage cues below) or use the Pikes Peak Greenway Trail, on the other side of the creek, to traverse the final flat leg back to the start. (Mark Dabling was a Colorado Springs police officer who was shot in the back during a traffic stop in 1982.) Dabling Boulevard is usually a pretty decent bike route, although some drivers think it is their personal Formula One tryout course. There is a tempting chicane, you have to admit.

Just 1.4 miles on Dabling brings you right back to the start, for a loop of less than 12 miles total. Nice and quick, this one. However, this loop is nicely situated on the Monument Creek multiuse path (MUP)—aka Pikes Peak Greenway Trail, aka Santa Fe Trail—so it can be reached easily from downtown or combined with other Colorado Springs rides.

Miles and Directions

0.0 Start from the parking area west of Corporate Drive near its intersection with Woodmen Road. Go out to Corporate Drive and take a left (north).

0.1 Take a left on Woodmen Road. This is the busiest section of the loop by far. Usually it is okay to travel in the right lane of Woodmen for these few blocks—there is more space than is immediately apparent. Those who feel uncomfortable with this should cross Woodmen as a pedestrian and head west on the sidewalk.

0.4 Take a right on Woodmen Road. (Woodmen takes a sharp right here; the road straight ahead becomes Rockrimmon Boulevard.)

5.3 Still on Woodmen, pass the Blodgett Peak Open Space Park.

6.1 Woodmen Road becomes Centennial Boulevard.

7.5 Turn left on Vindicator Drive.

8.7 Cross Rockrimmon Boulevard and continue straight on Tamarron Drive.

9.5 Take a right on Saddle Mountain Road.

9.9 Take a right on Delmonico Drive.

10.2 Go left on Rockrimmon Boulevard briefly.

10.3 Take a left on Mark Dabling Boulevard.

11.7 Arrive back at the parking area.

Ride Information

Information

Colorado Springs and Pikes Peak Convention and Visitors Bureau, 515 South Cascade Avenue, Colorado Springs; (877) 745-3773 or (719) 635-7506; www.coloradosprings -travel.com.

Restaurants

Margarita at Pine Creek, 7350 Pine Creek Road, Colorado Springs; (719) 598-8667. One of the Springs' most interesting dining experiences for almost 30 years. Reservations please, a bit up-scale with a Bohemian twist. Located on the extreme north side of town.

La Casita, 295 North Nevada Avenue, Colorado Springs; (719) 599-7829. The northern branch of the now-famous patio cafe.

Accommodation

Hearthstone Inn, 506 North Cascade Avenue, Colorado Springs; (719) 473-4413. Bed and breakfast just north of downtown Colorado Springs.

Maps

The Map of Greater Colorado Springs (Macvan Productions).

6 Denver–Colorado Springs Classic

This is an ambitious ride linking downtown Denver with downtown Colorado Springs. Almost half the mileage of this point-to-point adventure is on fully separated bicycle paths.

Start: Confluence Park, downtown Denver.
Length: 75.4-mile point-to-point.
Terrain: Rolling hills on Perry Park Road. The so-called New Santa Fe Trail is primarily flat, with some very sharp little dips and turns as it crosses Air Force Academy land.
Traffic and hazards: The biggest hazard of this ride is the U.S. Highway 85 portion. The highway has a ton of traffic, and it's somewhat narrow, without any significant shoulder in stretches south of the Louviers crossroads. The highway is currently under construction and it is unknown how it will turn out, but we can hope that the new highway will be much better for cycling. Perry Park Road is becoming a rather busy road with new development in the area. It is still a good ride, though the shoulder could be wider. The New Santa Fe Trail is a generally smooth gravel mega-path, with occasional sandy sections and bumpy stuff, even a few very short, steep sections that might require walking. The continuation of the same trail as it enters Colorado Springs is in poor condition, and parts are currently under construction.

Getting there: From downtown Denver go west on 15th Street, under the railroad tracks and over the Platte River, and take the first left after the river onto Platte Street. Park in the free lot by the REI flagship store. It will probably be just as easy, and more enjoyable, to ride to the bike path from a home base in Denver rather than drive and park. From points north or south of Denver, take Interstate 25 to exit 211. Go north on Water Street, under Speer Boulevard, and park in the lot next to or across the street from the REI store.

The Ride

This is the western passage between Denver and the Springs, linking two very long sections of bicycle-pedestrian path with the excellent Perry Park Road. Unfortunately, the route is not all happy-go-lucky the whole way. Immediately south of Denver, cyclists get hung out to dry. There are a few options, but no good ones. In this situation it is best to just take the most direct route, in this case US 85, the continuation of Santa Fe Drive south of C-470. Between Denver and Sedalia the highway is generally straight, nondescript, and too narrow for comfort. This is a very

Bison

well-used commuter route for folks who live in Douglas County, one of the fastest-growing counties in America over the last two decades. Of course, avoid the damn thing during rush hours. On weekends the road is part of the only route from Denver to the Rampart Range Road, so it's packed with dirt bikers in pickups with trailers. You could certainly put one of those little mirrors to good use on this section of highway.

If you don't mind losing the glory of going downtown to downtown, drive to Sedalia and start the ride there, parking in the dirt lot north of the second set of tracks, on Plum Avenue. Starting in Sedalia solves the US 85 problem, but also cuts out quite a lot of pleasant riding—about 16 miles of cruising on the intersection-less Platte River Trail. Trade-offs, life is full of trade-offs. It's strange that the ride through Denver is an easy section, traffic-wise. It is also the fastest way to get to the southern edge of the metro area, for the same reason.

Perry Park Road between Sedalia and Palmer Lake brings some relief. You can get a sense of what Perry Park used to be, a quiet country road, dipping and meandering along the range—a perfect cycling road. These days Perry Park has too much traffic volume to be perfect, but it's still a nice ride. The landscape is truly spectacular, green buttes with rocky crowns, rolling grassland. Watch for Monkey Face

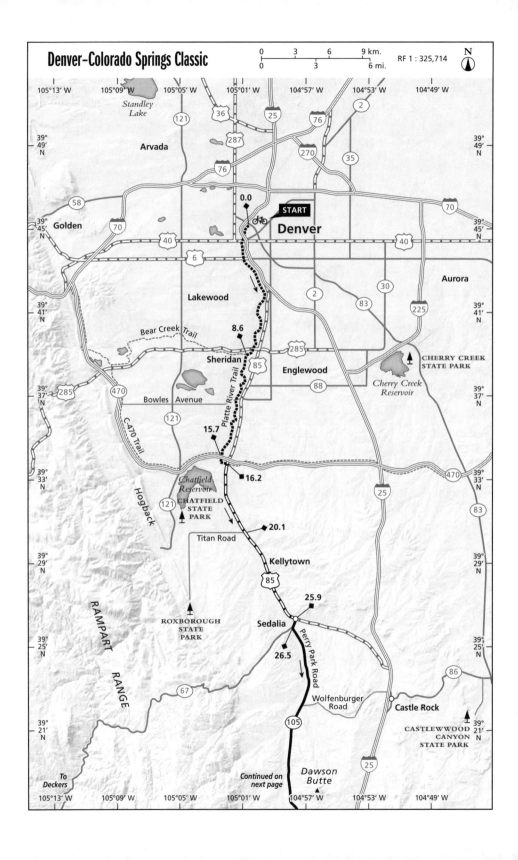

Denver–Colorado Springs Classic

RF 1 : 325,714

0 3 6 9 km.
0 3 6 mi.

N

105°13′ W 105°09′ W 105°05′ W 105°01′ W 104°57′ W 104°53′ W 104°49′ W

Standley Lake

121

36

25

76

2

Arvada

287

270

76

35

0.0

START

🚲 **Denver**

58

70

40

6

Lakewood

40

Aurora

2

30

83

225

39°
49′
N

39°
45′
N

39°
41′
N

Bear Creek Trail

8.6

Sheridan

85

285

Englewood

88

CHERRY CREEK
STATE PARK

Cherry Creek Reservoir

39°
37′
N

470

285

Bowles Avenue

121

Platte River Trail

15.7

16.2

C-470 Trail

39°
33′
N

470

25

83

Chatfield Reservoir

121

CHATFIELD
STATE PARK

20.1

Titan Road

Hogback

39°
29′
N

Kellytown

85

ROXBOROUGH
STATE PARK

25.9

Sedalia

26.5

Perry Park Road

39°
25′
N

86

Castle Rock

CASTLEWOOD
CANYON
STATE PARK

39°
21′
N

RAMPART RANGE

67

105

Wolfenburger
Road

25

To Deckers

Continued on next page

Dawson Butte

105°13′ W 105°09′ W 105°05′ W 105°01′ W 104°57′ W 104°53′ W 104°49′ W

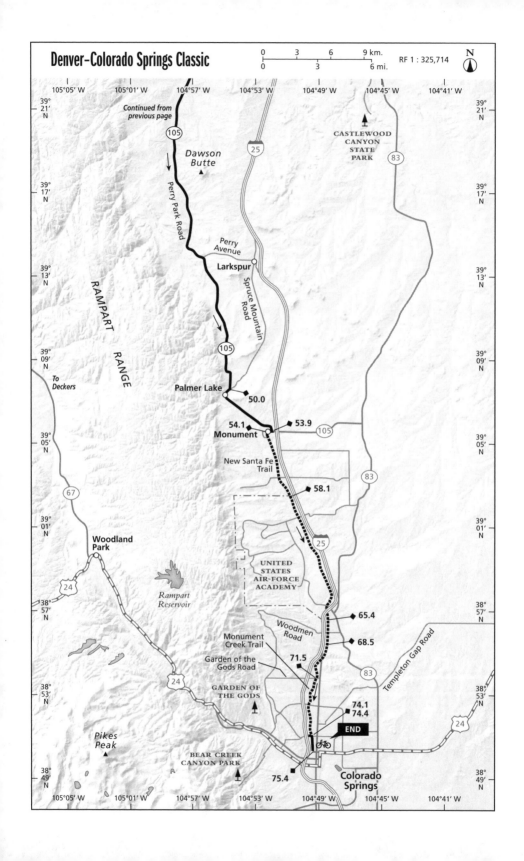

Denver–Colorado Springs Classic

RF 1 : 325,714

N

0   3   6   9 km.
0   3   6 mi.

Continued from
previous page

105

*Dawson
Butte*

CASTLEWOOD
CANYON
STATE
PARK

83

25

Perry Park Road

Perry
Avenue

Larkspur

Spruce Mountain Road

RAMPART

RANGE

*To
Deckers*

105

Palmer Lake ◆ 50.0

54.1 ◆ 53.9
Monument

105

New Santa Fe
Trail

◆ 58.1

67

UNITED
STATES
AIR-FORCE
ACADEMY

25

Woodland
Park

◆ 65.4

24

*Rampart
Reservoir*

Woodmen
Road

◆ 68.5

Monument
Creek Trail

71.5

83

Templeton Gap Road

Garden of the
Gods Road

24

GARDEN OF
THE GODS

74.1
74.4

END

*Pikes
Peak*

BEAR CREEK
CANYON PARK

24

75.4

**Colorado
Springs**

Mountain to the east. Greatly complicating the search for Monkey Face Mountain is the fact that several nearby formations look like monkey faces. Take your pick.

About 24 miles south of Sedalia, ride into Palmer Lake. The lake seems to have dried up, but at least the town is still there. There's a nice little ice-cream and hot dog place on the right as the road curves to the east. The New Santa Fe Trail, the multiuse path (MUP) that will usher you all the way to Colorado Springs, actually starts right near the lake, but you'll continue on the road as it curves east and bombs down a long hill into Monument. The path crosses the road, but it's probably easier to continue into town, through the first light, then take a right on Third Street. Find the trailhead for the New Santa Fe Trail a few blocks west.

The first thing you're going to notice about this trail is its surface: dirt. The second thing you're likely to notice is that the dirt surface is surprisingly smooth and fast. If you get the typical tailwind on this slight downhill, forget about it. It's a blast. Once the path enters Air Force Academy land, it has a habit of diving into a ravine or two and getting squirrelly with deep gravel. There are a few short segments that would be better tackled on a mountain bike, but nothing long enough to break the deal. Considering the alternatives, this dirt trail is a clean and efficient way to approach Colorado Springs.

The United States Air Force Academy was established on these grounds in 1954. Part of the reason this site was chosen over others around the nation was the nearby mountain range, which provides challenging flying conditions for the young cadets. The Santa Fe Trail cuts right through Academy land and is still open to the public, for the time being.[1] You are asked not to leave the path.

The Monument Creek Trail into Colorado Springs, fairly recently connected to the Santa Fe, is a distressing mix of bad asphalt and bad gravel surface. One can expect that improvements will be made piecemeal, when and if money becomes available, to bring the path out of the dark ages. By the time you read this, the whole length of path could be laid out with clean white concrete, 12 feet wide. Yeah, right. Despite its ugly surface the beauty of this facility lies in its complete separation from the street grid. Instead of stopping at lights or stop signs, or running smack into six-lane highways, this MUP drifts right under all of it, all the way into downtown Colorado Springs. So we can forgive a little bad surface. Those who detest the bad surface can jump off at Mark Dabling Boulevard or any number of places farther south. (Actually, those who detest riding on bad surfaces might want to move to Switzerland or someplace like that.)

---

[1] The road into the Academy is open to the cycling public between the North Gate and the cadet area only. The rest of the Academy's excellent roads are controlled-access, unfortunately, due to the new security paradigm. The Academy loop has been a favorite of local riders for a long time, even before it was used for the World Championship Road Race in 1986. On an unseasonably cold day, Moreno Argentin took the race, beating Greg Lemond, Bernard Hinault, et al. I was lucky enough to be there that day. Great disappointment accompanied the realization that I would not be able to include the Academy loop in this guide.

The United States Air Force Academy land from the Santa Fe Trail

Miles and Directions

0.0 Start riding south on the Platte River Trail from the REI store at Confluence Park, Denver. Start your odometer at the bike rack on the east side of the building.

8.6 Cut left across the bridge, toward the golf course, to continue south. (The right fork is the Bear Creek Trail. The mileage on the nearby sign is totally off.)

11.6 Here you can go straight or take a left and cross the bridge—it doesn't matter. You have to cross the river here or a little bit farther on. I took a left here.

12.1 Continue straight here (the other fork at mile 11.6 rejoins from the right).

15.7 After passing under the highway, take a left onto the C-470 Trail east.

16.2 At South Santa Fe Drive/US 85, take a right. This could be a rude awakening, traffic-wise. Climb for about 1 mile. There is adequate shoulder, for the most part, all the way to the Louviers crossroads.

20.1 Cross under Titan Road.

25.9 Take a right onto Highway 67 at Sedalia.

26.1 Pass Plum Avenue and cross over the second set of tracks. **Option:** To circumvent the problem of traffic on US 85, start the ride here, which will cut the classic to 49.6 miles. Just park in the dirt parking lot to the west.

26.5 Take a left onto Perry Park Road.

50.0	At the junction with County Line Road, take a right and roll toward the town of Palmer Lake.
53.9	After the road goes through a traffic light and turns southward, in the business district of Monument, take a right onto Third Street.
54.1	Turn left onto the New Santa Fe Trail.
58.1	Enter United States Air Force Academy grounds. Stay on the trail for the next 7 miles.
62.6	Somewhere in here, get ready for an unrideable little climb or two unless you're on a mountain bike. These sections are very short.
65.4	Exit the Air Force Academy installation.
67.1	Turn left at the fork.
67.5	Join the asphalt path.
67.6	Turn right across the bridge.
68.5	Go right across the bridge. (There is a full-service bike shop right here, to the left.) There will be several points south of here where it will be possible to jump off onto nearby streets.
70.9	Pass the dirt jumping park and the skate park.
71.5	Pass the intersection with the Templeton Gap Trail.
72.3	Cross Polk Street.
72.8	Get onto the road here and follow the signs, then back onto the trail immediately, continuing south. (Portions of the trail through here seem on the verge of falling off the edge of the earth or being constructed anew. One senses that the route could change slightly through this section.)
73.1	Roll through Monument Valley Park. (Ignore the many spur trails to the right.)
74.1	Go under Uintah Street, then left up to the road. Ride up the hill on Uintah.
74.4	Take a right on Cascade Avenue.
75.4	Arrive at downtown Colorado Springs, at the corner of Bijou Street and Cascade Avenue.

Ride Information

Information

Denver Metro Convention & Visitors Bureau, 1555 California, Suite 300, Denver; (800) 233-6837; www.denver.org.

Colorado Springs and Pikes Peak Convention and Visitors Bureau, 515 South Cascade Avenue, Colorado Springs; (877) 745-3773 or (719) 635-7506; www.coloradosprings -travel.com.

Restaurants

The B & E Filling Station, 25 Highway 105, Palmer Lake; (719) 481-4780. In Palmer Lake, an old house converted to intimate dining. Going there in bike clothes is definitely pushing it. A little pricey, reservations advised.

Villa at Palmer Lake, 75 Highway 105, Palmer Lake; (719) 481-2222. Pizza! Pasta! Yeah.

Poor Richard's Feed and Read, 324½ North Tejon Street, Colorado Springs; (719) 632-7721. Bookstore and food combined, just north of downtown Colorado Springs on Tejon. A Springs tradition.

Little Bangkok, 109 East Pikes Peak Avenue, Colorado Springs; (719) 442-6546. Small, casual, family-run Thai restaurant in downtown

Colorado Springs, across from Acacia Park near the Peak Theater. The food is very, very good.

Everest Nepal Restaurant, 28 East Bijou Street, Colorado Springs; (719) 473-3890. Friendly place downtown with exotic and tasty food.

José Muldoon's, 222 North Tejon Street, Colorado Springs; (719) 636-2311. Casual Mexi-merican in a dark cavern of a space, downtown across Tejon from Acacia Park. Beeg, beeg margaritas.

Accommodation

Hearthstone Inn, 506 North Cascade Avenue, Colorado Springs; (719) 473-4413. Bed and breakfast just north of downtown Colorado Springs.

Maps

Delorme: Colorado Atlas & Gazetteer: Pages 40, 50, 51, 63.

Denver and Golden

Before 1858 the area near the confluence of Cherry Creek and the Platte River on Colorado's Front Range was a well-known camp for Indians from several different tribes, who were generally happy to socialize and trade with the trappers and various sorts of mountain men who also frequented the area. When gold flakes winked at prospectors from the banks of Cherry Creek, however, that was all she wrote. The floodgates opened. A mob of speculators came across the prairie in a continuous westward flow, destination: Front Range. The lure of precious metals and get-rich-quick land deals sparked a bloody war with the natives, who were doomed to lose, and gave birth to multiple new settlements on this strip of land where the Rockies sprout abruptly from the plains.

Denver boomed as the center of commerce for the Colorado Territory's explosive mining economy, providing everything from haircuts to smelting. Since 1870 every rail line, from the hundreds of serpentine narrow-gauge lines twisting down from the highest mines to the larger lines fed like rivers by the smaller ones, flowed right into downtown Denver. Locomotives pulled an unending stream of newcomers from the east as well. For a few decades there was probably no town in the world with more energy. It was an unruly mess of unbridled speculation, prostitution, and vigilante justice. That was Denver's moment.

If you look at a photograph from Denver in the 1890s, you'll probably notice bicycles leaning against shop windows and people on bicycles cruising the dirt streets, sharing the road with a crowd of pedestrians, horse-drawn carts, and electric streetcars. Denver was one of the original bike towns. When America rediscovered bicycles in the early 1970s, this rediscovery came to Denver and the rest of the Front Range in a big way. Today it would be too much to say that Denver reveres the bicycle, but certainly there are more bike lovers here than in the typical American city. A sizable population of recreational riders joins an even bigger number of everyday bike users on their way to and from work. The traffic is frequently oppressive, but Denver has plenty of accommodating streets and has made a commitment to elaborate and thoughtfully constructed bicycle facilities to augment them. The result is that Denver is a great place to explore on two wheels—even if it is big, seething, and often frightfully smogged up.

In this section you will find a number of rides in and around the Bovine Metropolis. Some of these rides are on the bicycle paths, some are on the roads, and some use a combination of both. There are also several rides in the foothills west of the city with enough intensity to satisfy the climber in all of us. The excursions using Deer Creek Canyon are some of the nicest rides in the book, and Lookout Mountain west of Golden is a Front Range classic. Golden Gate Canyon is among the most difficult climbs in Colorado—if elevation gain is your goal, head there first. The hills are calling. From the Queen City of the Plains, you can heed the call or choose to ignore it completely.

7 Big South Suburban Bike Path Cruise

This ride takes you on a good-sized tour of south suburban Denver, primarily on fully separated multiuse paths (MUPs).

Start: Confluence Park, lower downtown Denver.
Length: 54.4-mile loop.
Terrain: False flats and rolling hills, generally shallow.
Traffic and hazards: Jordan Road, the connector between the E-470 Trail and the Cherry Creek corridor, is quite busy and not incredibly well suited for cycling. It is a bad road to ride after dark. The rest of the loop is on "bike paths," which carry an increased risk of minor collisions (see below). Clouds of gnats are a frequent annoyance on the MUPs. Even with the Jordan Road connector, this loop is a good ride for those hoping to avoid motor traffic.

Getting there: From downtown Denver go west on 15th Street, under the railroad tracks and over the Platte River, and take the first left after the river onto Platte Street. Park in the free lot by the REI flagship store. It will probably be just as easy, and more enjoyable, to ride to the bike path from a home base in Denver rather than drive and park. From points north or south of Denver, take Interstate 25 to exit 211. Go north on Water Street, under Speer Boulevard, and park in the lot next to or across the street from the REI store. The mileage cues for this ride begin on the east side of the REI and attached Starbucks, in front of the bike rack.

The Ride

Denver is blessed with a relatively extensive network of bicycle paths. Many of these paths can be classified as "fully separated facilities," meaning they are separated from the rest of the traffic grid. Whereas most paths must cross roads at intersections, the fully separated MUP flows under all crossings, like urban freeways. Often these paths are built alongside rivers or canals that already pass beneath the grid. This allows cyclists to ride for miles—sometimes a dozen miles or more in Denver—without ever having to deal with motor traffic.

This happy situation leads many to believe that the MUPs are tantamount to highways for bicycles. They do seem that way sometimes, but in fact, the MUPs are more like sidewalks than highways, as pedestrians hold the right-of-way on these facilities. Frequent interactions with pedestrians, often accompanied by their four-legged companions, and with other cyclists, most of whom are beginners, keep the bike paths sketchy and unpredictable. The current wisdom among cycling gurus is that riding a fully separated MUP brings a somewhat elevated chance of a minor collision compared with street riding, while the absence of car-bike interactions on the separated MUP reduces the risk of deadly injury. MUPs that are *not* separated from the traffic grid, and therefore must cross streets frequently, are probably more dangerous than streets in terms of both minor mishaps and car-bike collisions.[1] Even the fully separated paths are not immune from deadly wrecks. In 2003 a man died after a head-on collision with another rider on one of Denver's south suburban bicycle paths.[2] That particular section of path is featured in this ride—it was not the path that caused the tragedy, but a lack of awareness on the part of the riders.

So, those who use Denver's fully separated bicycle facilities for reasons of safety may be deluding themselves. But the paths remain extremely useful tools for urban transportation—by passing under all major streets while cutting across the city, these paths let cyclists avoid stopping at red lights and stop signs. Stopping is a bigger deal for a cyclist than a motorist. Flowing on the path is a much more pleasant way to travel and, if the path is headed in the right general direction, saves massive amounts of time as well. The paths' tendency to cut through the city on a diagonal tack adds to their usefulness, as it frees us from the tyranny of the right-angle street layout. Diagonals are precious in the game of urban route finding, though not so much for recreational riding.

Those who embark on this loop will have plenty of time to think about MUPs and will undoubtedly form a strong opinion about them by ride's end. From Confluence Park near downtown Denver, where Cherry Creek flows into the South Platte, Denver's two crown-jewel bicycle paths take off toward the distant suburbs: One path heads to Cherry Creek Reservoir to the southeast, the other to Chatfield Reservoir, south-southwest. This big wedge of a loop works nicely in either direction. Somewhat arbitrarily, we'll choose the counterclockwise option and head south on the Platte River Trail to begin.

The Platte River valley near downtown is ground zero for central Denver's new urbanist future. The planners have packed a lot of "attractions" near the Confluence, with more to come. On the left, across the water, is the multicolored Elitch's amusement park. You barely have time to clip in before rolling past the Ocean Journey aquarium, the acclaimed Children's Museum, and the absurdly named Invesco Field at Mile High—the new diaphragm-shaped football stadium. Soon the shiny stuff falls by the wayside, and the Platte River cruise becomes a tour of Denver's industrial

---

[1] While the vast majority of cyclists' accidents and injuries result from solo wipeouts, the vast majority of cyclists' fatalities result from car-bike collisions. Cycling fatalities of any sort are quite rare, relative to both motorists' fatalities and the bulk of cycling-related injuries. Attempts at quantifying the relative danger of riding on different types of facilities should be taken with a grain of salt. John Forester claimed in *Bicycle Transportation: A Handbook for Cycling Transportation Engineers* (Cambridge, Mass.: MIT Press, 1994) that a cyclist on a bicycle path is 2.6 times more likely to be involved in an accident than a rider on a street (p. 9). Forester's claim had to do with "side paths" and older-style bike paths, and probably does not translate well to Denver's modern fully separated facilities. Just figure that the paths are probably not as safe as you think they are and proceed from there.

[2] Marilyn Robinson, "Bicyclist Killed in Collision," *Denver Post,* 16 October 2003. The article quotes a Littleton police sergeant as saying the path is 5 feet wide in the area of the accident. In fact, the path is about 10 feet wide.

Elitch's amusement park from beneath the Speer Boulevard bridge

underbelly. You'll see two power plants, a cement plant, the garbage relay station, and a massive salvage yard, all bathed in the smell of sewage treatment. The Platte itself has been the ultimate beast of burden.

As if that weren't enough for delicate bikies to deal with, there are also . . . the gnats. Hovering over the banks of the Platte River are intermittent clouds of otherwise innocuous bugs. Encountering these clouds is almost inevitable during gnat season—about six months out of the year—and feels like somebody is standing off to the side of the path tossing handfuls of rice at your face. Mmm, protein.

The continuation of the Platte River Trail south of the Denver city limits is called the Mary Carter Greenway Trail. (It is typical around here that the same path changes names several times along its length, so try not to get too bent out of shape about the name of whatever path you happen to be on at any given time.) South of the Bear Creek turnoff after mile 8.6, the land around the MUP really opens up. Here it is easy to forget that you're still smack in the middle of a sprawling sea of city. As you approach the C-470 highway, you are poking around at the very edges of south suburban Denver, having already emerged from Lakewood, Englewood, and Littleton. Denver's suburban explosion since World War II has been completely off the hook.

Big South Suburban Bike Path Cruise

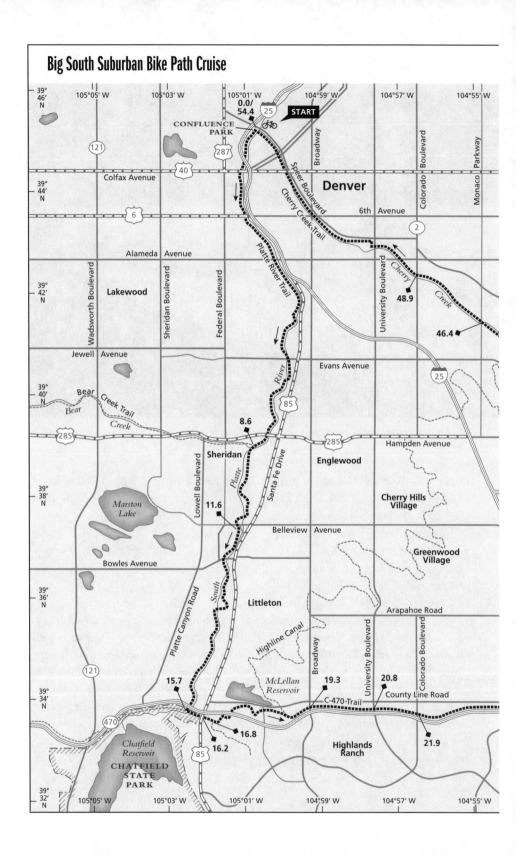

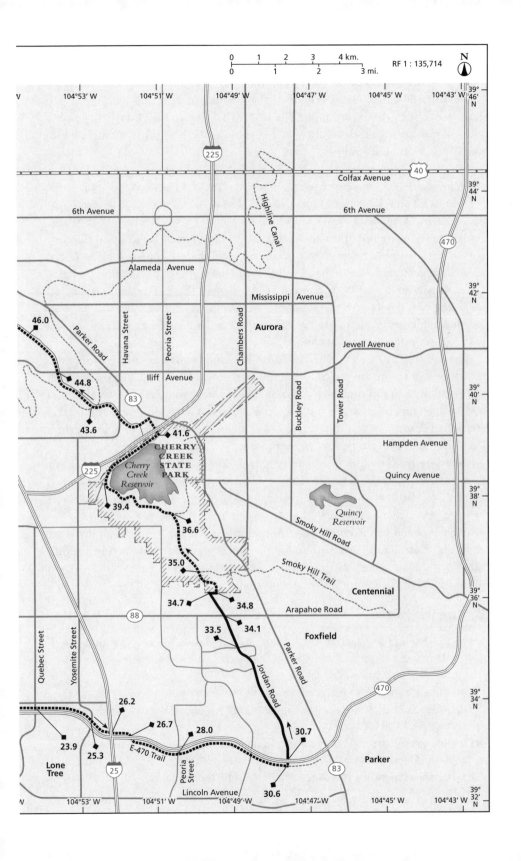

Take a left when the southward path runs into another MUP running east-west along C-470. Here it's called the C-470 Trail, but without warning the same path becomes the Highline Canal Trail, then the Centennial Trail, and then the E-470 Trail. Just go with the eastward flow. The C-470/E-470 path has a lot of sharp rollers and will make itself felt, especially with a headwind. This is usually the toughest section of the loop, headwind or not.

At mile 16.2 something really weird happens: The path crosses Santa Fe Drive at a regular intersection instead of passing under it. That was quite a run of carless riding you had. This intersection breaks the spell. The remainder of the E-470 path features a series of similar crossings, with long stretches of unbroken path in between.

It is unfortunate that you have to turn north onto Jordan Road when the time comes to turn north, rather than turning onto another nice, wide bike path. For years area cyclists have had a dream—that the section of bike path south of Cherry Creek Reservoir would be connected all the way to the E-470 path, creating an unbroken MUP loop. At the time of this writing, however, the path sections remained unlinked. Riders must use the roads to reach the Cherry Creek Trail, and Jordan provides the most direct link.

Entering Cherry Creek State Park from the south, you have some options as to how you want to circumvent, or loiter around, the reservoir. Roads and paths go left and right. You can roll clockwise or counterclockwise around the reservoir and not notice much difference in terms of required exertion. The mileage cues assume that you turn left south of the reservoir and roll around its west side. This allows for a long, fast descent on the path north of the dam.

North-northwest from the Cherry Creek Reservoir, the extremely popular Cherry Creek Trail cuts a diagonal through dense residential areas, helping cyclists avoid some of the worst traffic in town. The final 10 miles or so into Confluence Park are quite fast, with the path slightly downhill beside Cherry Creek.

Well, how did you like it? It's rare to find such a lengthy trip through the heart of a major metropolitan area with so little car-bike interaction. After a ride like this, you'll likely have gained an appreciation for the advantages of the fully separated MUPs, and a recognition of their imperfections.

Miles and Directions

0.0 From the east side of the REI store at 15th and Platte Streets in lower downtown Denver, start riding south on the Platte River Trail, a wide concrete bike path that runs alongside the Platte River on the west side.

1.3 Ignore the paths to the right (the Lakewood Gulch Trail and an unnamed spur).

8.6 Intersect with the Bear Creek Trail, turn left (south), and cross the river. Cut south through Englewood Golf Course.

11.6 Here you can go straight or take a left and cross the bridge—it doesn't matter. You have to cross the river here or a little bit farther on. I took a left here.

12.1 Continue straight here (the other fork from mile 11.6 rejoins from the right).

15.7 Take a left onto the C-470 Trail east.

16.2 Cross Santa Fe Drive, probably after waiting for a stoplight for the first time on this ride.

16.8 Turn left, joining the Highline Canal Trail.

17.7 Stay left at the fork (the right fork heads to Lucent Boulevard).

19.3 Cross Broadway.

20.8 Cross University Boulevard.

21.9 Cross Colorado Boulevard.

23.9 Cross Quebec Street.

24.3 Cross Acres Green Drive.

25.3 Cross Yosemite Street. Here you have to cross to the south side of the exit ramp to resume on the path.

26.2 Under I–25 and various off-shoots.

26.7 The path spills out onto a road. Take a right onto this road momentarily, cross under E-470, and resume on the path south of the highway.

28.0 Cross Peoria Street.

30.6 Take a left on Jordan Road.

30.7 Cross back under E-470.

33.5 Still rolling north on Jordan Road, cross East Fremont Avenue.

34.1 Cross Arapahoe Road.

34.7 Take a right on East Caley Avenue.

34.8 Take a left onto the bike path again (headed north). Here you are entering Cherry Creek State Park.

35.0 Stay left (the Smoky Hill Trail branches off here).

36.6 The trail spills out onto the road. Take a left onto the road or cross and continue on the path, which will meander around a bit but basically follows the road.

39.4 The road arrives at the west edge of the park at Dayton Road. Take a right on Dayton.

39.5 Cross East Union Avenue and get on the concrete path, headed east. You'll be back in the fully separated realm for a while. The path passes Village Greens Park and its parking lot and descends rapidly in the open space between the dam and I–225.

41.6 Hang a left at the fork. Swoop down a steep hill and go under I–225.

43.6 Stay right as the Highline Canal Trail (again!) branches off to the left.

44.8 The path goes under Iliff Avenue in a sort of cloverleaf.

46.0 The path abruptly turns right and crosses Cherry Creek on a bridge. On the other side of the creek, you have the choice to turn left onto the street or continue on the path, which twists pointlessly through the park beside the street.

46.4 Cross Monaco Parkway.

47.0 Cross Holly Street.

48.2 Pass the Four Mile Historic Park.

48.9 Pass under Colorado Boulevard and enter the Cherry Creek district.

54.4 Arrive back at Confluence Park.

Ride Information

Information

Denver Metro Convention & Visitors Bureau, 1555 California, Suite 300, Denver; (800) 233-6837; www.denver.org.

Restaurants

Wazee Supper Club, 1600 15th Street, Denver; (303) 623-9518. High-quality pizza in lower downtown.

Wahoo Fish Taco, 1521 Blake Street, Denver; (303) 623-0263. California-style Mexican food and a surf-inspired atmosphere. Good cheap food downtown.

Paris on the Platte, 1553 Platte Street, Denver; (303) 455-2451. Sandwiches, coffee, etc., in a casually hip bookstore/cafe. Very close to Confluence Park.

Rocky Mountain Diner, 800 18th Street, Denver; (303) 293-8383. Large portions of hearty western-style American food, including the ubiquitous buffalo meatloaf. In the heart of downtown in one of Denver's oldest surviving buildings, the "Ghost Building."

Fontano's Chicago Subs, 1623 California Street, Denver; (720) 956-1100. Open 'til 3:00 P.M. every day but Sunday. Get down there. Best meatball sub I've ever had.

16th Street Deli, 500 16th Street, Pavilions Mall, Denver; (720) 956-0440. The "half" sandwich is big. The "whole" is a real sandwich. Worth the trip uptown.

Tommy's Thai, 3410 East Colfax Avenue, Denver; (303) 377-4244. Quite cheap for good quality food and the whole town knows it. A few miles east of downtown on Colfax.

Mizuna, 225 East 7th Avenue, Denver; (303) 832-4778. This highly touted restaurant has been called the best in Denver. Upscale, reservations.

Le Central, 112 East 8th Avenue, Denver; (303) 863-8094. Authentic French cuisine, moderately priced. Reservations recommended.

Platte River Bar & Grill, 5995 South Santa Fe Drive, Littleton; (303) 798-9356. The Platte River bike path passes right by the back door of this place.

Maps

Delorme: Colorado Atlas & Gazetteer: Pages 40-41 C-1-4, D-1-4.

8 Bear Creek-Morrison Half-Century Cruise

This moderate half century departs from downtown Denver and reaches to the geologically spectacular foothills around Morrison and the Red Rocks amphitheater. The ride cuts through the heart of Denver without encountering motor traffic by following fully separated multiuse paths (MUPs) for most of its length.

Start: The intersection of the two MUPs, Cherry Creek Trail and the Platte River Trail (which, of course, is also very near the confluence of Cherry Creek and the Platte), just east of the REI store in central Denver.

Length: 48.2-mile loop.

Terrain: Gently rolling and flat terrain through Denver, then some moderate climbs on and around Dakota Ridge near Morrison.

Traffic and hazards: Much of this route utilizes multiuse paths that are very popular but nonetheless provide cyclists with the swiftest and safest way to connect with the outskirts near Morrison. Hazards on the path include joggers, walkers, staggering transients, dogs, other cyclists, and yourself. A narrow and well-used MUP demands just as much attention as a high-traffic roadway. Keep your head up and your eyes peeled. The sections of road along this route have moderate, occasionally heavy traffic. The road uphill and north out of Morrison between Red Rocks and the hogback can seem uncomfortably narrow in a few spots. Cars travel at high speed along Morrison Road, but the shoulder is wide.

Getting there: From downtown Denver go west on 15th Street, under the railroad tracks and over the Platte River, and take the first left after the river onto Platte Street. Park in the free lot by the REI flagship store. From points north or south of Denver, take Interstate 25 to exit 211. Go north on Water Street, under Speer Boulevard, and park in the lot next to or across the street from the REI store. The mileage cues for this ride begin on the east side of the REI and attached Starbucks, in front of the bike rack.

The Ride

Taking off from Confluence Park and the LoDo REI store[1] on a wide, smooth concrete path, this ride cruises south beside the Platte River, past power plants, around hobos, and through clouds of gnats, until the sight of downtown Denver has been miniaturized on the horizon. Despite its real-world shortcomings, the Platte River path is fast and much loved by Denver cyclists. You could follow the Platte River Trail from downtown all the way south to Chatfield Reservoir, a distance of more than 15 miles, and connect with paths headed east or west along the edge of the metroplex. For this ride, however, you'll take off to the west on the novel Bear Creek path after a mere 8 miles beside the Platte, still ensconced in urban density.

---

[1]The REI flagship store occupies the same hulking building that used to house the workings of Denver's old cable car system, and, after the rails were torn out, the Forney Transportation Museum.

Looking north up the C-470 Trail

Riders who are new to this route may feel as if they have embarked on a very interesting adventure. The Bear Creek bike path is creatively routed as it cuts through the borough of Englewood like a hot knife through butter, utilizing the back parking lots of strip malls and grocery stores, slipping through the narrow passages between the gulch of Bear Creek and backyards, charging through long strips of suburban park. Like its better-developed cousins, the Platte River Trail and the Cherry Creek Trail, the Bear Creek Trail is a very useful tool for cyclists because it dives under all major boulevards on its journey west and there is very little mandatory stopping. The surface of the Bear Creek throughway leaves something to be desired in comparison to Denver's two main MUPs, but it remains passable even on the most fragile road bike. Eager cyclists need to keep in mind, however, that any multiuse path like this is the domain of the pedestrian. As with any sidewalk, the cyclist is obligated to yield to all peds. There may even be a few times when the rider must slow to walking pace behind a group stretching across the trail. For the most part these encounters are rare along this route, but there are hot spots of pedestrian activity, especially in the parks near miles 10.5 and 12.0 and the big open field after mile 13.0. If you are one of those devoted vehicular cyclists, it is quite possible you will hate the Bear Creek Trail with every fiber of your being.

The farther it travels from the urban core, the less direct the Bear Creek path becomes. A wildly meandering bike path—is it a sign of civilization's decline or of its advancement? At mile 16.0, up against yet another golf course, you can continue down the golf club road to find the path again or jump on Morrison Road for a much more direct attack on the town of Morrison. The ride described here uses Morrison Road for this leg and the much longer and more scenic bike path for the return trip. Either way will get you there, over a 300-foot climb.

The little town of Morrison is a hub for many ride possibilities. In this case you'll veer right at the first opportunity, before you really enter the town, and head north up a long, steady, and straight climb just west of the Dakota Ridge. The so-called hogback is a vestige of a slab of rock that was originally created from sedimentary deposits laid down flat a few hundred million years ago. When the Rockies were formed, the slab was shoved upward at an obscene angle, along with the more famous red rocks to the west.[2] Differential erosion has since carved this spectacular landscape by removing some rock formations at a faster rate than others.[3]

In the 1870s the area's new inhabitants from the east discovered stuck in the hogback whole dinosaur skeletons from the Jurassic. The huge skeletons were removed to museums, but today there are outdoor exhibits explaining exposed fossils and tracks if you wish to check them out. The dinosaur track exhibit on the east side of the hogback is worth stopping for, even in the middle of a satisfying descent.

Having crossed the hogback, head south on the heavily cracked but fast C-470 bike trail on the east side of the highway. This route takes you past the famous Bandimere Speedway nestled against Dakota Ridge. At Morrison Road you can head east and backtrack all the way home or continue south on the bike path as it crosses a big open area (by Soda Lakes) and loops around the south side of Bear Creek Reservoir. The route described in this chapter continues south on the path, making the crossing of Morrison Road the intersecting point of a figure eight.

This section of path around Bear Creek Reservoir is far from the most efficient means of returning to town, but it certainly is worth a look. The path is usually nearly empty as it rolls pleasantly past Soda Lakes and around the reservoir, through chirping wetlands and high grasses. There is one sharp, twisting climb and a corresponding descent before the path ends at the golf course access road. Continue down this road to the same place you saw at mile 16.0, where you find the Bear Creek path again, headed south around a condo complex. If you're tired here, it will feel like a long, plodding 16 miles back to lower downtown.

If you're looking for a change of scenery, leave the path and head into Denver's expansive residential grid. There are countless ways to get home on the streets and

---

[2]The roads through Red Rocks Park offer a tempting side-trip opportunity for those looking for more challenge. The climb on the south side of the park leading up to the upper parking lot above the amphitheater is a brutal lung buster. The rest of the roads are moderate.

[3]Halka Chronic, *Roadside Geology of Colorado* (Missoula, Mont.: Mountain Press, 1980), pp. 76–78.

Bear Creek-Morrison Half-Century Cruise

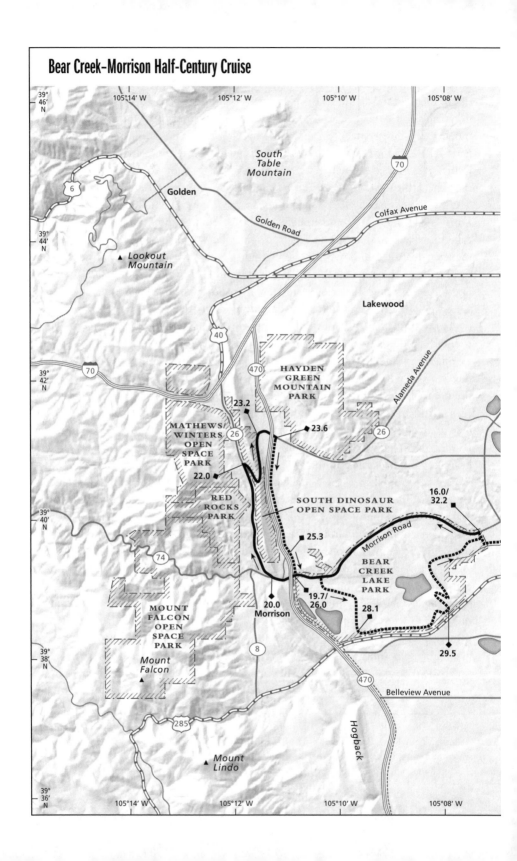

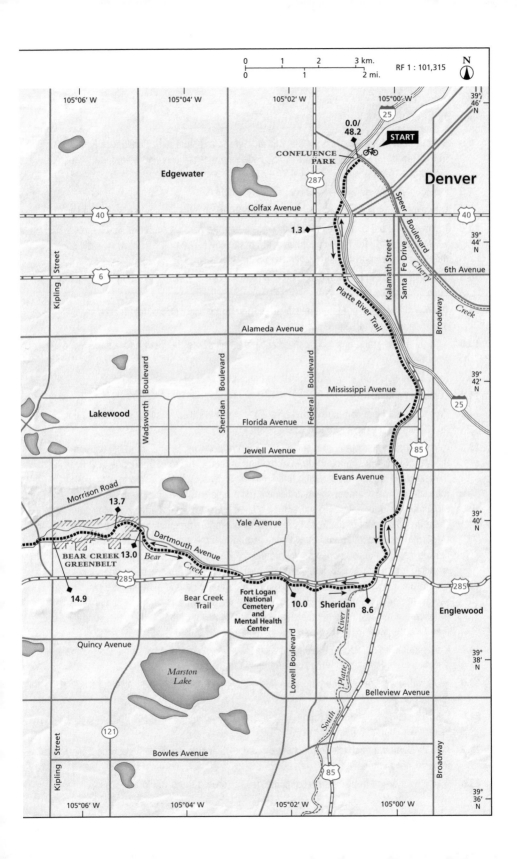

RF 1 : 101,315

N

105°06' W
105°04' W
105°02' W
105°00' W

39° 46' N

0.0/ 48.2

START

CONFLUENCE PARK

Edgewater

287

Denver

Colfax Avenue

40
40

39° 44' N

1.3 ♦

6
6

Kipling Street

6th Avenue

Santa Fe Drive
Kalamath Street
Speer Boulevard
Cherry
Broadway

Platte River Trail

Alameda Avenue

Cherry Creek

Wadsworth Boulevard
Sheridan Boulevard
Federal Boulevard

Mississippi Avenue

39° 42' N

25

Lakewood

Florida Avenue

Jewell Avenue

85

Evans Avenue

39° 40' N

Morrison Road

13.7

Yale Avenue

Dartmouth Avenue

BEAR CREEK GREENBELT

13.0

Bear Creek

285

285

14.9

Bear Creek Trail

Fort Logan National Cemetery and Mental Health Center

10.0

Sheridan

8.6

Englewood

Lowell Boulevard

Platte River

Quincy Avenue

Marston Lake

39° 38' N

Belleview Avenue

Kipling Street

121

South Platte

Bowles Avenue

85

Broadway

39° 36' N

105°06' W
105°04' W
105°02' W
105°00' W

countless dead-ends keeping you from getting there. Those who don't know the street layout will surely get caught in the net.

Miles and Directions

0.0 Start in front of the bike rack on the east side of the REI store near Confluence Park. Ride south down the Platte River Trail, the wide strip of white concrete following the west side of the Platte River.

1.3 Continue straight as other paths connect on the right.

8.6 Veer right onto the Bear Creek Trail. (The Platte River Trail continues south over a bridge.)

10.0 The trail spills out onto a road. Carefully cross the road and jog south about 10 meters, where the Bear Creek MUP continues south of the creek. The trail is choppy as it slips through the greenway behind Mullen High School.

10.6 Turn right, cross a narrow bridge, then head left through a park likely to be playing host to multiple barbecues.

11.4 The trail passes behind a commercial strip. There are grocery stores, fast-food chains, and even a bike shop along this stretch.

13.0 As if you could stand any more convenience, the trail passes very close to a convenience store here.

13.7 Pass an intersection with another MUP to the left.

13.9 Continue straight.

14.9 Cross a street here, continue on the MUP. (This street is called "Kipling," but it is not the real Kipling, a big boulevard just west of here.)

16.0 Here the path spills out onto a street, and you are faced with a choice: to continue on the MUP (which can be found down at the end of the nearby road that leads west past the golf club) or jump on Morrison Road, the big highway a few steps north of you. Both routes lead to the same place, but they are quite different. Morrison Road is a straight, moderate climb for about 1.5 miles, then a short coast down to the town of Morrison. There is a good deal of traffic, but the shoulder is ample. The continuation of the Bear Creek path meanders around the golf course and over the sharp hill to the south, then cruises through the wide-open space around the Bear Creek Reservoir. The path route to Morrison is almost twice as long as the Morrison Road route from this location. The elevation gain is about the same, although the climb on the path is more intense (which you might not guess from the mileage). Although either way will work in both directions, to follow the mileage cues here, continue west on Morrison Road on the westbound leg, then take the MUP route on the return leg (see mile 26.0 below).

19.7 Cross under C-470. Pedal past the convenience store and around the bend. (You will be approaching this point from the north a bit later in the ride.)

20.0 Veer right just before entering the town (Mount Vernon Road). Stay right again at stops at miles 20.1 and 20.2.

22.0 Take the sharp right here, headed back southeast, climbing the hogback. This road is called West Alameda Parkway.

23.2 After crossing the hogback and rushing down the other side, curve right past the Dakota Ridge Visitor Center.

23.6 Take a right onto the bike path. (Using the nearby Rooney Road would also work.)

25.3 Take a right onto the road here. Pass under the highway. The path reappears on the other side of C-470—you can use the path or just stay on the road as it curls south and cruises past Bandimere Speedway all the way to Morrison Road.

26.0 Cross Morrison Road and jump on the bike path just opposite.

26.3 Turn right here, staying on the bike path. The path will climb a bit, twisting but heading in a general southward direction.

28.1 Stay left as the path forks.

29.5 Stay left as the path forks again.

29.6 Turn right at the top of a steep climb.

30.1 After a fast descent with tight turns, the path spits you out onto a virtually unused service road.

31.6 Pass through the golf club parking lot.

32.2 The road connects to Morrison Road here. This is the same spot you passed at mile 16.0. This time find the Bear Creek Path and begin backtracking.

48.2 Arrive back at the start.

Ride Information

Events/Attractions

Dakota Ridge Visitor Center, 16831 West Alameda Parkway, on the east side of the hogback; (303) 697-3466; www.dinoridge.org. A low-key building with some explication of the area's geological history, and a parking lot.

Bandimere Speedway, located north of Morrison Road on the east flank of the hogback; (303) 697-6001; www.bandimere.com. A world-famous drag strip—bring earplugs if the alcohol- or nitro-burning cars are running.

Red Rocks Amphitheater (www.redrocks online.com) hosts an endless variety of concerts and events. You can literally ride your bike right onto the stage if nothing's going on (but you've got to climb a big hill to get there). Located north of Morrison and west of Road 93, behind those giant red rocks. Entrance off Road 93, or Morrison Road just west of town. Ticketing is handled by Ticketmaster; (303) 830-TIXS; www.ticketmaster.com.

Restaurants

Wazee Supper Club, 1600 15th Street, Denver; (303) 623-9518. High-quality pizza in lower downtown.

Wahoo Fish Taco, 1521 Blake Street, Denver; (303) 623-0263. California-style Mexican food and a surf-inspired atmosphere. Good cheap food downtown.

Paris on the Platte, 1553 Platte Street, Denver; (303) 455-2451. Sandwiches, coffee, etc., in a casually hip bookstore/cafe. Very close to Confluence Park.

Morrison Inn, 301 Bear Creek Avenue, Morrison; (303) 697-6650. Mexican food in Morrison, right on the main drag.

Dream Cafe, 119 Bear Creek Avenue, Morrison; (303) 697-1280. After a ride I dream of food. Sometimes during a ride. Lunch, dinner, coffee drinks. Closed Mondays.

Willy's Wings, 109 Bear Creek Avenue, Morrison; (303) 697-1232. If you like tiny chicken parts, Willy's is the place.

Blue Cow Cafe, 316 Bear Creek Avenue, Morrison; (303) 697-5721. Breakfast and lunch, ice cream and shakes.

Maps

Delorme: Colorado Atlas & Gazetteer: Page 40 C1, C2.

9 Morrison MUP Cruise

This is a unique southwest Denver metro loop starting from Morrison, ridden almost entirely on fully separated multiuse paths (MUPs).

Start: Morrison.
Length: 34.9-mile loop.
Terrain: There are some surprisingly tough rollers along the C-470 Trail. The rest is quite flat.
Traffic and hazards: This loop is almost entirely car-free. That's a happy thought.

Exercise special care, however, as the chance of running into something is actually greater on the path than it is on the street. Remember also that bike paths like these are actually bicycle-pedestrian paths on which the pedestrians always have the right-of-way.

Getting there: From central Denver and points north, take Interstate 70 or 6th Avenue west to C-470, go south on C-470 to the Morrison exit, then go west into Morrison on the main drag (Highway 8/Highway 74/Morrison Road). From south-central Denver take U.S. Highway 285/West Hampden Avenue west to C-470; take C-470 north briefly to the Morrison exit, then north, as the highway curves around the city, to Morrison. From extreme-south Denver and points south, take C-470 west all the way to the Morrison exit. Once in Morrison turn around and park in one of the spaces next to Bear Creek. Start the ride by riding east along Morrison Road (there is a good "sidepath" heading out of town on the south side of the road by the parking spaces), cross Soda Lakes Road, and turn right onto the Bear Creek Trail across from Rooney Road. Reset the odometer as you begin riding the Bear Creek Trail from Morrison Road.

The Ride

Over the decades the idea of separate facilities for cyclists has been a serious point of contention within the cycling community. To some, the very concept of a separate facility for bicyclists, whether it be a painted line on the street or some kind of bicycle-pedestrian path, is something to be fought against tooth and nail. The proliferation of separate facilities, they say, is a sign of the end-times for cyclists' right to the roadways. To some others, who never want to ride their bikes on the streets in the first place, the thought of separate facilities fills them with joy and comfort.

Around metro Denver this ongoing debate has been complicated mightily by the presence of several MUPs that don't conform to the conventional wisdom. Instead of spitting riders out at busy intersections every other block, they flow unbroken under major streets. Instead of being skinny and made of asphalt, they are wide and made of smooth, durable concrete. When it's all said and done, instead of being good-for-nothing recreational paths, they are put to use on a daily basis by commuters and other transportational cyclists, as well as by those just looking for a fun ride. Even in Denver there are plenty of questionable facilities. But the proliferation

C-470 Trail

of these well-designed paths gives us hope for the future. Denver is far ahead of many other big cities in this regard.

This loop gives riders a chance to roll on a nearly car-free loop in southwest Denver and to check out long sections of three different mega-paths in the process. For one magical stretch this route takes riders right through the guts of the metro area for 13 miles without crossing a single street. It really is a sight to behold.

Starting from Morrison, your first section of MUP takes you south across the bucolic open space around Soda Lakes. Watch for coyotes, and veer right onto the C-470 Trail for an extended southward cruise. The C-470 Trail is a straight shot beside the freeway (although not so close that it's really noticeable). The terrain is not flat. The path speeds primarily downhill and fast with occasional challenging humps. Wind direction will have a strong influence on how quick you feel on the exposed C-470 Trail. The condition of the surface is also an issue. Once nice and smooth, this Portland cement concrete surface is badly faulted and lends some unwelcome roughness to the ride. It's not a fully separated path, but almost, forcing riders to cross five streets on its 9-mile arcing journey around the southwest edge of the Denver metro area.

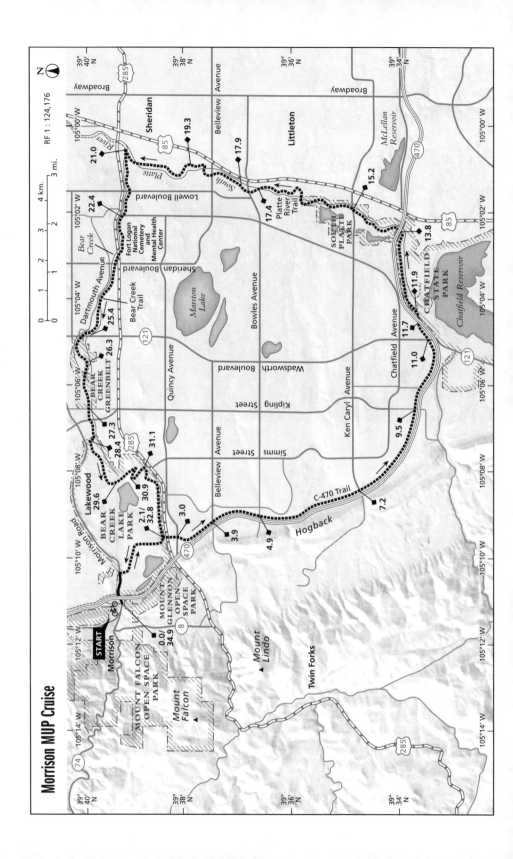

Morrison MUP Cruise

RF 1 : 124,176

The next part of this loop is northbound on the Platte River Trail—actually, it's known as the Mary Carter Greenway Trail down south, but if we have to use all the technical names for these different path sections, things get quite silly. This is the same trail that runs all the way from the C-470 Trail north into downtown Denver, sharing the floodplain with the Platte River and Santa Fe Drive/U.S. Highway 85. Call it what you want, but most folks around here call it the Platte River Trail. It's one of the favorites, very popular with recreational cyclists and commuters. On the south end it's not overrun with pedestrians, and cyclists can roll safely at a good clip. Just keep your head up, hold your line, and watch for riders coming in the other direction. As you approach downtown, the trail becomes more crowded with various sorts of pedestrians. On this loop, however, you'll turn off the Platte Trail and onto the Bear Creek Trail before you get too close to central Denver.

The Bear Creek Trail is an interesting ride; it follows the culvert of Bear Creek through the backyards and back lots of Sheridan and Lakewood, twisting sharply, darkly shaded and tucked away. This path meanders uselessly through a park or two—such fanciful routing is part of what makes strict utilitarian cyclists grumble about MUPs. But the Bear Creek Trail remains a useful tool even for the utilitarians, as it is almost completely separated from the street grid and therefore avoids red lights and other traffic-related delays. Pedestrians—who have the legal right-of-way, remember—can be a problem where this trail passes through strips of suburban parkland. You know how it is: You've had a few beers, you're heavily loaded with about six pounds of charred meat, and you're just not thinking about looking both ways before you cross the bike path. Give these guys a wide berth, wider if the Broncos lost that week.

The section of the Bear Creek Trail west of the Fox Hollow golf club is something else entirely. The land opens up. After climbing about 300 vertical feet above the golf club, you find yourself on top of the highest hill in the immediate vicinity, looking out at Bear Creek Reservoir and the accompanying open space, which is more than ten times as big as the reservoir itself. The nearest house is distant. A thrilling dive to the lowlands starts the final phase of this loop, across the blowing fields between the reservoir and Soda Lakes. Even those who hate the very idea of bicycle paths would have to enjoy that last unique segment of the Bear Creek Trail.

Miles and Directions

0.0 Start by turning south onto the bike path off Morrison Road, across from Rooney Road.

0.3 Turn right here, staying on the bike path. The path will climb a bit, twisting but heading in a general southward direction.

0.5 Stay right.

0.8 Cross a small road, and stay right.

2.1 Take a right at the fork.

2.9   After crossing over US 285, the path spills out onto pavement. Continue straight, passing a convenience store.

3.0   Cross West Quincy Avenue and continue south on the bike path.

3.9   Cross Belleview Avenue.

4.9   Cross West Bowles Avenue.

7.2   Cross West Ken Caryl Avenue.

9.5   Cross Kipling Parkway.

11.0   The path dives under Wadsworth Boulevard. Watch for the pinch-flat-causing and rim-bashing lip of concrete as you go into the tunnel.

11.7   Go left here (the path will curl back around to the south and go under C-470).

11.9   Stay left at the fork at the top of the hill, continuing on the C-470 Trail east.

13.8   Continue straight. (The right fork is the continuation of the C-470 Trail east; straight ahead the trail morphs into the Mary Carter Greenway Trail, which heads back under C-470 and north alongside the Platte River.)

15.2   Crossing under Mineral Avenue, ignore the spur trails heading off right and left.

17.4   Continue straight here. (You can actually take a left here across the river or continue straight, it doesn't matter; you'll have to cross over the river eventually anyway, and you'll end up in the same place.)

17.9   Go left across the bridge (don't go straight to Prince Street).

19.3   Pass the intersection with the Big Dry Creek Trail.

21.0   North of the Englewood Municipal Golf Course, cross the river again and take a left onto the Bear Creek Trail.

22.4   Cross the road (carefully!) and jog south about 10 meters to continue on the Bear Creek Trail. The trail surface leaves something to be desired on this section behind Mullen High School.

22.9   Turn right across the bridge. On the other side of the creek, take a left into a long park.

23.8   The path passes behind a shopping complex with a McDonald's and a bike shop.

25.4   Pass a convenience store and go under Wadsworth Boulevard.

26.3   Continue straight (not right across the bridge).

27.3   Cross Kipling Street.

28.4   The path spills out onto a road. Go west here on the road toward the Fox Hollow golf club. **Option:** To shorten the loop in a no-nonsense style, get on Morrison Road here and chug over the hill and straight into Morrison. This option cuts the rest of the mileage and scenery by about half.

29.6   After the road winds through the golf course, it eventually points back east and dead-ends. There you will find the continuation of the Bear Creek Trail, at the bottom of a tough little climb.

30.9   At the edge of the mesa, take a sharp left and descend.

31.1   Stay right as another trail comes in on your left.

32.8   Take a right at the fork and begin backtracking on the same route you rode in on.

34.9   The path spills out onto the road near Morrison.

Ride Information

Restaurants

Morrison Inn, 301 Bear Creek Avenue, Morrison; (303) 697-6650. Mexican food in Morrison, right on the main drag.

Dream Cafe, 119 Bear Creek Avenue, Morrison; (303) 697-1280. After a ride I dream of food. Sometimes during a ride. Lunch, dinner, coffee drinks. Closed Mondays.

Willy's Wings, 109 Bear Creek Avenue, Morrison; (303) 697-1232. If you like tiny chicken parts, Willy's is the place.

Blue Cow Cafe, 316 Bear Creek Avenue, Morrison; (303) 697-5721. Breakfast and lunch, ice cream and shakes.

The Fort, 19192 Highway 8, Morrison; (303) 697-4771. Eat Old West food in a replica of an Old West fort. Located south of Morrison a few miles on Highway 8, near its intersection with US 285.

Platte River Bar & Grill, 5995 South Santa Fe Drive, Littleton; (303) 798-9356. The Platte River bike path passes right by the back door of this place.

Maps

Bicycling the Greater Denver Area Route Map (Mapsco).

10 Deer Creek Canyon-Evergreen Challenge

This satisfying chunk of a ride proves that you don't have to go to Boulder to find nice canyons to conquer. Southwest of Denver, Deer Creek Canyon climbs about 9 solid miles on its way to South Turkey Creek Road near U.S. Highway 285. But this route goes above and beyond Deer Creek, tackling North Turkey Creek Canyon and gaining another thousand feet. Bomb down to Evergreen and enter Bear Creek Canyon, a gradual descent all the way into Morrison. From Morrison pick up an interesting and fast section of bike path that takes you back to the start.

Start: The bottom of Deer Creek Canyon Road near its intersection with South Wadsworth Boulevard, at the extreme southwest of the Denver metro area.

Length: 43.0-mile loop.

Terrain: From the red rocks of the foothills to fresh pine forests and back again. Long, gradual climbs and descents, with a few steep ones thrown in for good measure.

Traffic and hazards: Deer Creek Canyon is a well-used route for commuters in a god-awful hurry to get home. Avoid rush hours, if possible. Some tight curves in the canyon produce the typical frustrations for motorists who want to pass and can't. But this is a very popular bike route with generally good-natured motorists and ordinary surface hazards (ordinary except for the occasional rattlesnake at the bottom of Deer Creek Canyon).

Getting there: The start is located at the extreme southwest corner of the Denver metro area, near the intersection of Wadsworth Boulevard and C-470, west of Chatfield Reservoir. C-470 is part of a loop freeway around the city, so it may be the best route to take from many parts of town. From central Denver drive south on Interstate 25 or any major boulevard to C-470, go west

Descending Bear Creek Canyon

on C-470 to the Wadsworth Boulevard exit, drive south a quarter mile, and turn right onto Deer Creek Canyon Road. Park in the dirt parking lot there by the side of the road. (Although this is a makeshift parking area, it is legal, and the traditional spot for Deer Creek Canyon riders to park their vehicles. It's likely there will be a half-dozen or so cars there already.)

The Ride

Spilling out onto the rolling plains at the extreme southwestern tip of Denver's sub-urban sprawl, Deer Creek Canyon provides some of the finest road biking on the entire Front Range. Serious roadies from all over the region make the trip here to enjoy the hill. Most drive to the mouth of the canyon, but due to the proximity of southern Denver's excellent network of bike paths, many ambitious individuals actu-ally ride to the start from their home bases around the metro area.

This high-quality loop starts out on the flat, not far from the intersection of C-470 and Wadsworth Boulevard, at the bottom of Deer Creek Canyon Road. The road taxies for a few miles to the red rocks of the canyon entrance. On the right is the shiny Lockheed Martin plant immortalized in Michael Moore's *Bowling for Columbine;* on the left, a satellite of Denver's Botanic Gardens.

The real climb starts after mile 3, rather gradually at first, and is sustained for over 5 miles. The early stages of the climb are typical: big, round turns on a moderate grade beside a tumbling river. Very nice stuff.

Unfortunately, as many commuters live in Deer Creek Canyon and points west, rush hour tends to bring some pretty intense traffic to what would otherwise be an ideal cycling road. Thus, the best time to attempt this ride is in the middle of the day on a weekday. Weekends are noticeably busier, and rush hours can be bad. Commuter traffic is generally much more cutthroat compared to the relatively light-hearted weekend action.

Just after the 6-mile mark, the road climbs into a small hamlet called Phillipsburg and forks into South and North Deer Creek Canyons. This particular ride uses the right, or north, fork. The south fork clings to the side of a surprising gorge, and eventually ends up in the town of Conifer on US 285. The north fork tops out in just over 2 miles, getting progressively harder until the top. Both the north and south forks include some steep pitches, but the north fork is generally considered to be more tame than the southern route. That's small consolation when you're struggling to turn a 39 x 23 tooth gear on the north fork. In fact, it's debatable which route is actually tougher.

Before mile 9 you crest the top and coast down to South Turkey Creek Road. That's always a big commitment—descending off the back of a long climb—because you know you will have to either climb back out of wherever you're going or establish a homestead and live down there forever.

A quick spin down South Turkey Creek Road brings you to the mouth of Turkey Creek Canyon and the bottom of another nice canyon climb. (About a mile below the turnoff to North Turkey Creek Canyon is the quaint tourist attraction of Tiny Town. Call me crazy, but I think the side trip is worth it. Miniature towns, we need more of them.) North Turkey Creek is a pleasant but dark canyon that features another 5 miles or so of moderate climbing and moderate traffic. By the time you reach the junction with County Road 73 at mile 17, you have already conquered the high point of the loop. CR 73 falls steeply into Evergreen—which is essentially a bedroom community for Denver but nonetheless tosses up a down-home Main Street for the passers-through and offers plenty of lunching opportunities.

Bear Creek Canyon gives riders about 11 miles worth of very gradual descending, with decent surfaces and an ample shoulder. As you drop toward Morrison, notice the landscape turn from evergreen forest to the more dry and austere setting of the Front Range proper.

Out of Morrison this ride enters a distinctly different phase. Here you abandon the roads and jump on a well-developed network of multiuse paths (MUPs). The bike path (first a section of the Bear Creek Trail, and then the C-470 Trail) ushers you through a vast open space around Bear Creek Reservoir, by the Soda Lakes, then hugs C-470 for the long trip south along the hogback. The C-470 Trail is fast, primarily downhill with a few short, sharp climbs, but it's also heavily cracked and

Deer Creek Canyon-Evergreen Challenge

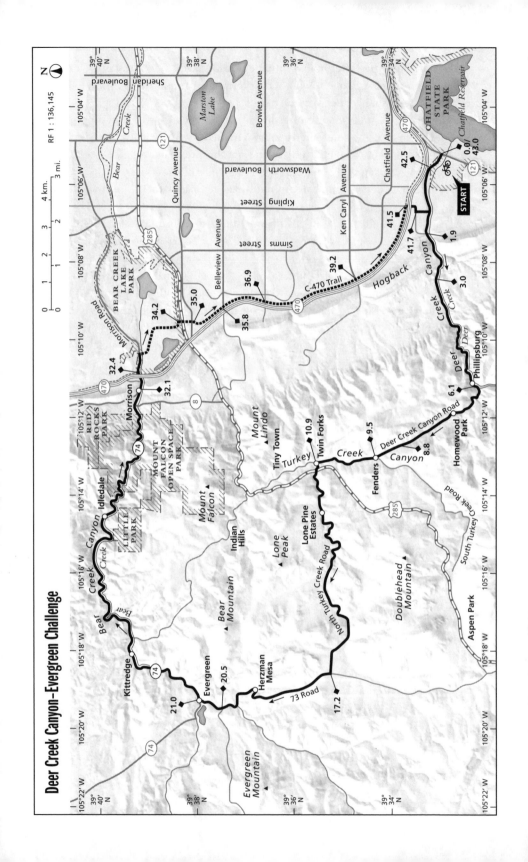

RF 1 : 136,145

N

somewhat less than smooth. Watch out for snakes sunning themselves cluelessly on the warm concrete surface. Getting on the bike path after a long descent, you can trick yourself into thinking that the day's suffering is as good as over. But this 10-mile strip of sharply rolling MUP manages to dish out its own brand of late-ride punishment. A stiff headwind can be devastating at this stage.

It would seem logical to simply stay on the path until Wadsworth Boulevard, then head south back to the start at Deer Creek Canyon Road. Unfortunately, the path doesn't intersect with Wadsworth, but goes under it; to exit the path at Wadsworth requires an untidy bit of fence hopping. So instead you'll leave the path at Kipling Street, and head to the start/finish, using a section of suburban bike path that seems to have been designed exactly for that purpose.

All told, beginning or intermediate riders are likely to find this loop quite difficult, while old hands may find it rather moderate.

Miles and Directions

0.0 Start riding west up Deer Creek Canyon Road from the parking area near Wadsworth Boulevard. Reset your computer at the nearby speed limit sign.

1.9 Turn left at the stop sign.

3.0 Go left at the fork here. (The right fork on South Valley Road leads to the Lockheed Martin plant.)

6.1 Here the road splits into North and South Deer Creek Canyons. Take the right fork.

8.8 Reach the top of a big climb.

9.5 Arrive at a T-intersection with South Turkey Creek Road. Take a right.

10.9 Turn left onto North Turkey Creek Road, under US 285, starting a gradual climb.

17.2 Turn right onto CR 73 and start a high-speed descent into Evergreen.

20.5 Head straight through the intersection with Buffalo Park Road.

21.0 Veer right onto Highway 74. Begin a long, steady descent to Morrison.

32.1 After passing through Morrison, turn right onto the bike path. Take an immediate left where the path splits, headed east. The path goes under C-470.

32.4 Take a sharp right turn here (going straight leads to a parking area).

32.6 Stay right.

34.2 Turn right at the fork. This is a crucial turn; don't miss it! The trail climbs and curves around, passing over US 285.

35.0 The bike path dumps you onto pavement. Continue straight (south at this point).

35.1 Pass a convenience store on your right, cross West Quincy Avenue, and rejoin the path directly opposite, continuing south beside C-470.

35.8 Cross West Belleview Avenue.

36.9 Cross West Bowles Avenue.

39.2 Cross West Ken Caryl Avenue.

41.5 The path, which has curled around to the east by now, arrives at South Kipling Street. Take a right onto South Kipling, headed south under C-470.

41.6 Ride straight through an intersection with West Ute Avenue.

41.7 Take a left onto West Vandeventor Drive into a suburban enclave.

42.1 Before West Vandeventor turns north, find the bike path on the right and get on it, headed south.

42.5 The path spills out onto Deer Creek Canyon Road. Take a left.

43.0 Return to the start.

Ride Information

Events/Attractions

The Denver Botanic Gardens at Chatfield Arboretum, 8500 West Deer Creek Canyon Road; (303) 973-3705. Open to the public from 9:00 A.M. to 5:00 P.M.

Tiny Town Railroad and Museum, Tiny Town; (303) 697-6829; www.tinytownrailroad.com. On South Turkey Creek Road, about 1 mile north of the intersection with North Turkey Creek Road. What is it? It's a tiny town. Some of the 3-foot-high miniatures are replicas of Colorado's famous buildings. It makes even normal-sized people feel quite large. Open Memorial Day through Labor Day.

Restaurants

Anderson's Deli, 5071 Highway 73, Evergreen; (303) 674-4123.

River Sage Restaurant, 4651 Highway 73, Evergreen; (303) 674-2914. Meatless meals a specialty.

The Local Grind, 32214 Ellingwood Trail #105, Evergreen; (303) 670-6773. Give 'em a break—all the cutesy coffee shop names have been taken already! This one also serves sandwiches.

Morrison Inn, 301 Bear Creek Avenue, Morrison; (303) 697-6650. Mexican food in Morrison, right on the main drag.

Dream Cafe, 119 Bear Creek Avenue, Morrison; (303) 697-1280. After a ride I dream of food. Sometimes during a ride. Lunch, dinner, coffee drinks. Closed Mondays.

Willy's Wings, 109 Bear Creek Avenue, Morrison; (303) 697-1232. If you like tiny chicken parts, Willy's is the place.

Blue Cow Cafe, 316 Bear Creek Avenue, Morrison; (303) 697-5721. Breakfast and lunch, ice cream and shakes.

LET'S GET READY TO RUMBLE Centerline rumble strips have been installed on two very popular cycling routes in Jefferson County: Deer Creek Canyon Road and Golden Gate Canyon Road. A rumble strip, not nearly as sexy as it sounds, is a series of depressions carved into the street, forming a strip of bumps designed to vibrate drivers out of their stupor when they drive over it. These particular rumble strips were placed right on the centerline in hopes of keeping drivers confined to their lanes in the tight curves of these narrow mountain roads, the reason being, of course, that very bad things are known to happen when vehicles drift too far inside on blind curves. Confining drivers to their proper lanes has the added benefit of limiting their speed—getting wild drivers to slow down has been the biggest challenge in these canyons.

There are many cyclists, however, who view these rumble strips as a problem. Since Deer Creek and Golden Gate are both narrow, almost completely shoulderless roads as it is, drivers

Close up of the centerline rumble strip

have already exhibited problems passing single cyclists in the turns. With the strips in place, many were concerned that drivers would be even more unwilling to pass or would do so unsafely just to avoid hitting a rumble strip.

After riding these roads with rumble strips and without, I personally don't detect much difference in the way motorists pass, which is to say most of them give plenty of room when they are able to pass and wait patiently when they can't. The vast majority of drivers still move well into the other lane to pass, which means now you can hear their vehicles bumping reassuringly across the strip as they approach. The frequency of uncomfortably close passes, which has always been rare but not rare enough, does not seem to have increased noticeably since the strips were installed. The difference now is that close passes are telegraphed by the silence of the vehicles in question.

But what if you, the cyclist, should happen to encounter one of these rumble strips yourself? Well, you will know it immediately. What provides a minor vibration to a car driver will violently jar a bicycle and possibly cause equipment damage or a wipeout. When descending at speed, rumble strips can be a serious problem. On the other hand, crossing into the wrong lane in blind curves at high speed is more dangerous than hitting a rumble strip at high speed.

If these strips perform as advertised, keeping drivers from cutting corners and encouraging them to drive at appropriate speeds, then they probably represent a net safety boon for cyclists as well as drivers and motorcyclists. The future addition of actual shoulders for these roads, as promised by the powers that be, will effectively counter any minor increase in close passes due to the strips.

11 South Deer Creek Canyon Challenge

A Front Range classic in a small package, this loop into the first stand of mountains southwest of Denver is strenuous, popular, and gorgeous.

Start: The bottom of Deer Creek Canyon Road near its intersection with South Wadsworth Boulevard, at the extreme southwest of the Denver metro area.
Length: 33.4-mile loop.
Terrain: The primary feature of this ride is a long, moderate-to-difficult climb. This is followed by rolling terrain and a long descent interrupted by a sharp half-mile climb.
Traffic and hazards: Deer Creek Canyon is a well-used route for commuters in a god-awful hurry to get home. Avoid rush hours, if possible.

Some tight curves in the canyon produce the typical frustrations for motorists who want to pass and can't. But this is a very popular bike route with generally good-natured motorists and ordinary surface hazards (ordinary except for the occasional rattlesnake at the bottom of Deer Creek Canyon). Shoulders in the canyon are small to nonexistent, and yet lanes are wider than they could be. U.S. Highway 285 has heavy traffic, but the shoulder is very wide for most of that stretch.

Getting there: The start is located at the extreme southwest corner of the Denver metro area, near the intersection of Wadsworth Boulevard and C-470, west of Chatfield Reservoir. C-470 is part of a loop freeway around the city, so it may be the best route to take from many parts of town. From central Denver drive south on Interstate 25 or any major boulevard to C-470, go west on C-470 to the Wadsworth Boulevard exit, drive south a quarter mile, and turn right onto Deer Creek Canyon Road. Park in the dirt parking lot there by the side of the road. (Although this is a makeshift parking area, it is legal, and the traditional spot for Deer Creek Canyon riders to park their vehicles. It's likely there will be a half-dozen or so vehicles there already.) It is also possible to park in many rather accommodating spots along Deer Creek Canyon Road between this spot and the fork after mile 6, cutting as much as 12 miles off the total distance, but still leaving a nice ride with a good climb.

The Ride

Deer Creek Canyon is a classic climber's route that splits into two classic climber's routes, one north and one south. I guess you'll just have to ride them both. Here we have the south route, which is a bit more spectacular visually than the north route and quite similar in terms of difficulty.

The high-grade road

Unfortunately, as many commuters live in Deer Creek Canyon and points west, rush hour tends to bring some pretty intense traffic to what would otherwise be an ideal cycling road. Thus, the best time to attempt this ride is in the middle of the day on a weekday. Weekends are noticeably busier, and rush hours can be bad. Commuter traffic is generally much more cutthroat compared to the relatively light-hearted weekend action.

The route starts with a 6-mile run-up to the fork at the settlement of Phillipsburg: You cross the flats beside the Denver Arboretum, then wind steadily up Deer Creek Canyon beside the small creek. The lower section of the climb is manageable but undeniable. At Phillipsburg hang a left onto the road with the sign that says HIGH GRADE ROAD. The grade actually softens after the turn. Dozens of nice homes are nestled into the slopes beside the road. I saw a bobcat come down and casually saunter across the pavement here, probably looking for an unsuspecting pet to snatch.

After a few miles of gentle rise, the road makes a 180-degree turn, leaves the residential zone, and points up. Another sharp turn back to the southwest and our road has grown a guardrail by necessity, as it climbs next to a rocky chasm. This is one of the classic, most memorable sections of paved road in Colorado. It's also a bit painful. The toughest stretch comes as the road climbs away from the gorge up the side of

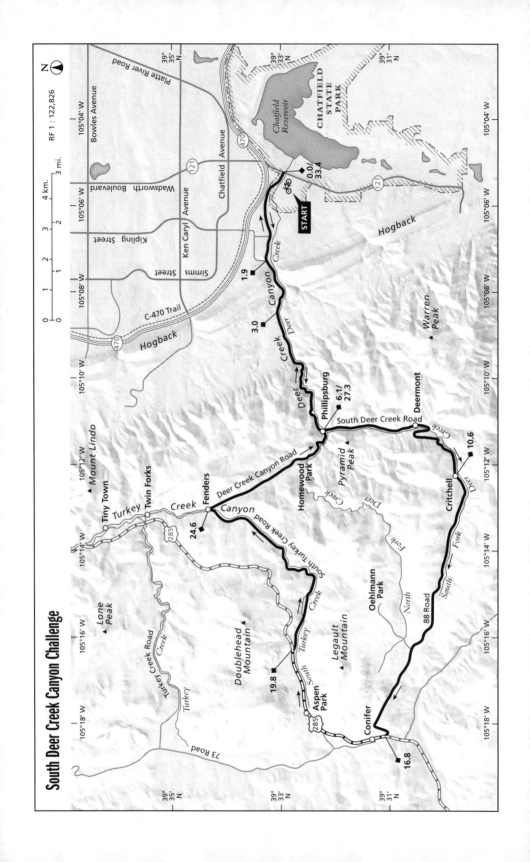

South Deer Creek Canyon Challenge

RF 1 : 122,826

N

START

Chatfield Reservoir

CHATFIELD STATE PARK

Hogback

Hogback

Platte River Road

Bowles Avenue

Wadsworth Boulevard

Chatfield Avenue

Ken Caryl Avenue

Kipling Street

Simms Street

C-470 Trail

Deer Canyon Creek

Deer Creek

Deer

Phillipsburg

South Deer Creek Road

Deermont

Creek

Critchell

Deer

Fork

North

South

Fork

88 Road

Oehlmann Park

Legault Mountain

Deer Creek

Homewood Park

Pyramid Peak

Deer Creek Canyon Road

Fenders

Turkey Creek

Twin Forks

Tiny Town

Mount Lindo

Lone Peak

Warren Peak

Turkey Creek Road

Turkey

73 Road

Doublehead Mountain

South Turkey Creek Road

South Turkey Creek

Aspen Park

Conifer

0.0/33.4

1.9

3.0

6.1/27.3

10.6

16.8

19.8

24.6

105°04' W
105°06' W
105°08' W
105°10' W
105°12' W
105°14' W
105°16' W
105°18' W

39°35' N
39°33' N
39°31' N

0   1   2   3 mi.
0   2   4 km.

the canyon. Slopes here are respectable, but not as harsh as those found on Magnolia, Flagstaff, Sugarloaf, Golden Gate, the top of Left Hand, or Four Mile to Gold Hill. This hill tops out relatively soon, in fact, leaving the road to cross several miles of rolling terrain before the eventual descent to Conifer and US 285. I usually don't like riding on the freeways, but this section of US 285 between Conifer and Aspen Park is fast and accommodating. (Those wanting to extend the ride can cross under US 285 at Conifer and begin a long cruise toward Evergreen; you can then continue all the way through Evergreen and descend to Morrison, or take a right before Evergreen and loop back toward Deer Creek via Turkey Creek Canyon.)

After US 285 rushes past the giant hot dog[1] and the collection of scattered houses known as Aspen Park, exit onto South Turkey Creek Road near the Meyer Ranch Open Space. The sign points the way to Tiny Town—that's your road.

South Turkey Creek Road is a sustained cruise following a lush valley, downhill all the way and very pleasant. (You might want to come back up here someday and ride this in the other direction.) Pass several roads on the right before turning at Deer Creek Canyon Road at mile 24.6. The first thing you notice here is a big hill staring you in the face. A half mile later you're at the top and could potentially coast all the way down the remainder of Deer Creek Canyon.

Should you feel the need for more miles, there's always the option of turning at the Phillipsburg fork and doing the loop again. Ambitious riders can also start the ride from central Denver, ride to and from Deer Creek (usually on the Platte River Trail), and pack on another 35 or so miles.

Miles and Directions

0.0 Start riding west from the dirt parking area at the bottom of Deer Creek Canyon Road. Reset your odometer at the speed limit sign.

1.9 Turn left at the stop sign.

3.0 Stay left at the fork.

6.1 At the Phillipsburg fork take a left onto the road with the HIGH GRADE ROAD sign. This is South Deer Creek Road.

10.6 The road is now Pleasant Park Road.

16.8 At the stop-signed intersection by the freeway, take a left and then a quick right to get on US 285.

19.8 Turn right onto South Turkey Creek Road. The sign here should mention Tiny Town. Do not turn on Meyer Road.

24.6 Turn right on Deer Creek Canyon Road and begin a modest climb. (Do not turn on Hilldale Road.)

27.3 Pass the fork at Phillipsburg. Backtrack to the start.

33.4 Arrive at the start/finish.

---

[1] The Coney Island Hot Dog Stand, inside a giant hot dog, is a well-known landmark along US 285.

Ride Information

Restaurant

The Coney Island Hot Dog Stand, Aspen Park; (303) 838–4210. The hot dog–shaped building on US 285 in Aspen Park. No address given, no address necessary.

Maps

Delorme: Colorado Atlas & Gazetteer: Pages 40 D-1, 50 A-1.

12 Golden Gate–Coal Creek Classic

Perhaps the most difficult climb on the Front Range takes you to the beautiful, undulating terrain of the Peak-to-Peak Highway. Tackle another difficult climb on Highway 72 before the cruise down Coal Creek Canyon. Who would've thought that a mere half century could beat you down like this?

Start: The intersection of Golden Gate Canyon Road and Highway 93, 1 mile north of Golden.

Length: 52.5-mile loop.

Terrain: Several long, difficult climbs that can seem relentlessly steep. Psychologically unhelpful false summits and fast descents provide only partial relief on this tough half century into the Front Range mountains.

Traffic and hazards: The roads here are not as accommodating for cycling as many of the favorite Front Range routes. Golden Gate Canyon is not blessed with a good shoulder and does not see nearly as many riders as, say, Left Hand or Deer Creek. This is probably a good place to use a mirror. And that's coming from a guy who doesn't own a mirror and rarely thinks about them. The Peak-to-Peak Highway section (Highway 119) is not as pampered and baby smooth as the section near Estes Park, but it's still decent with a wide shoulder. Highway 72 can be problematic. The section from Wondervu down Coal Creek Canyon is narrow, heavily trafficked, and choppy with road damage.

Getting there: From Denver go west on 6th Avenue all the way to Golden. 6th Avenue goes under Interstate 70 and C-470, crosses Colfax Avenue, passes the hulking Jefferson County Justice Center (known to area delivery drivers as "the Taj"), and curls around to the north. Stay on this highway as it crosses U.S. Highway 6 and becomes Highway 93 (the Foothills Highway). About 1 mile north of US 6, turn left off of Highway 93 onto Golden Gate Canyon Road. Park immediately in the makeshift parking area at the road's edge. (Note: It is also possible to park 1.2 miles up Golden Gate Canyon Road at Galbraith Park.)

The Peak-to-Peak Highway south of Rollinsville ▶

The Ride

Golden Gate Canyon Road is serious business. One does not oil up the three-speed, put on a floppy hat, and go for a jaunt up Golden Gate Canyon. If you want a picnic, this ain't it. This road serves up the brutality in industrial-sized portions.

The notorious Golden Gate climb comes in three parts, separated by descents. The first climb, starting right away, lasts 6.5 miles and tops out at Guy Hill Road. It is an eye-opener, but not overly difficult. After a fast mile-long downhill, the road points up again, big time, for part two. This is the hardest section of the entire loop. The slope quickly ramps up, flirts with percent grades in the teens, and continues with this madness for what can only be described as a long time. In fact, the steep grade persists for around 3 miles. All but the most fit climbers will cry uncle on this one.

Near mile 11.0 the gnarly hill tops out and the road rolls swiftly to Golden Gate Canyon State Park. Here begins climb number three, not as bad as part two, but exacting a toll on legs that are still dead from the previous climb. You finally reach the Peak-to-Peak Highway after 17 miles on Golden Gate Canyon Road. By this point you have already gained a net of almost 3,000 feet but have in fact climbed 1,200 or so more vertical feet than that!

You scarcely have time to congratulate yourself for a gutsy performance, though, as the terrain on the Peak-to-Peak is anything but flat. Headed north for this beautiful but tough 10-mile section, you start with a fast descent, then climb, then descend, then climb. . . . Ozzy was right: There is no rest for the wicked.

After the turnoff on Highway 72, the terrain is fast, gentle, and forgiving, which will certainly be appreciated even if you don't know what's coming next. Swoop down into Pinecliffe, crossing railroad tracks and South Boulder Creek near mile 31.9. *Uh-oh.* When you're riding in the mountains, crossing a creek can be an ominous sign of things to come. Here the crossing is ominous indeed, as the road beyond gains elevation with a vengeance. Wasn't this supposed to be the *downhill* part of the loop? There are some descents in the mix, but the general attitude of the road between Pinecliffe and Wondervu is unmistakably uphill. Very uphill. At this point in the ride, it's bound to hurt.

What you are doing here is climbing out of one canyon, the canyon of South Boulder Creek—which runs down and carves Eldorado Canyon—and into another canyon, that belonging to Coal Creek. Wondervu sits at the very top of the hill. The road tips over immediately, right in front of the Wondervu Cafe. There is some steep stuff at first, then the road follows Coal Creek into typical round, fast canyon turns. The road is narrow, not to mention poorly surfaced for long sections, and you might find yourself with some traffic bottled up behind you momentarily. Perhaps by the time this book goes to press, Highway 72 will be given a thorough makeover. But this road has been one of the messiest around in terms of cracks, chuckholes, crumbling edges, and various forms of massive road damage. The bumps on Highway 72 can make the washboard dirt roads around here look pretty

Golden Gate-Coal Creek Classic

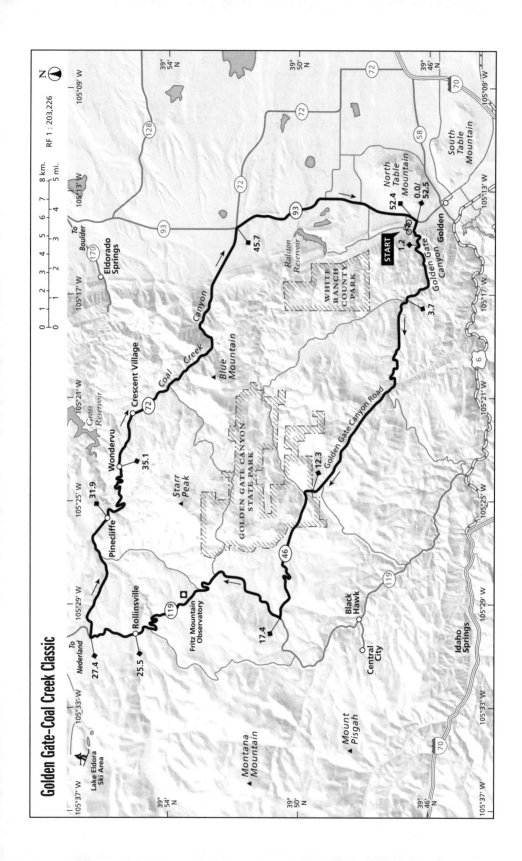

tame. Smoothing out the Coal Creek descent, and dealing with the traffic, takes a lot of finesse.

At the end of Coal Creek Canyon, Highway 72 spills out onto the flats (Rocky Flats, to be exact), and the road is straight. Since a hard wind is often blowing out of the hills, the road is often very fast as well. Unfortunately, it's narrow. During afternoon commutes lines of cars coming up the road cause problems by preventing downstream cars from passing cyclists (because there is scarce open road to pass) and by causing downstream cars to pass cyclists too closely. The best way to avoid this problem is to get down the canyon before rush hour. The final leg of this route goes by quickly—rolling terrain on the Foothills Highway, with its wide shoulder, heavy traffic, and unexciting scenery. You'll undoubtedly feel a strong sense of accomplishment while rolling up on the start/finish.

This loop is a real leg breaker that garners a "classic" designation at only 52 miles. It might be best to save this ride for the cooler autumn months so you can avoid getting hammered by Colorado's midday summer sun while plodding up the climbs. If you take this approach, be sure to pack the appropriate cold-weather gear, lest you freeze your nipples off on the descents.

Miles and Directions

0.0 Start riding west up Golden Gate Canyon Road from the makeshift parking area near the intersection with Highway 93. Reset the odometer at the nearby sign that says WHITE RANCH PARK.

1.2 Pass Galbraith Park (an alternate parking and start/finish here).

3.7 Pass Crawford Gulch Road.

12.3 Enter Golden Gate Canyon State Park (no fee required).

17.4 Finally reach Highway 119 (Peak-to-Peak Highway). Turn right and head north. First, however, check out the awesome views to the south.

23.8 Pass the Fritz Mountain Observatory.

25.5 Roll through Rollinsville.

27.4 Take a right on Highway 72.

31.9 At Pinecliffe ride over the tracks and South Boulder Creek. Begin a tough climb.

35.1 Reach Wondervu.

45.7 Turn right on Highway 93.

52.4 Turn right on Golden Gate Canyon Road.

52.5 Arrive back at the start/finish.

Ride Information

Maps

Delorme: Colorado Atlas & Gazetteer: Pages 39 A, B-7; 40 A-1.

13 Denver–Golden Cruise

Find your way from Confluence Park in lower downtown Denver to the town of Golden, 12 miles west. This route uses accommodating cycling roads to slice through Denver to the 32nd Avenue corridor.

Start: Confluence Park, lower downtown Denver.
Length: 12.2-mile point-to-point.
Terrain: After climbing out of the Platte Valley, this route is virtually flat, with one short hill on 32nd Avenue between Simms and Youngfield Streets.

Traffic and hazards: This route uses accommodating cycling roads when possible, but 32nd Avenue is heavily traveled and lacks a comfortable shoulder for the most part. It is, however, a very popular bike route. The trip through Denver features wide curb lanes, but constant intersections.

Getting there: From downtown Denver go west on 15th Street, under the railroad tracks and over the Platte River, and take the first left after the river onto Platte Street. Park in the free lot by the REI flagship store. It will probably be just as easy, and more enjoyable, to ride to the bike path from a home base in Denver rather than drive and park. From points north or south of Denver, take Interstate 25 to exit 211. Go north on Water Street, under Speer Boulevard, and park in the lot next to or across the street from the REI store. The mileage cues for this ride begin at the intersection of Platte and 15th Streets. Platte becomes Water Street and then 23rd Avenue.

The Ride

One of the big problems with Denver is its location—out on the flat plains. They didn't name it the Queen City of the Plains for nothing. So, central Denverites who like to climb big ol' hills on their bicycles find themselves gazing westward across the rooftops toward Golden and the hills beyond. The closest real hill to downtown Denver is Lookout Mountain, just west of Golden. If we get up in a high building, we can see Lookout Mountain out there, spiked with radio and cell towers. So near, yet so far.

Golden is a nice little town—a real town, not a post-suburban construction—that offers bike shops and restaurants and *free beer* in addition to hills. What are you waiting for?

Those who aren't familiar with the route and try to just wing it, thinking they will find their way to Golden somehow, are almost certain to run into some route-related trouble. There are dozens of bottlenecks and dead-ends, and really only one single cycling-friendly road that goes all the way through: 32nd Avenue, which is the key to almost any Denver-to-Golden route.

Perhaps the tidiest route to Golden (via 32nd) begins on Platte Street/Water Street west of the Platte River. From the corner of 15th and Platte Streets, ride south past the REI and the Ocean Journey aquarium. The road curves around to the west,

crossing over I–25 (watch for frantic on- and off-rampers), and becomes 23rd Avenue. A few blocks' worth of hill takes you out of the valley and due west toward the real hills. Crossing I–25, the "Valley Highway," and escaping the Central Platte Valley tends to involve much more hassle.

Before 23rd runs into Sloan's Lake, go north on one of the streets there—Perry Street is good—and resume westward travel on 26th Avenue, another relatively bike-friendly street. Legend has it that Thomas Sloan, who owned a farm on this site in the 1860s, created this lake by accident when he was trying to dig a well. Accidental or not, it's a nice lake.

There is a good reason to delay your rendezvous with 32nd Avenue—west of Wadsworth Boulevard, 32nd narrows considerably, while 26th offers a wide shoulder. Between 26th and 32nd, from Wadsworth to Kipling Street, is land occupied by Crown Hill Cemetery and Crown Hill Lake, another lake ringed by a popular multiuse path. Beyond Kipling our route cuts up to 32nd on Simms Street. You've got to get on 32nd at some point, and Simms is as good a place as any, especially as it allows you to take advantage of a short diagonal section. Since the start of the ride, you have passed through the layers of Denver's short history like the rings of a tree: neighborhoods built in the nineteenth century, then neighborhoods built in the early twentieth century, the 1920s and 1930s, and now the 1950s. And you're only about halfway to Golden.

The section of 32nd around the Applewood Golf Course and Rolling Hills Country Club gets a little dicey, with not much room for cyclists and some frantic drivers around rush hour. It is, nonetheless, a very popular cycling route. Most of the trip has been arrow-straight, but at around mile 10 the road goes into a series of big curves. The surroundings are more rural than suburban as 32nd curls around the base of South Table Mountain. This is the last remaining enclave of open land between Denver and Golden.

The Coors complex soon comes into view, often sporting plumes of industrial effluent. Not long after you see it, you smell it. Mostly it is the wholesome smell of beer being created, but there are some less sumptuous things going on in this valley. The Coors plant here is sprawled out over a large area, and creates porcelain products, glass bottles, and aluminum cans in addition to cold barley pops. The best way to view the plant and the rest of Golden is to climb a ways up Lookout Mountain. The brewery operation can also be seen from the inside on the famous free Coors tour. Yes, there is free beer to be had at the end of the tour. Unfortunately, you are not allowed to take a backpack inside the brewery—therefore, you will not be able to follow through on your plan to abscond with several souvenir six-packs.

32nd Avenue has turned into 13th Street. At the intersection of 13th and Ford Street here in Golden, ambitious riders have plenty of opportunities before them.

◀ *Looking over Interstate 25 toward downtown*

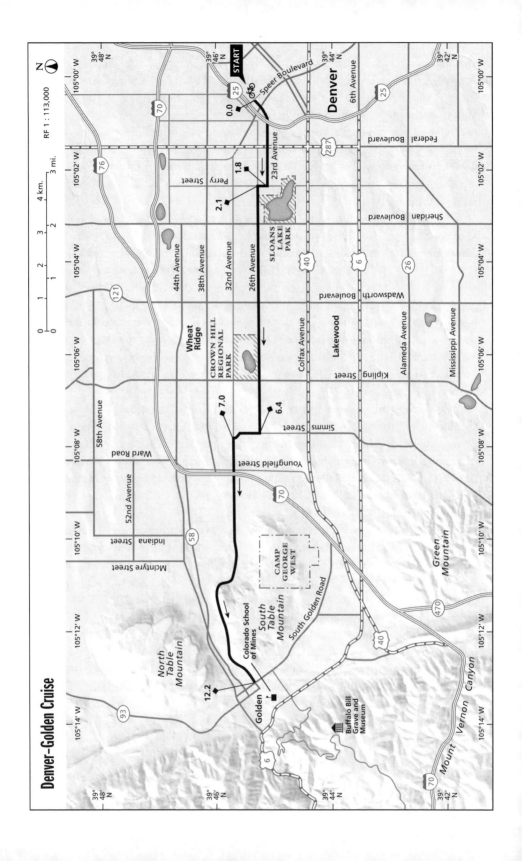

Denver-Golden Cruise

RF 1 : 113,000

START

Of course, the classic climb of Lookout Mountain looms above. You are really at the base of Lookout when you are at this intersection by the Coors plant, and the climbing begins from right here. To start the climb roll straight through downtown Golden, head up the steep slope and through the Colorado School of Mines campus, and regroup at the intersection of 19th Street and West 6th Avenue. Nineteenthth becomes Lariat Loop—that's the road you want. (You might find these low slopes of Lookout to be the hardest part of the climb. Often the first steep slopes of a climb are painful because the rider has not yet warmed up properly—the system is still in shock.)

Many other rides are well within reach from the Coors plant. North off Highway 93 are the entrances to two great canyon climbs: Coal Creek and Golden Gate. Highway 93 (the Foothills Highway) would be glad to take you all the way into Boulder, no problem, if you don't mind sharp hills, high winds, and lots of traffic. To the south connections are possible to Red Rocks, Morrison, the C-470 Trail, and the Bear Creek Trail, to name a few popular options. The C-470 Trail is in the process of being extended into Golden, which will greatly ease the current southward passage and will create a load of brand-new options; to the northwest of town, another path takes off from West 44th Avenue and follows Interstate 76 all the way to Commerce City. It is easy to rack up 70 miles or so on these loops around the west Denver metroplex.

Miles and Directions

- **0.0** Start from the corner of 15th Street and Platte Street (which will become Water Street) and ride southwest. Water Street curves around to the west, crosses I-25, and becomes West 23rd Avenue.
- **1.8** Turn right on Perry Street.
- **2.1** Turn left on West 26th Avenue (navigating past Sloan's Lake).
- **6.4** Turn right on Simms Street.
- **7.0** Turn left on West 32nd Avenue.
- **12.2** Arrive in Golden at the corner of 13th and Ford Streets.

Ride Information

Events/Attractions

Tours of the Coors Brewery are conducted Monday through Saturday from 10:00 A.M. to 4:00 P.M. No tours on Sundays, and no backpacks allowed. Walking tours take approximately ninety minutes. From the parking lot southeast of 13th and Ford Streets in Golden; (303) 277-BEER.

Restaurants

Wazee Supper Club, 1600 15th Street, Denver; (303) 623-9518. High-quality pizza in lower downtown.
Wahoo Fish Taco, 1521 Blake Street, Denver; (303) 623-0263. California-style Mexican food and a surf-inspired atmosphere. Good cheap food downtown.

Paris on the Platte, 1553 Platte Street, Denver; (303) 455-2451. Sandwiches, coffee, etc., in a casually hip bookstore/cafe. Very close to Confluence Park.

Rocky Mountain Diner, 800 18th Street, Denver; (303) 293-8383. Large portions of hearty western-style American food, including the ubiquitous buffalo meatloaf. In the heart of downtown in one of Denver's oldest surviving buildings, the "Ghost Building."

Fontano's Chicago Subs, 1623 California Street, Denver; (720) 956-1100. Open 'til 3:00 P.M. every day but Sunday. Get down there. Best meatball sub I've ever had.

16th Street Deli, 500 16th Street, Pavilions Mall, Denver; (720) 956-0440. The "half" sandwich is big. The "whole" is a real sandwich. Worth the trip uptown.

Tommy's Thai, 3410 East Colfax Avenue, Denver; (303) 377-4244. Quite cheap for good quality food and the whole town knows it. A few miles east of downtown on Colfax.

Mizuna, 225 East 7th Avenue, Denver; (303) 832-4778. This highly touted restaurant

has been called the best in Denver. Upscale, reservations.

Le Central, 112 East 8th Avenue, Denver; (303) 863-8094. Authentic French cuisine, moderately priced. Reservations recommended.

Woody's Woodfired Pizza & Watering Hole, 1305 Washington Avenue, Golden; (303) 277-0443.

Golden Pizza Shoppe, 2501 Ford Street, Golden; (303) 279-5610.

D'Deli, 1207 Washington Avenue, Golden; (303) 279-8020. Sandwiches and soups, right smack downtown.

Accommodation

Table Mountain Inn, 1310 Washington Avenue, Golden; (303) 277-9898; www.tablemountain inn.com. This 74-room hotel includes a well-liked Southwestern restaurant, serving breakfast lunch and dinner 365 days a year.

Maps

Delorme: Colorado Atlas & Gazetteer: Page 40 C-1-2.

14 Lookout Mountain Cruise

A short but strenuous climb of one of the locals' favorite hills, this version of the beloved Lookout Mountain ride includes a back-side loop and a bonus climb.

Start: Beverly Heights Park parking area, about 0.4 mile up Lariat Loop Road from 6th Avenue/U.S. Highway 6, west of Golden.

Length: 15.1-mile lariat.

Terrain: A moderate but lengthy climb on a well-designed tourist road. The back-side climb is steeper but shorter. Total elevation gain is about 1,600 feet.

Traffic and hazards: The descent has the potential for danger, like any mountain descent. Ride within your limits and make sure your equipment is functioning. Surface conditions are generally good, but watch for rough road and potholes on the lower part of the descent as you reenter the residential zone.

Getting there: From Denver take 6th Avenue west all the way past Golden. The road goes past the hulking Jefferson County Justice Center and curls around to the north. Turn left on Lariat Loop

Late afternoon on Lookout ▶

Road (this road becomes Lookout Mountain Road) due west of the town of Golden and drive up the hill. As Lariat Loop curves back to the south, find the parking area on the east side of the road at Beverly Heights Park.

The Ride

Today you've got an appointment with Lookout Mountain. Lookout is a well-known and well-loved climb for area residents. It's the closest real climb to Denver, so riders from the city reach for it often when they need to satisfy their thirst for climbing. Sometimes people will ride out to Lookout from Denver; sometimes people just want a climb, and they don't want any flat stuff to spoil the fun. Here's a good little ride with no distracting flat sections.

The actual base of Lookout Mountain is down in Golden. So we are really cheating by starting up on the mountain a ways; in fact, we are cutting out some of the toughest climbing. That's okay; everybody does it. You'll still get a good workout, and it won't take long at all.

The Lookout Mountain Highway (aka Lariat Loop) was constructed as a tourist road when the novelty of travel by auto was still in high bloom. As such, the road is carefully laid out to minimize grades, snaking all over the mountain. Heading south at first, Lariat Loop quickly switches back toward the north and contours up the east face of the mountain, gaining altitude steadily but mercifully. Views—of Golden, the Coors Brewery, North and South Table Mountains, the Denver conurbation, and the eastern plains—are already rewarding just a mile or so up the road. The end of the first third of the climb is marked by the big flat switchbacks on the north side, where you can peek over the edge and see US 6 down in the canyon below.

The next phase of the climb brings you back onto the east face, much higher up than you were before. You might see some paragliders jumping off and floating down to the open field next to the freeway, and on this more exposed section of road, you might really feel the wind that keeps them aloft. The road false-flattens again and rolls to a saddle where the footpath/mountain bike trail crosses for the second time. Here begins the final phase of the climb. After another series of switches, the road meanders up moderate grades toward the summit and the Buffalo Bill Museum and Grave. Buffalo Bill Cody was a real-life cowboy, frontier scout, marksman, prospector, and Pony Express rider who became a caricature of himself later in life, traveling around the country with his Wild West Show. It was Buffalo Bill's wish that he be buried atop Lookout Mountain, and that he was in 1917. Good choice, Bill.

Most cyclists turn around at the turnoff for the overlook parking area at mile 4.2. The road, however, keeps chugging along. Follow it for a while and see what happens. It rocks and rolls along the top of the foothills, dipping into valleys and climbing out, reaching its high point some distance after Lookout Mountain and the Buffalo Bill turnoff.

At mile 6.8 hang a left onto the highway and descend to Paradise Road. You're at the bottom of a fairly serious climb here. But then, you wouldn't have attempted

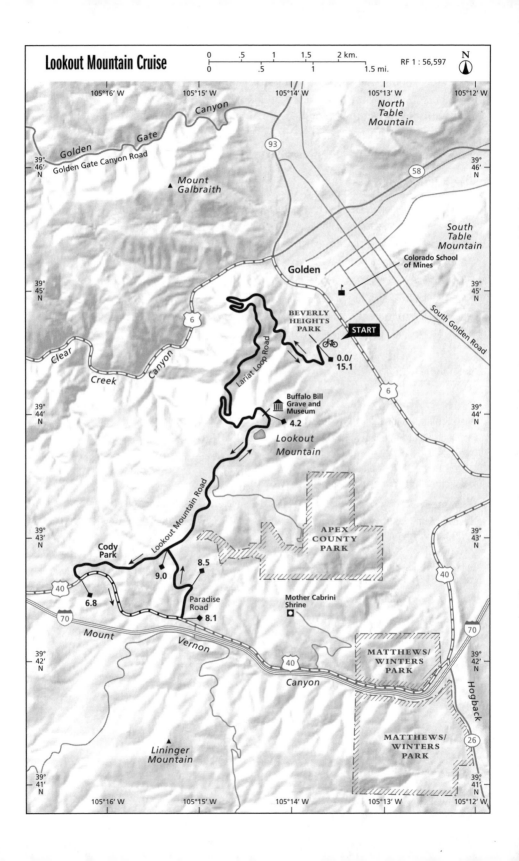

Lookout Mountain Cruise

RF 1 : 56,597

N

North Table Mountain

Canyon

93

58

Golden Gate

Golden Gate Canyon Road

▲ *Mount Galbraith*

South Table Mountain

Golden

Colorado School of Mines

6

BEVERLY HEIGHTS PARK

Lariat Loop Road

START

🚲

South Golden Road

■ **0.0/ 15.1**

Clear

Creek

Canyon

Buffalo Bill Grave and Museum

🏛

◆ **4.2**

6

Lookout Mountain

Lookout Mountain Road

APEX COUNTY PARK

Cody Park

◆ **8.5**

40

◆ **9.0**

Paradise Road

Mother Cabrini Shrine

▫

40

◆ **6.8**

70

◆ **8.1**

Mount

Vernon

40

Canyon

70

MATTHEWS/ WINTERS PARK

Hogback

▲ *Lininger Mountain*

MATTHEWS/ WINTERS PARK

26

this ride at all if you didn't like climbing at least a little bit. Ascend through the Paradise Hills subdivision back to Lookout Mountain Road (same as Lariat Loop Road), completing your little back-side loop. This economy-sized climber's loop is nicely situated for multiple repetitions. For that matter, if you're still feeling good when you arrive at the parking lot from which you started this ride, why not turn around and do the whole thing again?

Miles and Directions

0.0 Start riding up the hill from the dirt parking lot. The lot is located about 0.4 mile above the road's intersection with 6th Avenue/US 6.

4.2 Pass the road leading to the Buffalo Bill museum.

6.8 Take a left on U.S. Highway 40, goin' down.

8.1 Take a left on Paradise Road.

8.5 At the fork either way will work. I went left on Charros Drive.

9.0 Back at Lookout Mountain Road, take a right and retrace your path back to the start.

15.1 Finish at the Beverly Heights Park parking lot.

Ride Information

Events/Attractions

Buffalo Bill Museum and Grave, 987½ Lookout Mountain Road, Golden; (303) 526-0747; www.buffalobill.org/home.htm. Buffalo Bill Cody is buried amidst photographs and artifacts, and a bathroom. Admission is $3.00.

Restaurants

Woody's Woodfired Pizza & Watering Hole, 1305 Washington Avenue, Golden; (303) 277-0443.
Golden Pizza Shoppe, 2501 Ford Street, Golden; (303) 279-5610.
D'Deli, 1207 Washington Avenue, Golden;
(303) 279-8020. Sandwiches and soups, right smack downtown.

Accommodation

Table Mountain Inn, 1310 Washington Avenue, Golden; (303) 277-9898; www.tablemountaininn.com. This seventy-four-room hotel includes a well-liked Southwestern restaurant, serving breakfast lunch and dinner 365 days a year.

Maps

Delorme: Colorado Atlas & Gazetteer: Page 40 C-1. *Bicycling the Greater Denver Area Route Map* (Mapsco).

15 Tour de Downtown Ramble

Starting from City Park, this route takes you right through downtown, proceeds through the Auraria campus and into the industrial zone, and loops back to the start via pleasant, mansion-lined 7th Avenue. This is an easy route with some real urban traffic.

Start: Denver's City Park.

Length: 10.4-mile loop.

Terrain: Central Denver is quite flat. This ride features one noticeable climb, about 2 blocks long.

Traffic and hazards: There is fairly heavy traffic on all roads on this loop through the center of Denver's densely packed urban core. Some of the roads have painted bike lanes. Parked cars and their associated Door Zones are a constant companion. Don't ride in the DZs, within about 3.5 to 4 feet of any parked car. The condition of road surfaces in central Denver leaves something to be desired—keep your eyes forward.

Getting there: Denver's City Park is bordered by York Avenue on the west, Colorado Boulevard on the east, East 23rd Avenue and the Municipal Golf Course on the north, and East 17th Avenue on the south. It is nicely accessible by bike from much of Denver. In a car use Colorado Boulevard from the north or south and Colfax Avenue from the east or west.

The Ride

Denver's City Park was designed in the popular style of the early twentieth century—wide open lawns, flower gardens, lakes, fountains, neoclassical statues and colonnades, groups of trees, all deliberately placed. All details have been carefully determined. This is a prime example of the heavy-handed landscape architecture of the City Beautiful movement, which defines the scenery in much of central Denver. All big American cities have such parks, and we are lucky to have them.

Start the ride in the southwest quadrant of the park, across from East High School. Here you will find a mysterious statue of a woman amidst a traffic circle and a fountain. The fountain was donated to the city in 1918 by Joseph Addison Thatcher, a prominent local banker. The unique sculpture is worth a look. It is actually of three different figures, representing loyalty, learning, and love. From the fountain head south, across busy East 17th Avenue, and parade across the front of East High School. The grounds of the old high school were designed as part of the park; the road is called City Park Esplanade. Turning right onto 16th Avenue, you are headed right at downtown. 16th has a painted bike lane, partially in the off-limits Door Zone of parked vehicles. Although the bike lane is a help, 16th remains an extremely sketchy urban street due to cross traffic. The biggest problem by far on 16th is that of motorists failing to see the stop signs or failing to notice approaching traffic when restarting from a stop sign. Basically, cyclists traveling down 16th

need to assume the worst from all other road users and anticipate their mistakes. Keep an eagle eye on the flanks. With all its problems 16th is still the best street for approaching downtown from the east.

Nearing downtown, you'll jog to the north a few blocks, crossing in front of 1700 Lincoln, the skyscraper known as the "Cash Register Building" because . . . well, look at it. Turn left on 18th Avenue, swoop down downtown Denver's only hill, and shoot into downtown. The corner of 18th and Broadway is funky and dangerous. The road cuts at an angle to the right here—the central downtown street grid is askew—where cyclists usually have a head of steam coming off the hill. Cyclists need to be assertive here and move carefully into the lane before the intersection— to avoid the nasty grate on the right, to avoid being squeezed off by bad drivers, and to avoid pedestrians and other cyclists who often fly out randomly from behind the blind corner created by a church.

Roads in downtown Denver are almost exclusively one-way streets. The other available one-way street going west (actually northwest) through the central downtown area is 15th Avenue, but for quite a while now, 18th has been the friendlier conduit in that direction.[1] On a slight downhill 18th takes you past several more skyscrapers, some of which are named for telecommunications companies with legendary accounting techniques. A bike lane appears on this street west of Champa Street. Most cyclists really appreciate the segregated space—just watch for the 6-inch drops around the manholes.

At the west end of downtown, 18th dead-ends at Wynkoop Street. Wynkoop is named for a real Colorado hero: a United States cavalry officer who made an earnest effort to create a lasting peace with the Arapahoe and Cheyenne in 1864, before hundreds were massacred at Sand Creek and peace became impossible. Ride it with style to honor his memory. Is it WINE-koop or WIN-koop? Those in the know say *wine*-koop.

Wynkoop, the lowest cross street on the old downtown grid, has seen a lot of action in the last 140-odd years. Back then visitors to town could expect to meet a whole cast of hucksters as soon as they stepped off the train at Union Station and started walking up 17th Street. Sure, there were a lot of warehouses and things down here (check out the brickwork on the Icehouse refrigerated warehouse at 18th and Wynkoop), but Denver's real contribution came in the form of prostitutes, alcohol, and gambling. Such proud origins!

After a very brief lap through LoDo, come back up and turn onto historic Larimer Street, headed toward the Auraria campus. Auraria includes the University of Colorado Denver branch and Metro State College.

◀ *Downtown Denver*

---

[1]Much of the problem on 15th has been ongoing construction work, which may be completed when this book goes to press. Also, there are many city bus routes that use 15th and only a few that use 18th.

Tour de Downtown Ramble

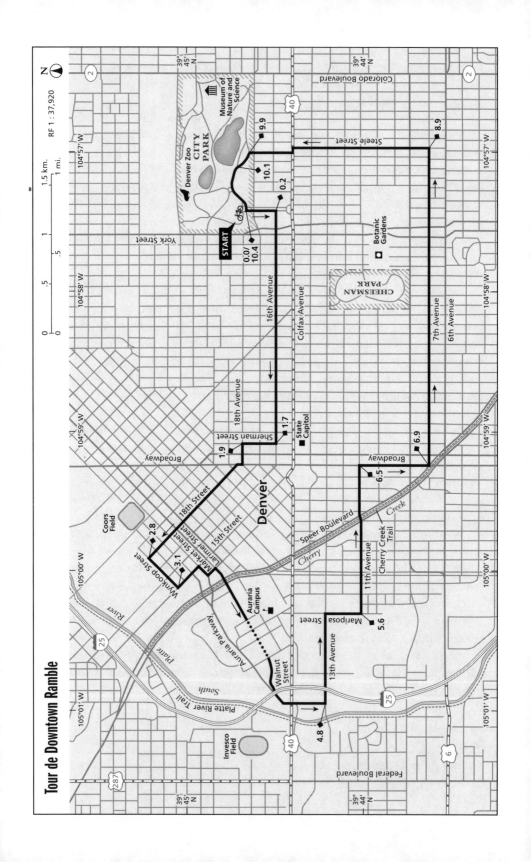

RF 1 : 37,920

N

2

39° 45' N
104°57' W

Denver Zoo
CITY PARK
Museum of Nature and Science

9.9
10.1
0.2

York Street

START

0.0/10.4

16th Avenue

Colfax Avenue

CHEESMAN PARK

Botanic Gardens

7th Avenue
6th Avenue

Steele Street

8.9

40

39° 44' N
Colorado Boulevard
2

104°57' W

18th Avenue

Sherman Street
1.7
1.9

State Capitol

104°59' W

Broadway

Denver

18th Street
15th Street
Market Street
Larimer Street

Coors Field

2.8
3.1

Wynkoop Street

Auraria Campus

Walnut Street

Speer Boulevard

Cherry Creek

Cherry Creek Trail

11th Avenue

6.5

6.9

Broadway

104°59' W

13th Avenue

Mariposa Street

5.6

Platte River Trail

South Platte River

Auraria Parkway

25

105°00' W
105°01' W

Invesco Field

287

40

4.8

25

Federal Boulevard

39° 45' N
104°58' W

39° 44' N
104°58' W

6

105°00' W

0   .5   1   1.5 km.
0   1 mi.

Here I have routed you right through the campus. This requires you to dismount for a few minutes' walk. The members of the campus security squadron are extremely motivated to catch and detain anybody who thinks they can get away with riding a bike through the dismount zone. I seriously dare you to try it. These guys hate freedom. Those who can't stand the thought of walking their bikes—wearing the wrong shoes, perhaps—can jump off onto the Cherry Creek path at 14th Street and Larimer and take the path southeast to 11th Street to rejoin the loop. Those who do this, however, will miss the coolest part of the loop, on Walnut Street. Walnut disappears under a vast web of freeway flyovers and spits you out by the old power plant. There are no multiuse paths (MUPs) on this loop, just good old-fashioned urban street action. Hazards along this picturesquely industrial section include four sets of railroad tracks, one set on Walnut and one set on 13th being true wheel mashers.

Emerging from the industrial backwater, the route makes its way to Broadway and the 7th Avenue corridor. Locals put 7th to use whenever possible, and you'll use it here for the bulk of your eastward travel, all the way to Steele Street. The first mile or so east of Broadway is tight but pleasant, with a short climb. East of Williams Street, 7th sprouts a bike lane. The massive old houses along the 7th Street corridor—not just a street but a corridor—are ripe with history and crowded with ghosts. In its day 7th was the most exclusive subdivision in the city. The appropriately stately structure at 750 Lafayette Street, for instance, is the Doud Mansion, in which Mamie Doud and a young Dwight Eisenhower were married. The house became Eisenhower's version of the Crawford ranch after Ike became president.[2]

Miles and Directions

0.0 Start from the fountain at the southwest side of City Park and begin riding south on City Park Esplanade. Immediately Cross East 17th Avenue and roll in front of East High.

0.2 Turn right on 16th Avenue. Head west, crossing multiple streets.

1.7 Turn right on Sherman Street.

1.9 Turn left on 18th Avenue.

2.8 Take a left on Wynkoop Street.

3.1 Turn left on 15th Avenue (headed back east-ish).

3.2 Turn right on Wazee Street.

3.3 Take the first left off of Wazee.

3.4 Turn left onto Market Street very briefly, then turn right onto 14th Avenue. (You have negotiated your way around some one-way messiness.) Traffic is often very heavy through here.

3.5 Turn right on Larimer Street. Then cross Speer Boulevard and enter the Auraria campus. Continue straight. **Option:** To avoid dismounting ahead, or perhaps just to make the loop less relentlessly urban, or just to shorten the darn thing a bit, cross Larimer and find the

---

[2]Nancy L. Widmann, *The East 7th Avenue Historic District* (Denver: Historic Denver, Inc., 1997), p. 44. The house is a half block north of 7th on Lafayette.

on-ramp for the Cherry Creek MUP. Take the path southeast and exit at 11th Street to rejoin the loop at mile 6.1 below.

3.8 Continue straight here at the end of the road, but dismount, lest you be sent to Guantanamo Bay.

3.9 Turn right onto the street, then make a quick left after a half block, going around the parking garage. This is Walnut Street.

4.0 Cross 7th Avenue.

4.3 Cross a particularly bad set of tracks.

4.6 After the road curls to the west, take a left onto Zuni Street, headed south.

4.8 Turn left onto 13th Avenue.

5.0 Cross another bad set of railroad tracks.

5.4 Take a right onto Mariposa Street.

5.6 Take a left on 11th Avenue.

5.7 Cross Lipan Street and continue straight through the no-cars-allowed zone. Continue east on 11th.

6.1 Cross Speer Boulevard.

6.5 Turn right on Broadway. (To avoid traffic on the big boulevard, you can use Acoma Street, but only as far as 8th Avenue.)

6.9 Immediately after the shiny building, turn left on 7th Avenue. There is a bike shop 1 block on at 7th and Lincoln.

8.9 Turn left on Steele Street.

9.7 Cross Colfax Avenue, jog left a half block, and continue north on Steele Street.

9.9 Cross 17th Avenue and reenter City Park. Go left after entering the park.

10.1 Approaching a lake, take a left.

10.2 Go left at the traffic circle.

10.4 Arrive back at the start/finish statue.

Ride Information

Restaurants

Wazee Supper Club, 1600 15th Street, Denver; (303) 623-9518. High-quality pizza in lower downtown.

Wahoo Fish Taco, 1521 Blake Street, Denver; (303) 623-0263. California-style Mexican food and a surf-inspired atmosphere. Good cheap food downtown.

Paris on the Platte, 1553 Platte Street, Denver; (303) 455-2451. Sandwiches, coffee, etc., in a casually hip bookstore/cafe. Very close to Confluence Park.

Rocky Mountain Diner, 800 18th Street, Denver; (303) 293-8383. Large portions of hearty western-style American food, including the ubiquitous buffalo meatloaf. In the heart of downtown in one of Denver's oldest surviving buildings, the "Ghost Building."

Fontano's Chicago Subs, 1623 California Street, Denver; (720) 956-1100. Open 'til 3:00 P.M. every day but Sunday. Get down there. Best meatball sub I've ever had.

16th Street Deli, 500 16th Street, Pavilions Mall, Denver; (720) 956-0440. The "half" sandwich is big. The "whole" is a real sandwich. Worth the trip uptown.

Tommy's Thai, 3410 East Colfax Avenue, Denver; (303) 377-4244. Quite cheap for good quality food and the whole town knows it. A few miles east of downtown on Colfax.

Mizuna, 225 East 7th Avenue, Denver; (303) 832-4778. This highly touted restaurant has been called the best in Denver. Upscale, reservations.

Accommodation

Hotel Monaco, 1717 Champa Street, Denver; (800) 990-1303. High style amid the high-rises.

Maps

Bicycling the Greater Denver Area Route Map (Mapsco).

16 Cherry Creek Reservoir Ramble

The Cherry Creek bike path is the eighth wonder of the world. Use it to roll all the way from deep, dark downtown to Cherry Creek State Park and Reservoir. This is a great ride for those hoping to avoid car traffic.

Start: Confluence Park, lower downtown Denver.
Length: 33.7-mile lariat.
Terrain: False flats and rolling hills, generally shallow.

Traffic and hazards: The Cherry Creek bicycle-pedestrian path is a popular facility for all manner of pedestrians and cyclists. The downtown section of the path is particularly busy during lunch hour on weekdays. At all times keep your head up and your eyes forward.

Getting there: From downtown Denver go west on 15th Street, under the railroad tracks and over the Platte River, and take the first left after the river onto Platte Street. Park in the free lot by the REI flagship store. It will probably be just as easy, and more enjoyable, to ride to the bike path from a home base in Denver rather than drive and park. From points north or south of Denver, take Interstate 25 to exit 211. Go north on Water Street, under Speer Boulevard, and park in the lot next to or across the street from the REI store. The mileage cues for this ride begin on the east side of the REI and attached Starbuck's, in front of the bike rack.

The Ride

Here is a popular little ride that starts in the burgeoning Platte Valley—an area of old warehouses, open fields, and railroad yards that has been and continues to be transformed into a residential area for Denver's young professionals. The path shoots you all the way out to southeast suburbia, where you can peruse a state park near a good-sized body of water before heading back downtown. Those who detest waiting at intersections and jockeying for position on city streets will appreciate this route, which is almost entirely on well-designed MUPs (multiuse paths) and mellow sight-seeing roads.

Leaving Confluence, this trail cuts a no-nonsense diagonal right past downtown. North of Colfax Avenue, the path is split, with the pedestrians' and in-line skaters'

Another incredible sunset, seen from the Kennedy Ballfields

path on the opposite side of the creek. To the south of Colfax, expect to encounter joggers and all kinds of pleasure walkers if the weather is conducive. You'll see that this path is truly of the multiuse variety as you pass small groups of homeless sleeping under the bridges. It's all pretty benign and, at least before nightfall, yuppie approved.

For the most part this path is well designed, but there are some curious features. Note the occasional stretches where the edge of the path drops precipitously into a bed of sharp rocks. If you happened to look down at your shoe for a second and ride off the concrete slab to a crushing, bloody disaster among the rocks, you wouldn't be the first, unfortunately. Keep your head up! That is really one of the keys to avoiding all manner of MUP-related mishaps.

At mile 3.0 pass the Washington Street Falls; 0.2 mile beyond, there are more falls under Corona Street; then the path climbs out of the culvert and up to street level. The next stretch is directly adjacent to Speer Boulevard, which has at this point aligned itself neatly along the east-west axis in preparation for its becoming 1st Avenue, the main drag through the Cherry Creek shopping sector. The Cherry Creek MUP becomes, essentially, a "sidepath"—a glorified sidewalk. Sidepaths are often problematic for absentminded or beginner cyclists because they cross a load of intersections and thus lure unsuspecting riders into car-bike conflicts. But this side-path only crosses one intersection along this stretch, the entrance to the highfalutin Denver Country Club. The intersection sees an insignificant amount of traffic. After the country club watch for a series of sharp, blind corners as the path goes under University Boulevard.

The MUP splits into two routes as it skirts the back side of the Cherry Creek Mall, one of the few area malls that still has some bloom on its rose, then comes back together as it approaches Cherry Creek Drive North. (Near the reconvergence, at mile 4.8, notice an offshoot from the MUP that heads due south across Cherry Creek. Being the only bridge across Cherry Creek between University and Colorado Boulevards, this is the start of an important and much used southward cycling route. Keep this in mind for your other rides through the city.)

A fast and curvy section leads to this path's coup de grace: the underpass below Colorado Boulevard at mile 5.5. Traverse another underpass below Cherry Street, and you have been ushered quietly past some of the nastiest traffic in the Denver metro area, found in the municipality of Glendale.

You will likely have to stop at an actual intersection when the path reaches Holly Street near mile 6.8. The section beyond Holly is less useful, meandering next to a lake and through a park popular with dog- and toddler-walkers, Rollerbladers, etc. There is also a tricky little intersection or two through here—cyclists in a big hurry may opt for the parallel Cherry Creek Drive North.

The path runs into another intersection at the sizable Monaco Parkway at mile 7.4, then, just a few ticks later, cuts south across a bridge and begins to follow the south side of Cherry Creek, through clouds of gnats in early summer. Here the thoroughfare opens up again. The MUP corkscrews underneath Iliff Avenue, yet another major boulevard, at mile 9.0. At mile 9.5 there is an interchange of sorts with the Highline Canal Trail. (The "Highline Trail" is a dirt and asphalt-surfaced MUP that follows a wildly meandering canal as it snakes all over east Denver.) Follow the well-signed route to continue on toward the Cherry Creek Reservoir.

Mile 11.7 finds you at an actual hill as the trail climbs to the Kennedy Ballfields and a view of the dam to the south. The trail then swoops down and under Interstate 225, then back up the other side. This is not a terribly easy section. At the top of the second hill is an intersection with a path that cuts westward at the base of the dam. This is the beginning and end of the loop around the lake. Both directions are nice, but veering left will put you into the state park sooner than will the right fork. There is one road to cross here, then the path dives immediately into Cherry Creek State Park.

Once in the park, options abound. You might want to stop and check the map at mile 13.3, just inside the park's boundary, and decide which way to go. You could remain entirely on paths, or loop around on the moderately trafficked road, or use a combination. The route described here keeps you on the same path initially, on a straight shot to the "beach," where much atmosphere can be absorbed,

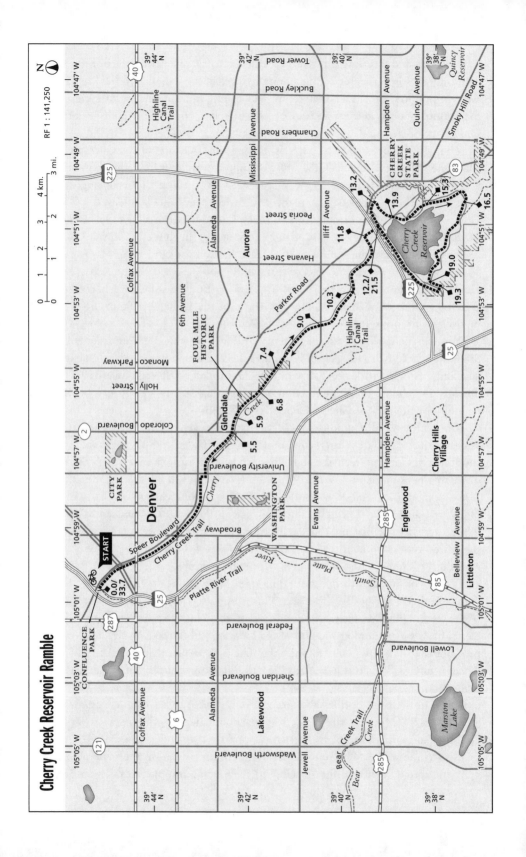

Cherry Creek Reservoir Ramble

RF 1 : 141,250

N

CITY PARK

Denver

CONFLUENCE PARK

START

0.0/ 33.7

Cherry Creek Trail

Speer Boulevard

Platte River Trail

Cherry Creek

5.5

5.9

6.8

7.4

9.0

10.3

Glendale

FOUR MILE HISTORIC PARK

University Boulevard

Highline Canal Trail

11.8

12.2/ 21.5

13.2

13.9

15.3

16.5

19.0

19.3

Cherry Creek Reservoir

CHERRY CREEK STATE PARK

Aurora

Washington Park

Englewood

Cherry Hills Village

Littleton

Lakewood

Marston Lake

Quincy Reservoir

before continuing with the loop on the road. Riders who aren't interested in soaking in atmosphere, or who just want to ride, might opt for a cleaner, faster route that bypasses the beach area.

Concerning the paths and roads in Cherry Creek State Park, it is worth noting that this area tends to be heavily infested with puncture vine, aka goatheads. The best way, perhaps the only way, to thwart their attack is to confine your travels to the established routes. And not just the established routes, but the middle of the established routes, if possible. The goathead is such an effective thorn that if it ends up out in the *middle* of the path it's going to be picked up quickly by a pedestrian or a cyclist. The result is that the middle of the path is usually swept clean of thorns by the poor suckers who came through before you.

At the time of this writing, some sections of the MUP around and near the lake were still under construction. Soon—perhaps by the time this book is in your hands, although with the current state of fiscal distress in the public sector it's hard to say— it will be possible to complete this ride entirely on MUPs, if you wish.

Miles and Directions

0.0 Start riding east on the Cherry Creek Trail from the REI store at Confluence Park. Reset the computer at the bike rack on the east side of the store. The first thing you will have to do from here is go east over the footbridge and take a left, which puts you on the trail.

5.5 Cross under Colorado Boulevard.

6.2 Pass the Four Mile Historic Park.

6.8 Here is an actual intersection to cross, Holly Street. You may want to jump on the street here (Cherry Creek Drive) after crossing Holly to bypass the next section through the Garland Park, which can be crowded with pedestrians and other hazards.

7.4 Reach another serious intersection at Monaco Parkway.

7.8 Turn right (south) across a bridge; the path continues on the south/west side of the creek.

9.0 Pass under Iliff Avenue; the path resumes on the north/east side of the creek.

9.4 The path splits. Go right over the bridge, back to the south/west side.

10.3 Continue straight at an intersection with the Highline Canal Trail. The HCT is a popular MUP, and while it can be quite useful for those who live very near it, as many do, its erratic snaking route makes it more of a recreational trail than a utilitarian one for cyclists.

10.5 Stay left.

11.8 After going up a hill, the path goes by the Kennedy Ballfields.

12.2 Take the left fork. You'll be coming back that other way later on.

12.7 Stay right.

13.0 The trail comes right up to I-225.

13.2 Cross Vaughn Way.

13.3 At the park map stay right. (There are plenty of route options once you're inside the park.)

13.9 Cross the road. This version of the route takes you right down to the beach on the bike path. If you want to avoid any shenanigans like that, take a left onto the road here.

14.4 Get on the road to the left.

14.5 Turn right onto a road.

14.6 Take another right.

15.3 Turn right.

16.5 Cross the bicycle path. **Option:** Get on the path here and it will meander by the road. The path is currently under construction, with the intention of linking up with the path on the north side of the dam. Estimated time of completion: unknown.

19.0 Stay left here. (The right fork goes to the marina.)

19.3 Across from Cherry Creek High, take a right on Dayton Street.

19.4 Cross the Cherry Creek Dam Road and get on the bike path on the other side.

21.5 Take a sharp left. This completes the loop around the reservoir. From here backtrack all the way to Confluence Park.

23.2 Stay right as the Highline Canal Trail comes in on your left.

25.9 The path abruptly turns right and crosses Cherry Creek on a bridge. On the other side of the creek, you have the choice to turn left onto the street or continue on the path, which follows a curvy line through the park beside the street.

26.3 Cross Monaco Parkway.

26.9 Cross Holly Street.

28.2 Cross under Colorado Boulevard.

33.7 Arrive back at Confluence Park.

Ride Information

Restaurants

Wazee Supper Club, 1600 15th Street, Denver; (303) 623-9518. High-quality pizza in lower downtown.

Wahoo Fish Taco, 1521 Blake Street, Denver; (303) 623-0263. California-style Mexican food and a surf-inspired atmosphere. Good cheap food downtown.

Paris on the Platte, 1553 Platte Street, Denver; (303) 455-2451. Sandwiches, coffee, etc., in a casually hip bookstore/cafe. Very close to Confluence Park.

Maps

Delorme: Colorado Atlas & Gazetteer: Pages 40–41, C-1–4, D-1–4.

17 Washington Park-Highline Canal Ramble

This is a really nice loop through the countrified suburbs of south-central Denver, utilizing the Highline Canal Trail, a meandering multiuse path (MUP).

Start: The west side of Washington Park in central Denver, from the parking area where Exposition Avenue enters the park from the west.
Length: 22.5-mile loop.
Terrain: Virtually flat in its entirety.
Traffic and hazards: The road around Washington Park is rife with wandering joggers, dogs, toddlers, you name it. It's kind of a mess, so watch out. The speed limit around the park is 15 mph, by the way. Franklin and Clarkson Streets are relatively quiet streets. The Highline Canal section is usually less congested than Denver's other main MUPs, but riders should not only expect crowds of pedestrians with dogs, they should be prepared to yield to them as well. The last phase of the loop, on Dahlia Street and Florida and Louisiana Avenues, features noticeably higher traffic intensity than the rest of the ride, but nothing too harsh.

Getting there: From downtown Denver go southeast on Speer Boulevard to Downing Street. Turn right and head south on Downing. Turn left into Washington Park at Exposition Avenue and park in the parking lot there near the park entrance. From outside Denver take Interstate 25 to the Downing Street exit and head north to Washington Park, entering at Exposition Avenue.

The Ride

I must confess a strong affection for this easy, flat loop through Denver's most deluxe suburbs. Starting from Washington Park, perhaps the finest of Denver's many excellent parks, this ride demands little from riders, and gives plenty. Traffic is generally mellow (rush hours excepted), neighborhoods are peaceful, and dogs are leashed and well fed. Best of all, the route wanders through an oasis in the city, the area between Cherry Hills and Greenwood Villages, which gives a decent impression of rural countryside. Surrounded on all sides by miles of dense middle-class suburbs, this is old farmland that has been subdivided into multimillion-dollar estates, but there are still open fields, ponds, horses, and other vestiges of the area's not-so-distant rural past. Snaking through this bucolic area, following one of the least direct routes imaginable, is the Highline Canal, an old irrigation ditch, and an accompanying bicycle-pedestrian path. If only it took a little longer to find its way through, this ride would be perfect.

There are a lot of serious riders out there who detest the idea of toodling along on any bicycle-pedestrian path. Bicycles belong on the street, they say, and only losers ride MUPs. Lordy, will those folks hate this ride! Not only is this an MUP, it's a pointlessly wandering, shamelessly recreation-oriented MUP. Although some, including the author, have found occasion to use sections of this path for straightforward transportation purposes, the Highline in general is good for nothin' but

The Highline Canal Trail

having fun. Toodling along is the name of the game here. Try it and you may agree that toodling on the Highline Canal Trail makes for a first-class riding experience.

This route uses Franklin Street to bolt south from Washington Park, then Clarkson Street to slip past the impenetrable Cherry Hills Village. Clarkson would be glad to take you all the way down to C-470, but you'll jump off and connect niftily to the Highline Canal Trail off a street called East Sunset Court (not to be confused with East Sunset Ridge, please). Join the ditch as it winds past the backyards of an affluent neighborhood (some houses with tennis courts, some with swimming pools, some lucky bastards with tennis courts and swimming pools) for a few miles. The Highline is quite different than the other big MUPs, because it meanders crazily, for one thing, but also because it is surfaced for much of its length with fine gravel. This actually makes the ride better than it would be if the path were paved, in the opinion of this author. The surface is smooth and slightly loose at the same time, giving a pleasant airy feel to the ride. It feels fast. If anything, the gravel/dirt surface is smoother than many asphalt streets.

The land really opens up around mile 8.0—fewer backyards, more open fields, fewer Range Rovers, more rusting tractors. This small loop somehow features something like 5 miles' worth of exceedingly pleasant, faux-rural wandering, right in the middle of the metroplex. The air is fresh, the birds are chirpin', and the rabbits are afraid of the coyotes.

By mile 14 you are sneaking up on Denver's middle-class core again. Your next nifty route-finding trick is to jump off the path early and use Dahlia Street to bypass the traffic clusterplotz around Hampden Avenue and Colorado Boulevard. Connect to the Highline Canal Trail again, a little more than a mile north, east of Mamie D. Eisenhower Park. This section of the Highline is, unfortunately, surfaced with asphalt, and it's much narrower than the section you had been enjoying previously. However, it helps out in a rather cool way—by passing seamlessly under Interstate 25, Denver's biggest route-finding nightmare.

The Highline Canal Trail continues on its way, to nowhere and everywhere, but jump off at mile 17.6 and get back into the street grid. There are many possible return routes from this point, but the route described here heads west to Dahlia Street again, uses it to cross Evans Avenue, then uses Florida Avenue to cross Colorado Boulevard on the way back to Washington Park.

Miles and Directions

0.0 Start from the parking area on the west side of Washington Park, where Exposition Avenue enters the park. Start riding south on the road that rings the park. Reset the odometer when you pass through the posts that restrict motor traffic.

0.8 As the road curls around the southern edge of the park, passing the tennis courts, turn right onto a path/sidewalk before the road turns back to the north. This little spur path will take you very briefly to Louisiana Avenue, which forms Washington Park's southern border.

0.9 Cross Louisiana Avenue and ride south on Franklin Street, passing South High School.

3.1 Cross Dartmouth Avenue.

3.3 Turn right on Floyd Avenue.

3.8 Turn left on South Clarkson Street.

6.4 Don't turn on East Sunset Ridge.

6.5 Turn left on East Sunset Court.

6.6 At the dead end of East Sunset Court, get on the bicycle-pedestrian trail. Less than 0.1 mile later, the trail runs into the Highline Canal Trail. Turn left onto the Highline Canal Trail.

8.0 Cross Long Road.

9.0 Stay left at the fork here. (There are many little spurs and connectors intersecting with the Highline Canal Trail, but this one is a more significant fork.)

14.0 Cross Quincy Avenue.

14.3 As the Highline Canal Trail makes a big sweeping left-hand curve, turn right and cross a bridge on another path.

14.4 Turn left on Dahlia Street, headed north.

15.6 Turn right onto the Highline Canal Trail again, just east of Mamie D. Eisenhower Park. Here the MUP is surfaced with asphalt.

16.3 The trail passes under I-25.

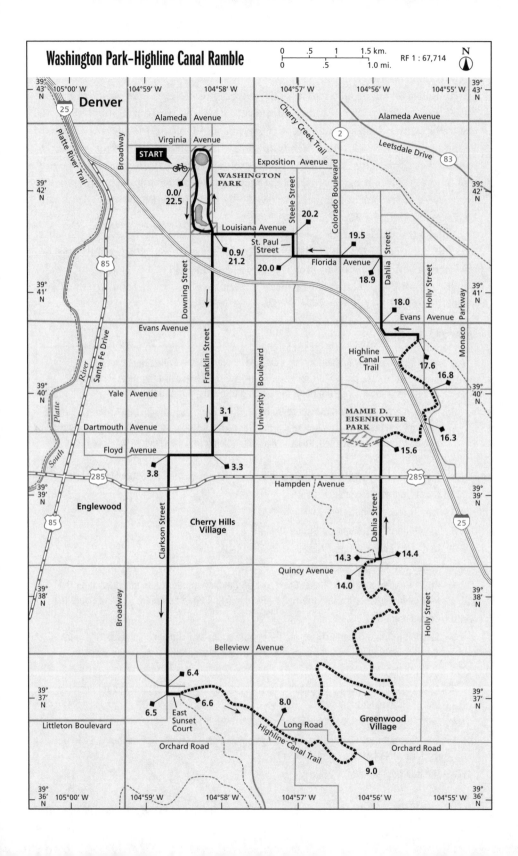

Washington Park–Highline Canal Ramble

RF 1 : 67,714

N

0   .5   1   1.5 km.
0   .5   1.0 mi.

Denver

Platte River Trail

Alameda Avenue

Virginia Avenue

START

Cherry Creek Trail

Alameda Avenue

Leetsdale Drive

Exposition Avenue

WASHINGTON PARK

0.0/22.5

Broadway

Louisiana Avenue

20.2

St. Paul Street

0.9/21.2

20.0

19.5

Florida Avenue

Steele Street

Colorado Boulevard

18.9

Dahlia Street

18.0

Evans Avenue

Holly Street

Monaco Parkway

Downing Street

Evans Avenue

Highline Canal Trail

17.6

16.8

Franklin Street

Yale Avenue

University Boulevard

MAMIE D. EISENHOWER PARK

16.3

Dartmouth Avenue

3.1

Floyd Avenue

3.3

15.6

3.8

285

Hampden Avenue

285

Englewood

Cherry Hills Village

Santa Fe Drive

South Platte River

Clarkson Street

Dahlia Street

14.3   14.4

Quincy Avenue

14.0

Broadway

Belleview Avenue

6.4

6.5   6.6

East Sunset Court

8.0

Long Road

Greenwood Village

Holly Street

Littleton Boulevard

Highline Canal Trail

Orchard Road

Orchard Road

9.0

16.8   Cross Yale Avenue.

17.6   Drop left off the trail on a semi-official-looking exit that leads directly to a residential neighborhood, at the corner of Iliff Avenue and South Grape Street. Head north on South Grape briefly.

17.7   Turn left on Warren Avenue.

18.0   Turn right on Dahlia Street.

18.9   Turn left on Florida Avenue, headed west.

19.5   Cross Colorado Boulevard.

20.0   Cross Steele Street and turn right on St. Paul Street. (This is just one option at this point, on your final approach to Washington Park. You can use just about any street to jog north to Louisiana, or just stay on Florida for as long as you can.)

20.2   Turn left on Louisiana Avenue.

21.2   Across from Franklin Street turn right onto the same little spur path that you used at the beginning of the ride. Head back into the park and turn right on the road. (You can't turn left here, as bike traffic is routed counterclockwise around the park.)

22.5   Arrive back at the start/finish.

Ride Information

Restaurants

Handlebar and Grill, 305 South Downing Street, Denver; (303) 778-6761. Yeah, that's really the name of it. And there really is a load of bike-racing memorabilia, including complete bicycles, hanging all over this place. Which helps you get over the fact that the food is mediocre. Quite close to Wash Park.

Tommy's Thai, 3410 East Colfax Avenue, Denver; (303) 377-4244. Quite cheap for good quality food and the whole town knows it. A few miles east of downtown on Colfax.

Mizuna, 225 East 7th Avenue, Denver; (303) 832-4778. This highly touted restaurant has been called the best in Denver. Upscale, reservations.

Angelo's, 620 East 6th Avenue, Denver; (303) 744-3366. Small, dark, family-run Italian place. Modestly priced.

Pete's Central One, 300 South Pearl, Denver; (303) 778-6675. Greek food at the corner of Alameda and Pearl, close to Wash Park. Pete owns several Greek restaurants in Denver—this is the best one.

Jerusalem Restaurant, 1890 East Evans Avenue, Denver; (303) 777-8828. Good Middle-Eastern food served up fast. Open late. A few blocks west of University Boulevard on Evans near the University of Denver. Hummus can you eat? 'Til you falafel.

Los Troncos, 6th. 730 East 6th Avenue, Denver; (303) 778-8533. Bolivian and Mexican food at this humble restaurant.

Maps

Delorme: Colorado Atlas & Gazetteer: Pages 39 A, B-7; 40 A-1. *Bicycling the Greater Denver Area Route Map* (Mapsco).

Boulder

he People's Republic of Boulder (as it is known to smart alecks statewide) provides an incredible home base for road cyclists. One of the best in the world, in fact. This is no secret. An incredible lineup of road and mountain bike racers, triathletes, fitness nazis, and other endorphin junkies have settled in Boulder over the decades, and they continue to flock here to make their dreamiest two-wheeled fantasies come true.

The real attraction, besides all the frighteningly beautiful people, of course, is the proximity to the mountains. Right out the back door, to the west, is a glorious array of beautiful hill climbs. These are the roads that make Boulder unequaled in its volume and quality of riding opportunities: Flagstaff, Magnolia, Sugarloaf, Four Mile, Sunshine, Left Hand, South Saint Vrain . . . These climbs can be mixed and matched and combined in hundreds of possible configurations. (In this guide, we won't shy away from using a few sections of dirt road to create new versions of these classic Boulder hill rides.) The eastern horizon is no slouch either, with rolling hills and dead-flat farmland stretching all the way to Kansas City. There are dozens of good bike roads out there. Just get on and ride, and don't stop 'til you're done.

Boulder is the land of no excuses. No matter what type of riding you crave, this is the center of it. But if you love long, tough climbs snaking from the foothills to the alpine heights, Boulder is nothing less than your paradise. Think of what incredible shape you'd be in, and how happy you'd be, if you could just stay here and ride these roads every day. If only you could manage the cost of housing, that is.

18 NCAR Ramble

Enjoy some of the finest views on the Front Range on this short, moderate climb to the campus of the National Center for Atmospheric Research (NCAR).

Start: The intersection of Broadway and Table Mesa Drive in south Boulder.
Length: 4.8-mile out-and-back.
Terrain: One continuous hill climb, moderate.

Traffic and hazards: The descent has the potential for dangerous speed. Traffic is slight once the road leaves the built-up area.

Getting there: This short ride is easily accessible by bicycle from anywhere in Boulder. From central Boulder, near downtown, the Mall, or the University of Colorado campus, the best way to get to Table Mesa Drive is probably to use the MUP (multiuse path) that travels south along Broadway. This north-south MUP branches off from the east-west Boulder Creek path near the southeast corner of Broadway and Arapahoe Avenue, across from the Wild Oats grocery store. Between Arapahoe and Table Mesa is a 2.6-mile section of MUP. From Denver take U.S. Highway 36 to the Table Mesa exit and drive west on Table Mesa Drive to Broadway. Park somewhere in the vast sea of parking southwest of Broadway and Table Mesa.

The Ride

When you get on a bike and ride up the big curl of a road leading to NCAR, you are riding on a work of functional art. And that's not just something cute to say; it's really true. The layout of the road was designed by the architect I. M. Pei in the 1960s as part of his larger plan for the scientific campus on the mesa. The road is deliberately indirect and lengthy on its way to the complex, a design feature that Pei hoped would add drama to the approach and impart a sense of significance to the whole enterprise.

Although Pei didn't know it, he made a great cycling road. The road doesn't go anywhere else, and it's not possible (even with this author's beloved dirt roads) to make any kind of loop with it, but it still deserves a place in this guide. Starting in the heart of modern suburbia—amidst a vast sea of parking lots near the bustling intersection of Broadway and Table Mesa Drive—get warmed up with a slight climb away from the retail madness into a residential neighborhood. This first phase culminates with a little out-of-saddle jump as the road abruptly leaves the residential area and is surrounded by open field. The climb is staring the foothills right in the face and settles into about a 6 percent grade, maddeningly steady, relentless if a headwind is blowing. As the road curls ever so slowly to the south, you might find that this silly little climb is giving you some trouble.

The Flatirons

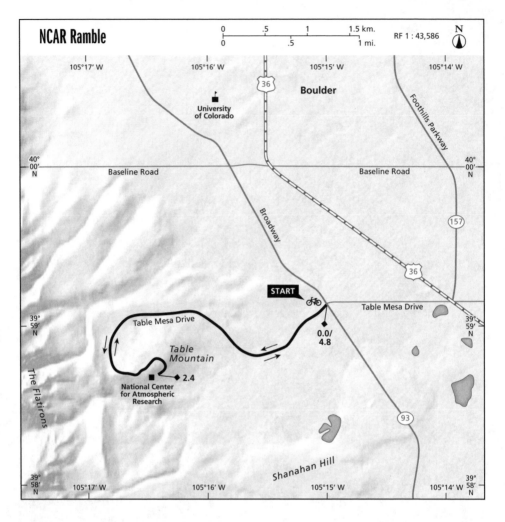

A common experience on the NCAR climb is to feel a strong and mysterious boost of energy as the road turns to the east—here it is flattened as well as turned windward for its final approach to the mesa top. On the mesa you can walk a bike along the hiking trails to prime hanging-out spots overlooking Boulder. The view is excellent. Looking back at Pei's NCAR is interesting as well.

I. M. Pei won the commission to design NCAR in 1961, beating out a number of better-known architects. The prevailing thought was that Pei, being young and hungry, would involve himself more fully in the project than some others might. That turned out to be correct. Pei slept on the mesa and engaged in long conversations about abstract concepts with Walter Orr Roberts, the visionary in charge of the project. Roberts had some unconventional ideas about architecture and what he wanted Pei to achieve with his design. Says Roberts: "Chaos is an integral part of creativity, and I wanted a building that would be somewhat chaotic, that would encourage random interaction, a place where if you wanted to go from point A to point B, there were five different choices, and no way to tell which was the best without a guide."

Pei's initial designs were rejected by Roberts—not chaotic enough. At the 1967 dedication Pei said, "We tried many buildings here, many designs, but they all fell apart." Even after that agonizing process, the finalized blueprint did not correspond to what stands on the mesa today, as the money ran out before a large portion of the complex could be finished. Omitted from the composition were two more towers, intended for the hillside on the south.[1]

The final product, nonetheless, is a striking sculptural form, reminiscent of Stonehenge and the cliff dwellings of Mesa Verde. And apparently it is chaotic as all heck: mission accomplished on that front. While the work was regarded as a triumph for Pei, he now feels this early design to be overly dramatic and sophomoric, and he is not alone in that judgment. What do you think?

I. M. Pei went on to design such diverse spaces as the Kennedy Library, the Rock and Roll Hall of Fame, and the glass pyramid addition to the Louvre. Pei has his elegant (yet derivative) mark on downtown Denver as well, having designed the Mies van der Rohe–inspired Mile High Center at 1700 Broadway, another of his very early works, and the building that currently holds the Adam's Mark hotel at 15th Street and Court Place, an homage to Le Corbusier.

Miles and Directions

0.0 Start from the corner of Table Mesa Drive and Broadway in south Boulder, riding west up Table Mesa Drive.

2.4 Top out at the NCAR complex.

4.8 Return to the starting point at Table Mesa and Broadway.

Ride Information

Events/Attractions

National Center for Atmospheric Research, 1850 Table Mesa Drive, Boulder; (303) 497-1173; www.ncar.ucar.edu/. According to the Web site, "NCAR is a federally funded research and development center. Together with our partners at universities and research centers, we are dedicated to exploring and understanding our atmosphere and its interactions with the Sun, the oceans, the biosphere, and human society." The NCAR visitor center is open to the public seven days a week and is free.

Restaurants

Mustard's Last Stand, 1719 Broadway, Boulder; (303) 444-5841. Quality fast-food burgers, Chicago-style dogs, veggie burgers, to go or consume on site. Where Boulder Creek flows under Broadway.

[1]Carter Wiseman, *I. M. Pei: A Profile in American Architecture* (New York: Henry A. Abrams, 1990), pp. 73-91.

Wild Oats Grocery and Deli. Two useful locations in Boulder: 1651 Broadway, (303) 442-0082; 2584 Baseline Road, (303) 499-7636. Big sandwiches, salad bar, refrigerated liquids, bathroom. This place is undeniably useful.

La Iguana Taqueria, 1301 Broadway, Boulder; (303) 938-8888. Heaping portions of Fresh-Mex on the Hill.

Jalino's, 1647 Arapahoe Avenue, Boulder; (303) 443-6300. Excellent pizza and sandwiches.

Bova's Pantry, 1325 Broadway, Boulder; (303) 449-0874. Grocery and deli on the Hill. Still wrappin' sandwiches after all these years.

Pasta Jay's, 1001 Pearl Street, Boulder; (303) 444-5800. Once the upstart restaurateur of the Front Range, Jay is now an institution.

Narayan's, 921 Pearl Street, Boulder; (303) 447-2816. Boulder has lots of great little restaurants serving up the exotic tastes of the Far East. This is one of the best.

Maps

Delorme: Colorado Atlas & Gazetteer: Page 40 A-1.

19 Boulder-Hygiene Cruise

This cruise takes you on a fast loop through the farm, ranch, and ranchette country northeast of Boulder. It's a flatland favorite.

Start: The intersection of Folsom Avenue/26th Street and Valmont Road in north-central Boulder. Choosing a start/finish for a ride like this is somewhat arbitrary. This corner is as good as any—there's a 7-11 store here at least—but the ride could begin just about anywhere around town.

Length: 30.1-mile loop.

Terrain: As flat as it gets for these parts. Flats and false flats spiced with rolling hills.

Traffic and hazards: Traffic volume is heavy along U.S. Highway 36 and Highway 119 (the Diagonal), and speeds are high. Shoulders along both stretches, however, are plenty wide. 75th Street has moderate traffic and can feel narrow when cars are passing in both directions. The portion of the loop within Boulder is along established bike routes with segregated bike lanes.

Getting there: From Denver and points south, take Interstate 25 north to US 36. Take US 36 northwest to the Foothills Parkway exit. Take Foothills Parkway (Highway 157) north to Valmont Road, then take a left (west) and go west about 15 blocks and run into this loop's start at Folsom Avenue/26th Street. From points north of Boulder, drive south on U.S. Highway 287 or I-25 to Highway 119 west to Boulder. Highway 119 spills out onto US 36 south (which is also 28th Street) at the northeast corner of town; take US 36/28th Street south to Valmont Road, then go west on Valmont 2 blocks to the start. Parking abounds in the surrounding residential area (not true for much of Boulder but true of this neighborhood). If you already have a home base in Boulder, don't drive to this loop. Ride the bike, of course.

Curious cows near Hygiene Road

The Ride

This ride starts in a promising fashion, by taking you on a tour of nearly the entire length of highway between Boulder and Lyons. Rolling north along the edge of the foothills, it requires a bit of discipline to keep pedaling right past the tempting eastbound turnoffs of Neva Road, Nelson Road, and Saint Vrain Road. The longer trip north pays off, as Hygiene Road is the class of the bunch. You're already descending a bit and moving fast when you make the turn onto Hygiene, which drops away and sends you hurtling on a 30 mph rip past prime cow country. The road makes a brief jog around Foothills Reservoir, but is essentially a straight shot all the way into Hygiene.

Crossing railroad tracks after 4 miles on Hygiene Road, make the right turn and head south on 75th Street. Should you need anything, there is a small store a half block to the north.

Hygiene, the town, sprouted in the 1880s around a sanitarium for tuberculosis patients. The Colorado Front Range, with its crisp, fresh air, was a favorite destination for Easterners seeking relief from TB and other respiratory ailments. This particular

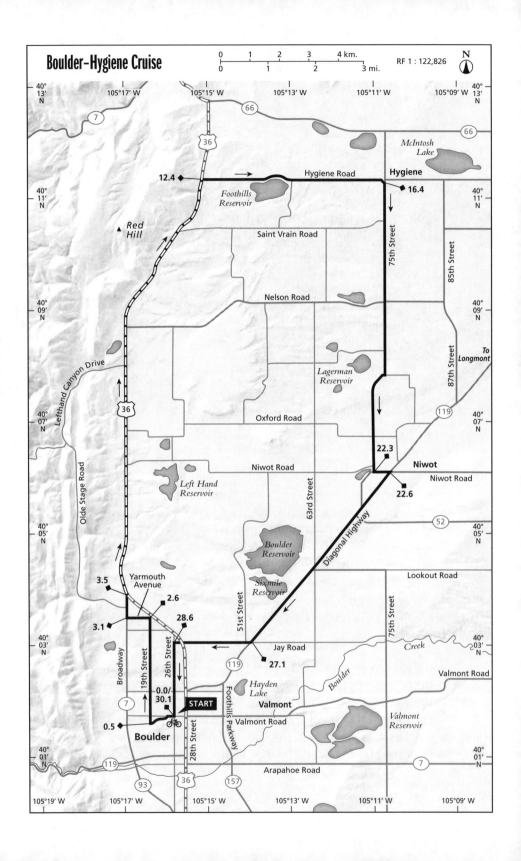

Boulder–Hygiene Cruise

RF 1 : 122,826

N

facility was run by a religious order known as the Dunkards, famous for their excessive dunking in baptism rituals. No, I am not making that up.

South out of Hygiene the intensity of traffic ramps up a little, with a slightly increased volume as well as a slightly skinnier road. The scenery is pretty intense out here as well—looking west across a brilliant green patchwork dotted with ponds and reservoirs with the mountains forming a jagged backdrop. Seventy-fifth is not blessed with a lot of curves, but it's still nice.

At mile 22.6 join the Diagonal and cut an angle straight to Boulder. The so-called Diagonal is a major highway, but the shoulder is huge. The endgame of this loop features a stellar way to slice back through north-central Boulder: Jay Road west to 26th Street south. Add 26th to Boulder's other highly functional north-south corridors, 4th and 19th Streets.

This loop has lots of obvious variations. It can easily be started from just about anywhere in Boulder. It could also skip Boulder in its near entirety with a minor change of route. The counterclockwise version works well, though perhaps not as well as the clockwise loop. Making that right turn at Hygiene Road off of US 36 and rocketing eastward across the prairie is what this ride is all about.

Miles and Directions

0.0 Start from the corner of Folsom/26th Street and Valmont Road. Head west up Valmont, which jogs south and becomes Balsam Avenue.

0.5 Take a right on 19th Street.

0.8 Pass Salberg Park.

2.6 On the north side of the trailer park, take a left on Yarmouth Avenue.

3.1 Turn right on Broadway, the main drag.

3.5 Turn left onto US 36.

12.4 Turn right on Hygiene Road.

16.4 Cross railroad tracks, then go right on 75th Street.

22.3 With the Diagonal Highway (Highway 119) in view, take a left onto Niwot Road.

22.6 Take a right onto Highway 119.

27.1 Turn right on Jay Road.

28.6 Turn left onto 26th Street. Continue south on 26th through a few strange intersections.

30.1 Arrive back at the intersection of 26th Street and Valmont Road.

Ride Information

Restaurants

Mustard's Last Stand, 1719 Broadway, Boulder; (303) 444-5841. Quality fast-food burgers, Chicago-style dogs, veggie burgers, to go or consume on site. Where Boulder Creek flows under Broadway.

Wild Oats Grocery and Deli. Two useful locations in Boulder: 1651 Broadway, (303) 442-0082; 2584 Baseline Road, (303) 499-7636. Big sandwiches, salad bar, refrigerated liquids, bathroom. This place is undeniably useful.

La Iguana Taqueria, 1301 Broadway, Boulder; (303) 938-8888. Heaping portions of Fresh-Mex on the Hill.

Jalino's, 1647 Arapahoe Avenue, Boulder; (303) 443-6300. Excellent pizza and sandwiches.

Bova's Pantry, 1325 Broadway, Boulder; (303) 449-0874. Grocery and deli on the Hill. Still wrappin' sandwiches after all these years.

Pasta Jay's, 1001 Pearl Street, Boulder; (303) 444-5800. Once the upstart restaurateur of the Front Range, Jay is now an institution.

Narayan's, 921 Pearl Street, Boulder; (303) 447-2816. Boulder has lots of great little restaurants serving up the exotic tastes of the Far East. This is one of the best.

Maps
Delorme: Colorado Atlas & Gazetteer: Page 30 C, D-1.

20 Boulder Creek-Gunbarrel Ramble

Head east and enjoy a modest 25-mile cruise completely devoid of serious climbing. This short tour cuts through the heart of Boulder on its very popular fully separated path, rolling out to the outlying suburbs and farm country northeast of town.

Start: The intersection of two major bicycle-pedestrian paths, southeast of the corner of Broadway and Arapahoe Avenue in Boulder.

Length: 24.7-mile loop.

Terrain: Slightly downhill on a very curvy, paved multiuse path, then flats and easy rollers on straight roads in farm country.

Traffic and hazards: The Boulder Creek bike path is often clogged and is always dangerous—riding it requires special care. Expect to yield often to pedestrians and slower cyclists, including children. The roads on this route carry a lot of cars—they are minor highways—but the shoulders are generally wide and many of the road segments here have explicitly labeled bike lanes. Overall traffic intensity is moderate. Road surfaces are good.

Getting there: As this loop starts on the Boulder Creek Trail, at its intersection with the Broadway bike path, it will probably be easiest to start the ride by cycling from somewhere in Boulder on one of these two paths. If driving in, take U.S. Highway 36 to the Foothills Parkway exit. Go north on Foothills Parkway to Arapahoe Avenue, and go west on Arapahoe to 13th Street. Take a right on 13th and park. The bike path flows through the park there and goes under Arapahoe. The start/finish is just on the other side of Arapahoe.

The Ride

There are infinite variations on this loop out of Boulder into the rolling farm country east and north of town. We'll shake things up a little this time by using the Boulder Creek bike path to get out of town onto familiar roads. The road network out there has been and still is much loved by the top-notch competitive riders who live in Boulder. This love is largely dependent on the wind direction at any given time.

Dodd Reservoir near Niwot Road and the Diagonal Highway

The Boulder Creek bicycle-pedestrian path—going out on a limb here—is probably the busiest of all the multiuse paths on the Front Range. Although it is a fully separated path that runs uninterrupted for a long distance, it is not a straight-forward bicycle highway where high speeds are feasible. Not only is it exceedingly—almost comically—busy at times, it has many tight, blind curves. Weekdays are a bit quieter. Anyone who rides this path should accept the fact that it will be a complete clustermunch. If you can make that leap of faith, you can then appreciate the path's positive points, of which there are many.

The 4.5-mile section of Boulder Creek Trail spits you out east of town at the Stazio Ballfields, a well-known spot to Lycra locals, as it is often used for criterium races. From here jump on Valmont Road, a popular cycling route for the eastbound crowd. Valmont flirts with actual curviness—a rare commodity out east—as it circumnavigates Valmont Reservoir.

The first serious northbound movement of this route comes courtesy of 75th Street, once a gritty, windblown country road, now looking quite suburban. The shoulder is wide. Cut back west on Lookout Road and zip down the hill into Gunbarrel. Yes, that's what it's called: Gunbarrel. Gunbarrel is not an actual town but an

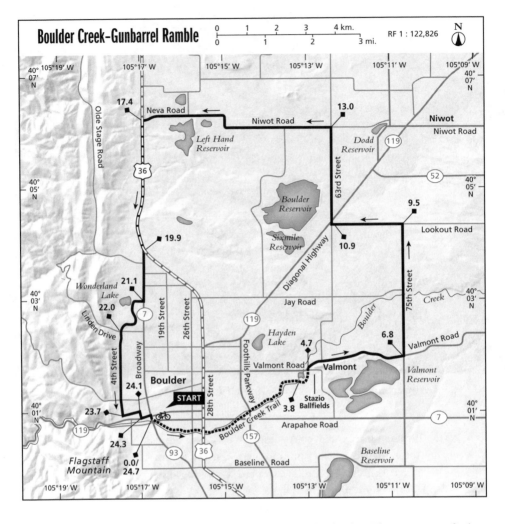

Boulder Creek-Gunbarrel Ramble

office/industrial park development with some attached suburbia. There you can find a huge grocery store and fast food if you need it, but not much else to catch your attention.

Traveling north on 63rd Street, pedal up some minor hills and out into more open country, irrigated fields flashing in the sun. Take a left onto Niwot Road at mile 13.0. (Riders looking for a little more variety might want to take an early left on Monarch Road, one of the area's many smooth dirt roads, and use that to cut over to Niwot Road.) Niwot does a little right-angle this-way-and-that on its 4.4-mile trip across the flats to US 36.

There are a few good ways to get back to the start/finish from the intersection of US 36 and Broadway. You could go east briefly—on Yarmouth Avenue, for instance—and take 19th Street all the way in. Or you could do as described in the mileage cues and take the pleasant 4th Street/Wonderland Hill Avenue passage down to west Boulder, then take the bike path to get back to the start/finish from the west. Either way is quite nice.

Miles and Directions

0.0 Start riding east down the Boulder Creek Trail from the major intersection with another path, the Broadway bike path, just south of Arapahoe Avenue and east of Broadway. Pass behind Boulder High.

3.8 Take a right as the bike path forks around a lake.

4.1 Take a left and cross the bridge to the Stazio Ballfields.

4.5 Spill out onto pavement and continue straight.

4.7 Take a left across the tracks, then a quick right, then join Valmont Road, headed east.

6.8 Take a left on 75th Street.

9.5 Turn left on Lookout Road.

10.9 Take a right on 63rd Street.

11.1 Cross the Diagonal (Highway 119).

13.0 Take a left on Niwot Road (this road becomes Neva Road later on).

17.4 Turn left onto US 36.

19.9 Take a right on Broadway and head back into Boulder.

21.1 Take a right on Quince Street.

21.5 Continue straight on the short bike path segment where Quince dead-ends. Then take a left on Wonderland Hill Avenue.

22.0 Cross Linden Drive and continue south on the bike path segment. At the end of this block-long path, continue straight south on 4th Street.

23.7 Take a left on Spruce Street.

24.1 Take a right on 9th Street.

24.3 Cross Canyon Boulevard and turn left onto the Boulder Creek bike path.

24.6 Stay right after the path dives under Broadway and enters a park. Go under Arapahoe Avenue.

24.7 Arrive back at the start/finish.

Ride Information

Restaurants

Mustard's Last Stand, 1719 Broadway, Boulder; (303) 444-5841. Quality fast-food burgers, Chicago-style dogs, veggie burgers, to go or consume on site. Where Boulder Creek flows under Broadway.

Wild Oats Grocery and Deli. Two useful locations in Boulder: 1651 Broadway, (303) 442-0082; 2584 Baseline Road, (303) 499-7636. Big sandwiches, salad bar, refrigerated liquids, bathroom. This place is undeniably useful.

La Iguana Taqueria, 1301 Broadway, Boulder; (303) 938-8888. Heaping portions of Fresh-Mex on the Hill.

Jalino's, 1647 Arapahoe Avenue, Boulder; (303) 443-6300. Excellent pizza and sandwiches.

Bova's Pantry, 1325 Broadway, Boulder; (303) 449-0874. Grocery and deli on the Hill. Still wrappin' sandwiches after all these years.
Pasta Jay's, 1001 Pearl Street, Boulder; (303) 444-5800. Once the upstart restaurateur of the Front Range, Jay is now an institution.
Narayan's, 921 Pearl Street, Boulder; (303) 447-2816. Boulder has lots of great little restaurants serving up the exotic tastes of the Far East. This is one of the best.

Maps

Delorme: Colorado Atlas & Gazetteer: Page 30 D-1.

21 Flagstaff-Coal Creek Challenge

Get in touch with your inner Lance on this very strenuous adventure through the mountains west of Boulder. It covers some of the steepest hills and roughest roads available. This ain't no downstream ride.

Start: Chautauqua Park, Boulder.
Length: 33.8-mile loop.
Terrain: Several pitches of ridiculous climbing characterize the first third of this ride. The rest is moderate climbing and descending and a rolling traverse along the easternmost foothills. Total elevation gain is about 2,800 feet.
Traffic and hazards: To make a loop using Flagstaff Road, this route necessarily incorporates a significant length of dirt road—about 6 miles' worth. If you want a magic carpet ride,

this isn't it. Traffic volume is moderate on Flagstaff Mountain, but motor traffic can feel oppressive on the low slopes where the narrow road makes passing difficult. (Meanwhile, the motorists are thinking that the bicycle traffic is oppressive.) Highway 93 is a heavily traveled commuter route. Shoulders range in and out—thinner sections can occasionally be a problem. It is not a good road to ride after dark, so start early. The end of the ride features a bike path with the attendant dangers.

Getting there: Chautauqua Park lies on the extreme western edge of Boulder, at the base of the Flatirons, along Baseline Road. Baseline Road is one of the main east-west boulevards south of the University of Colorado campus. Baseline is easy to find on a map because it traces the 40th parallel. From U.S. Highway 36 take the Baseline exit and drive west toward the mountains. The park entrance is on the south side of Baseline, west of 9th Street and directly across from Grant Street. Parking is available in the public lot, although it does fill up occasionally.

The Ride

For decades Boulder's bike-crazy population has used Flagstaff Mountain as its public proving ground. Between classes, after work, or first thing on a Saturday morning, local riders flock to the switchbacks of Flagstaff to suffer for their sins. Flagstaff is Boulder's little Alpe d'Huez.

Gross Reservoir

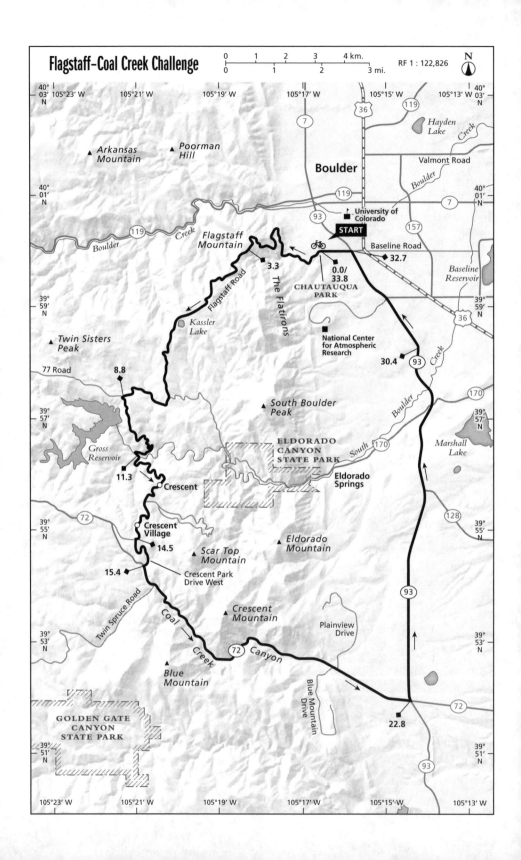

Flagstaff-Coal Creek Challenge

RF 1 : 122,826

N

0   1   2   3   4 km.
0   1   2   3 mi.

40°03' N 105°23' W   105°21' W   105°19' W   105°17' W   105°15' W   105°13' W 40°03' N

36

7

119

Hayden
Lake

Boulder
Creek

Poorman
Hill

Arkansas
Mountain

Valmont Road

Boulder

40°01' N

119

7

157

University of
Colorado

START

Baseline
Reservoir

Baseline Road

♦ **32.7**

119

Boulder   Creek

Flagstaff
Mountain

Flagstaff Road

The Flatirons

3.3

**0.0/
33.8**

CHAUTAUQUA
PARK

40°01' N

39°59' N

Kassler
Lake

National Center
for Atmospheric
Research

30.4
♦ 93

39°59' N

Twin Sisters
Peak

77 Road

8.8

South Boulder
Peak

ELDORADO
CANYON
STATE PARK

South   Boulder

170

Marshall
Lake

39°57' N

39°57' N

Gross
Reservoir

11.3

Crescent

170

Eldorado
Springs

128

39°55' N

72

Crescent
Village

14.5

Scar Top
Mountain

Eldorado
Mountain

93

39°55' N

15.4

Crescent Park
Drive West

Twin Spruce Road

Coal   Creek

Crescent
Mountain

Plainview
Drive

39°53' N

39°53' N

72   Canyon

Blue Mountain Drive

93

72

Blue
Mountain

GOLDEN GATE
CANYON
STATE PARK

22.8

39°51' N

93

39°51' N

105°23' W   105°21' W   105°19' W   105°17' W   105°15' W   105°13' W

Most of those who enjoy Flagstaff, however, turn around at the top of the first mountain, somewhere around mile 3.3. These riders miss out on a lot: Some of the most intense climbing on the Front Range and a whole rewarding adventure lie beyond. The short up-and-back version makes a fine ride, but the loop described here is truly memorable.

The staging area is at the foot of the Flatirons rock formation (the formation armors the east slope of Green Mountain), which is one of the proudest hunks of rock on the Front Range and ranks right up there with Maroon Bells as one of the most photographed vistas in the state. The slabs are particularly beautiful with a very light dusting of autumn snow. (The sight of snow at this altitude, however, is a bad omen for those attempting this loop.)

With scant opportunity for warm-up, this route quickly puts you onto a difficult hill. The first pitches of Flagstaff, the little mountain just north of the Flatirons, are attention grabbing. The early climb steepens to a relentless grade that shows mercy only after passing the overlook and fancy-dancy Flagstaff House restaurant about a mile up. Above the restaurant the climb is almost easy for a long while as it twists and turns severely to flatten the grade.

Traffic on the serpentine Flagstaff Road is usually pretty heavy. Hikers, picnickers, sightseers, overlookers, smoke dopers, and motorcycle racer wannabes all tend to act simultaneously on their urge to drive up Flagstaff. Rock climbers also swarm the mountain, because some of the world's most famous "bouldering problems"—Monkey Traverse, for instance—are just off the road. (These climbers are known to come right up to you—but don't feed them.) The traffic thins out dramatically after mile 3.3. Most of the other road users concern themselves with destinations on the eastern face of the mountain, except for the trail bikers, who are on their way to Walker Ranch Park near Gross Reservoir. There is also a small contingent of commuters using the road.

The degree of traffic and the personality of the hill strongly recall Lookout Mountain near Golden.

After cruising over the top of Flagstaff, past the point where the vast majority of riders turn around, this ride is really just getting started. A much more severe brand of hill lies in wait at mile 3.8. This one slaps you hard with percent grades in the high teens, then settles into a slope that, although not quite brutally steep, disappears into the distance in an intimidating show of length. Get set for a solid, unbroken mile of tough climbing, followed by an additional 4 miles of occasional flats, fast descents, and still more climbing. The worst (or best) of it is over by mile 5.

When the road finally approaches Gross Reservoir, an ominous sign looms above: NO OUTLET. Fear not; to escape the tyranny of an out-and-back route, cut a left onto the dirt road at mile 8.8. Now we're talkin'. Riders with cyclo-cross setups will fare better on this road, but such equipment is not a requirement. When in doubt, ride a bit slower and lighter than you normally would.

This road is no mere connector. It takes its time descending to water level, crossing South Boulder Creek, then chugs up the other side over a modest pass. It's a notable climb, exacerbated by the dirt surface with its washboard and chuckholes. Some of the 6 miles along this dirt road section seem extra long.

After about mile 14.5 cut left onto a deus ex machina of a road called Crescent Park Drive West and drop into Coal Creek Canyon on the smooth, comforting pavement of mountain suburbia. A perfectly placed convenience store awaits at the bottom of the hill, on Highway 72. This ride ain't over, so it's good to stock up here. May I recommend the Snickers-banana-Gatorade combination platter?

Descending Coal Creek is a bumpy ride due to road damage, and drivers can seem a bit impatient in the narrow curves, but it is otherwise nice. The typical round turns lead to a long fast straightaway as Coal Creek emerges from the last stand of foothills and spills onto the plains. On the west edge of the land once occupied by the nuclear trigger factory called Rocky Flats—now posing as a harmless empty field after the contaminated buildings were painstakingly removed piece by piece—take a left onto Highway 93 for the final stretch. Highway 93 is an up-and-down affair. Traffic is moderate to heavy, which would be no problem except that the paved shoulder disappears occasionally, leaving a sketchy dirt surface. After the day's previous 6 miles of dirt road, at least you know you have the skills to ride this shoulder if you need to. Another common theme along Highway 93 is wind. This road is famous for its gale-force crosswind coming out of the west.

You know what you need after all that? Another hill. The final climb up Baseline Road is a worthy finale. There is a shady spot of grass with your name on it in Chautauqua Park.

Miles and Directions

0.0 Start from the parking area at Chautauqua Park and begin riding west up Baseline Road. Mileage cues begin at the intersection of Grant Street (which is the street directly opposite the entrance to the park) and Baseline Road.

3.3 Pass the short spur road that leads to the overlook parking area at the top of Flagstaff Mountain. Take the short side trip if you feel good; it's a nice view.

3.8 The day's most brutal climbing is found through here.

8.8 Approaching Gross Reservoir, hang a left onto a dirt road. You'll climb a very short hill and pass to the east of the reservoir. There are beautiful views across the water.

11.3 Cross South Boulder Creek, then, at a fork in the road, take a left. (The right turn leads to the reservoir.) Modest climbing ensues.

14.5 Take a left onto paved Crescent Park Drive West and descend all the way to Coal Creek.

15.4 Take a left onto Highway 72 and roll down the canyon. Note the convenience store just downhill from this intersection.

22.8 Take a left onto Highway 93, headed north.

30.4 Somewhere through here, it is a good idea to move from the highway to the bike path (actually a multiuse path) near the road.

30.9 The path crosses under Broadway. Continue north.

32.7 Take a left onto Baseline Road. There is one last climb.

33.8 Arrive back at Chautauqua Park.

Ride Information

Events/Attractions

Chautauqua Park and Auditorium, 9th Street and Baseline Road, Boulder; (303) 442-3282; www.chautauqua.bouldernet.com. There's a whole big thing going on up here— concerts and lectures in the auditorium, classes in the academic building, food in the dining hall, and lodging in the cottages. That's not to mention the multiple hiking trails that spread out from here to the undeveloped west and south (no bikes allowed, strictly enforced), or the grade A, traditional, shady, green grass park that is so popular with local Frisbee players and sunbathers. Built in 1898, Boulder's Chautauqua was one of several such places around the country, part of the "Chautauqua movement," and today is one of only a few sites that have remained in continuous operation. From the Web site of the Colorado Chautauqua Association: "Before radio and television, the Chautauqua movement united millions in common cultural and educational experiences. Orators, performers, and educators traveled a national Chautauqua circuit of more than 12,000 sites bringing lectures, performances, concerts, classes, and exhibitions to thousands of people in small towns and cities." Some fairly big names play the auditorium these days.

Restaurants

Mustard's Last Stand, 1719 Broadway, Boulder; (303) 444-5841. Quality fast-food burgers, Chicago-style dogs, veggie burgers, to go or consume on site. Where Boulder Creek flows under Broadway.

Wild Oats Grocery and Deli. Two useful locations in Boulder: 1651 Broadway, (303) 442-0082; 2584 Baseline Road, (303) 499-7636. Big sandwiches, salad bar, refrigerated liquids, bathroom. This place is undeniably useful.

La Iguana Taqueria, 1301 Broadway, Boulder; (303) 938-8888. Heaping portions of Fresh-Mex on the Hill.

Jalino's, 1647 Arapahoe Avenue, Boulder; (303) 443-6300. Excellent pizza and sandwiches.

Bova's Pantry, 1325 Broadway, Boulder; (303) 449-0874. Grocery and deli on the Hill. Still wrappin' sandwiches after all these years.

Pasta Jay's, 1001 Pearl Street, Boulder; (303) 444-5800. Once the upstart restaurateur of the Front Range, Jay is now an institution.

Narayan's, 921 Pearl Street, Boulder; (303) 447-2816. Boulder has lots of great little restaurants serving up the exotic tastes of the Far East. This is one of the best.

Maps

Delorme: Colorado Atlas & Gazetteer: Pages 39 A-7, 40 A-1.

22 Magnolia Road-Nederland Challenge

Is Magnolia Road the toughest paved climb on the Front Range? There's only one way to find out. From Boulder loop straight up to the town of Nederland, then bomb down Boulder Canyon back to town. This ride is short on miles, but long on challenge.

Start: Eben G. Fine Park on the west side of Boulder, at the mouth of Boulder Canyon.
Length: 33.0-mile lariat.
Terrain: Magnolia is among the steepest paved climbs in Colorado. Total elevation gain for this ride is about 2,500 feet, which does not do it justice.
Traffic and hazards: The early part of this loop uses the Boulder Canyon bike path, so perhaps the biggest traffic hazard of the whole ride comes from other riders and pedestrians on the path, which has its share of tight, half-blind turns. Remember that pedestrians have the right-of-way on this and other "bike paths." The Canyon path is surfaced with gravel for most of its length; there are a few sections that are eroded and rocky, and there are some sharp bridge edges (pinch-flat alert), but for the most part the gravel path is accommodating for road bikes. You will then be ascending for 2 miles on the highway itself. In general,

the shoulder is wide and smooth enough for easy lane sharing with motorists. There is a short tunnel along this section that can be somewhat disconcerting. Magnolia Road itself is mellow, traffic-wise. But the pavement ends about 4 miles up, and the unpaved road tends to be rough, with occasional huge washboard. The condition of the surface will vary according to recent weather events and maintenance schedules. I have found Magnolia to be a bit rougher than the dirt roads around Gold Hill and will not recommend descending it on a road machine. Climbing it is usually okay, though. Descending Boulder Canyon on Highway 119 is notoriously sketchy. The steep section around Boulder Falls (about 25 miles into the ride) is particularly troublesome. The combo of high speed, young drivers, lack of space, and occasional gravel on the road can lead to disaster for beginning riders. Ride within your limits.

Getting there: This ride begins at Eben G. Fine Park in west Boulder. From anywhere in Boulder simply get on Arapahoe Avenue and head west, and eventually you will run into Eben G. Fine Park. From Denver drive or take the bus northwest up U.S. Highway 36 to Boulder. Take the Baseline Road exit and head west to Broadway. Take a right and go north on Broadway, past the University of Colorado campus, up and over the "Hill," then go left (west) on Arapahoe Avenue just past the Wild Oats grocery store. Follow Arapahoe west until it dead-ends at Eben G. Fine Park, where there should be some parking available, either on the street above the park or in the lower lot. Mileage cues begin at the boulder in the park on the west side, where the path exits westward.

The Ride

Magnolia Road. Magnolia. This is the name that is on your lips when you suddenly shoot awake from that frightening dream, shaking and drenched in cold sweat. You know the dream—you're standing on the pedals, climbing a road that gets ever

Magnolia

steeper, as if some giant beast from a Japanese monster movie is standing on the other side, pushing it over on you. The road gets steeper and steeper until you realize you are riding straight up, and then the road keeps going *past* vertical and you're falling, falling, and then you wake up, shaking and grabbing the air. *Magnolia.*

Or is that just me?

Anyway, damn, this road is steep. Go check it out.

Magnolia takes off up the side of Boulder Canyon, so follow the multiuse trail up Boulder Creek as far as it will take you—about 2 miles. When the trail runs out, jump on Highway 119 for a few more miles and watch for the obvious turnoff for Magnolia Road on the left. See that road going up the side of the mountain there?

The brutality begins immediately. Percent grades in the mid- to high teens usually come in bite-sized chunks on Colorado roads; here the steep stuff persists for miles, or so it seems. Take a look at your speedometer at around mile 5. My grandma can swim faster than that!

Magnolia does ease up eventually. Unfortunately, it eases at about the same time it turns to dirt. This section of dirt on Magnolia Road is quite rough and certainly won't be everybody's cup of tea. There are those who are riding on elite, paper-thin racing frames and wheels made of babies' whispers who may not want to subject their equipment to any extra stress; then there are those who simply hate a rough, loose surface, no matter what they're riding. Nobody who feels this way about dirt roads is required to endure this one—simply turn around. The ride will be a tough enough workout even as a 15-mile, all-pavement out-and-back. If you've come this far, however, with that ridiculous climb behind you, chances are you're not going to be too bothered by a bit of washboard. Might as well keep going. (For additional inspiration see "In Defense of Dirt" in the Introduction.)

Magnolia intersects the Peak-to-Peak Highway at a point very near the town of Nederland. Follow the Peak-to-Peak north, cruise down a series of fast, round turns, and enter bustling downtown Ned in a matter of minutes. Bustling is a bit of an exaggeration, but there will be opportunities for lunch, drinking whiskey, and doing laundry before heading down-canyon. If you're really lucky, your visit to Nederland will coincide with Frozen Dead Guy Days, the local festival honoring the cryogeni- cally frozen Bredo Morstøl, who currently resides in a Tuff Shed here, awaiting the march of science. When Morstøl's grandson first tried to house his grandfather's frozenness here, in 1994, the town council didn't like the idea. But the people of Nederland voted the bums out and brought in a new council that would support the concept of frozen dead guys. Today, the frozen Norwegian is one of the town's most distinguished and upstanding citizens. His festival features a pancake breakfast, coffin races, shed tours, and other bizarre activities.[1]

Out of Nederland the highway slips past picturesque Barker Reservoir. There is a nice little trail around the reservoir that is accessible from the road, if you feel the need to sit and stare at the water for a while. Highway 119 starts off nearly flat, then falls off the edge by Boulder Falls (about mile 25). This is one of the Front Range roads on which cyclists can achieve speeds in excess of 50 mph. With the narrow lanes here, however, and the concrete wall on your right, the sand and gravel on the road, the reckless drivers in varying states of inebriation, the inability of all parties to keep their vehicles within the confines of the lanes in the curves, etc., this is not the place to try for a new speed record. Highway 119, in fact, demands a sober, focused demeanor from drivers and cyclists alike. Bring your "A game" to Boulder Canyon, precisely because so many others won't. Try not to let any cryogenics-related risk compensation creep into your ride: *Oh, it's okay—if I have a head-on collision with a car, they'll just freeze me until science figures out a cure for massive head and organ trauma.*

Boulder Canyon flattens into a 30 mph cruise with huge round turns. Traffic is fairly heavy and getting heavier all the time.[2] The same could be said for traffic on the gravel bike path, which begins near mile 31. Things to watch out for on the path

---

[1]It should be noted that the festival is endorsed and supported by Morstøl's family. Unfortunately, it is highly unlikely that you will be riding this loop during Frozen Dead Guy Days, as the festival is held in mid-March. At this time of year, the dirt section of Magnolia Road is usually—not always—messy with recent snow and snowmelt.

[2]If they ever do unfreeze Bredo Morstøl, he is going to be pissed about all the traffic.

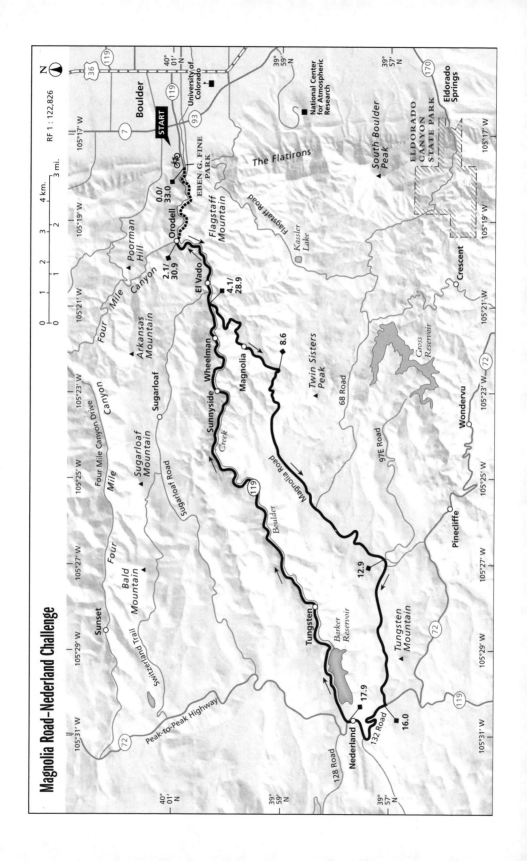

Magnolia Road–Nederland Challenge

include occasional ruts and rocks, sharp edges of bridges, blind turns, meandering joggers, and cyclists staring at their shoes.

When it's all said and done, what you remember most about this ride is the brutal, steep climb at the bottom of Magnolia Road. This road is a celebration of gravity and pain. You had to do it once. The question is, will you be back?

Miles and Directions

0.0 Start from Eben G. Fine Park, headed west up Boulder Canyon on the bike path. Reset the computer at the boulder on the west end of the park.

2.1 The path ends at the road (Highway 119). Carefully cross and start riding up the canyon on Highway 119. (Note: Do not start up Four Mile Canyon, which has its intersection very close by.)

4.1 Turn left onto Magnolia Road (County Road 132) and immediately begin a brutal climb.

8.6 The pavement ends, and so does most of the rough climbing.

12.9 Stay right at the fork.

16.0 Turn right onto Highway 72/Highway 119 (the Peak-to-Peak Highway) and descend into Nederland.

17.9 Continue through Nederland, sweeping right (eastbound) and staying on Highway 119.

30.9 Across from the entrance to Four Mile Canyon, take a right onto the bike path and continue down.

33.0 Return to Eben G. Fine Park.

Ride Information

Events/Attractions

Frozen Dead Guy Days, Nederland; www .nederlandchamber.org/FrozenDeadGuyDays/. Held over several days in the middle of March each year. It is somewhere between a blatant excuse for intoxication and an informative celebration of cryogenic possibilities.

Restaurants

Mustard's Last Stand, 1719 Broadway, Boulder; (303) 444-5841. Quality fast-food burgers, Chicago-style dogs, veggie burgers, to go or consume on site. Where Boulder Creek flows under Broadway.

Wild Oats Grocery and Deli. Two useful locations in Boulder: 1651 Broadway, (303) 442-0082; 2584 Baseline Road, (303) 499-7636. Big sandwiches, salad bar, refrigerated liquids, bathroom. This place is undeniably useful.

La Iguana Taqueria, 1301 Broadway, Boulder;

(303) 938-8888. Heaping portions of Fresh-Mex on the Hill.

Jalino's, 1647 Arapahoe Avenue, Boulder; (303) 443-6300. Excellent pizza and sandwiches.

Bova's Pantry, 1325 Broadway, Boulder; (303) 449-0874. Grocery and deli on the Hill. Still wrappin' sandwiches after all these years.

Pasta Jay's, 1001 Pearl Street, Boulder; (303) 444-5800. Once the upstart restaurateur of the Front Range, Jay is now an institution.

Narayan's, 921 Pearl Street, Boulder; (303) 447-2816. Boulder has lots of great little restaurants serving up the exotic tastes of the Far East. This is one of the best.

Neapolitan's, One West 1st Street, Nederland. Primo Italian in the casual atmosphere of Ned.

Maps

Delorme: Colorado Atlas & Gazetteer: Pages 29 D-7, 30 D-1, 39 A-6, 7.

23 Four Mile Canyon-Gold Hill Challenge

This ride climbs one of the toughest hills west of Boulder, and that's really saying something. Although touring some of the most scenic terrain on the Front Range, this loop is most highly recommended for those who want a punishing workout in a short ride. A long dirt road section further separates the wheat from the chaff. Delicate constitutions and frou-frou wheelsets will not be helpful.

Start: Eben G. Fine Park in west Boulder, at the mouth of Boulder Canyon.

Length: 21.4-mile loop.

Terrain: This baby is a no-nonsense climber's loop. Although much of the climbing is moderate at best, Captain Gravity makes up for it by dishing out major suffering in one long, continuous helping below Gold Hill, then rewards with a sweet descent.

Traffic and hazards: The bike path up Boulder Canyon, with its blind corners and moving obstacles, is probably the sketchiest part of the ride. Traffic is moderate in Four Mile Canyon and slight on the road to Gold Hill. Sunshine Canyon invites disaster with its speedy descent—expect drunk and distracted drivers to meet you on the way up.

Getting there: Eben G. Fine Park is located on the west edge of Boulder, at the mouth of Boulder Canyon. To get there from central Boulder, simply get on Arapahoe Avenue and head west until you run into the park. From Denver drive or take the bus northwest up U.S. Highway 36 to Boulder. Take the Baseline Road exit and head west to Broadway. Take a right and go north on Broadway, past the University of Colorado campus, up and over the "Hill," then go left (west) on Arapahoe Avenue just past the Wild Oats grocery store. Follow Arapahoe west until it runs into Eben G. Fine Park, where there should be some parking available.

The Ride

Do not be fooled by the low mileage of this loop. This is a toughie that only requires a few hours to complete, but also requires legs of thunder and an indomitable will. An adventurous spirit also helps, as a substantial portion of this loop is on dirt road.

Start the ride on the Boulder Canyon bike path out of Eben G. Fine Park, with its wonderfully located parking area on the extreme west end of Boulder. Years ago the legions of bicyclists who wanted to ride up Boulder Canyon were out on the high-speed road with cars; now there is a fully separated multiuse path (MUP) that takes bikes and peds all the way up to the mouth of Four Mile Canyon, dipping under the highway twice on the way up. It's nearly certain that the confinement of cyclists to the new facility has resulted in an *increase* in cyclists' accidents and injuries, and only part of that increased danger can be explained by booming numbers of cyclists in the canyon compared to the old days. Even with the increase in minor injuries and mishaps, it is also quite certain that the facility is an

Just one of many great dirt roads above Boulder

improvement over the old situation.[1] Crazy things, these MUPs. Like the streets, they defy simplistic judgments.

The path rises gently from Eben G. Fine Park, quickly shedding its smooth concrete surface after just a mile or so; beyond, the path is surfaced with gravel, but provides smooth travel for road bikes above a raging Boulder Creek—except for occasional rocks and a few sharp edges of bridges. At mile 2.1 the path abruptly turns and climbs to the road. Cross Highway 119 with care and find Four Mile Canyon Drive directly across.

Four Mile Canyon starts off flat, fast, and easy. A mile up the canyon you can look down and notice that you're still in the big ring. Steadily, the incline ramps up and becomes more and more serious. There is a sizable hill starting about 2 miles up—putting you up high where you can get a good look at the high mountains to the west—then a fast descent. Not long after this descent, at mile 7.1, the road forks decisively among a group of charming houses. This is the settlement known as Salina. To the left is the tiny hamlet of Wallstreet. The right fork is yours and will take you to Gold Hill, somewhat brutally.

---

[1] I can say this with good confidence, having ridden up Boulder Canyon to Four Mile Canyon hundreds of times in the pre-bike path era.

Four Mile Canyon–Gold Hill Challenge

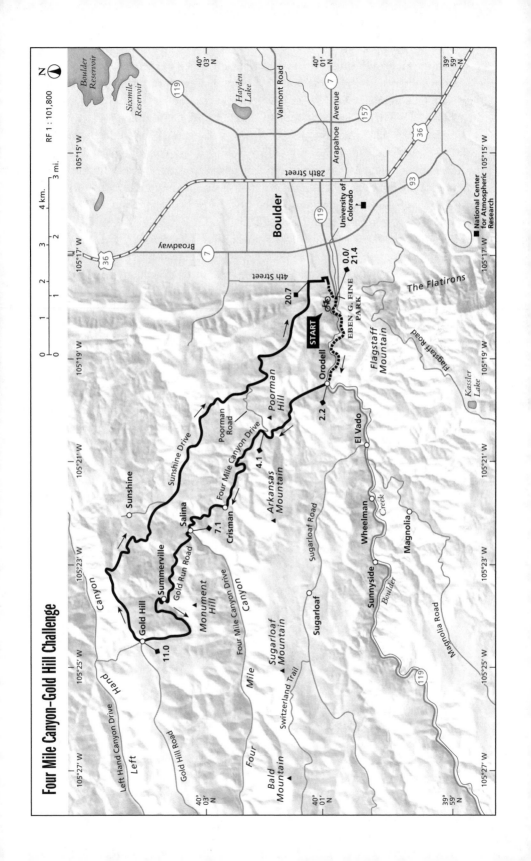

RF 1 : 101,800

N

So far the ride has been hilly, sure, but decidedly mellow, even easy, compared to what comes after the right turn at mile 7.1. Good luck with this steep, relentless, 3-mile wall. True climbers will love it. Everyone else will be chased by the Devil on the climb and will have nightmares for weeks afterward. Good times.

Don't be alarmed when the pavement goes away about a half mile above the fork. The au naturel road surface is bound to feature a sampling of typical dirt road hazards, potholes and washboard sections, but overall you are likely to find it quite accommodating for your delicate road machine. It may require some extra finesse to maintain out-of-the-saddle traction on the steepest parts of the climb. Triple chain rings can be very comforting in this regard.

Gold Hill is scattered with old hippies, artists, stray dogs, and other refugees from the seething urban rat race that is Boulder, Colorado. The residents, despite their best efforts, are inexorably linked to the larger town and its far-reaching energy.

From Gold Hill you can turn west and ride up to the Peak-to-Peak Highway, drop into Left Hand Canyon to the north, or climb east over a short hill to drop into Sunshine Canyon. All roads out of Gold Hill are of the unpaved variety. It might seem easiest to descend from here to Left Hand Canyon and get home that way, but remember, the Left Hand escape hatch drops you about 5 miles north of Boulder on U.S. Highway 36, whereas the Sunshine Canyon descent deposits you right in town near the start/finish.

Taking the route described in this chapter, you'll find the climb east out of Gold Hill to be relatively forgiving (luckily). Sunshine Canyon from near the top of Bighorn Mountain starts as a steep descent, still on fairly rough and rocky dirt, then transitions to an incredibly fast descent on pavement. This is one of those roads with 50 mph potential. As always, ride within your limits.

Sunshine is a classic climb, too. Try this loop backwards. For a much shorter and easier route using Four Mile and Sunshine Canyons, try the Poorman Road loop. Or, you can still enjoy the excellent Four Mile Canyon without the harsh climb to Gold Hill—simply turn around at Salina or even sooner, thus making a moderate, scenic, and very enjoyable out-and-back.

Miles and Directions

0.0 From Eben G. Fine Park on the west side of Boulder, at the mouth of Boulder Canyon on Boulder Creek, start riding up the wide concrete path headed west up the canyon on the south side of the creek. Reset the odometer at the big boulder as the path leaves Eben G. Fine Park.

2.1 The path turns sharply to the right and rises to the main road (Highway 119).

2.2 Cross Highway 119 and begin riding up Four Mile Canyon Drive (County Road 118), directly across from the path's terminus.

4.1 Pass Poorman Road. (Poorman connects to Sunshine Canyon via a steep dirt road climb.)

7.1 Take a right at the fork, following the signs to Gold Hill (County Road 89/Gold Run Road). The real climbing begins.

11.0 Arrive in Gold Hill. Take a right at the stop sign onto County Road 52/Sunshine Drive. The road climbs over the hill and descends on the same rough dirt surface for a time before turning back to pavement.

20.7 Back in Boulder, take a right onto 4th Street.

21.0 Turn right on Spruce Street, then left onto the waiting bike path.

21.1 Turn right on Pearl Street.

21.2 Hop onto the bike path again; it's right there. The path crosses under Canyon Boulevard, passes over Boulder Creek on a bridge, and enters Eben G. Fine Park.

21.4 Complete the loop; join a drum circle. A drum circle is an impromptu gathering of amateur percussionists who pound away on drums while sitting in a large circle. The drummers are generally accompanied by a scattering of hippie girls who dance and twirl around in a dreamy state until everybody's buzz wears off. Eben G. Fine Park is one of the world's epicenters of drum circle action.

Ride Information

Restaurants

Mustard's Last Stand, 1719 Broadway, Boulder; (303) 444-5841. Quality fast-food burgers, Chicago-style dogs, veggie burgers, to go or consume on site. Where Boulder Creek flows under Broadway.

Wild Oats Grocery and Deli. Two useful locations in Boulder: 1651 Broadway, (303) 442-0082; 2584 Baseline Road, (303) 499-7636. Big sandwiches, salad bar, refrigerated liquids, bathroom. This place is undeniably useful.

La Iguana Taqueria, 1301 Broadway, Boulder; (303) 938-8888. Heaping portions of Fresh-Mex on the Hill.

Jalino's, 1647 Arapahoe Avenue, Boulder; (303) 443-6300. Excellent pizza and sandwiches.

Bova's Pantry, 1325 Broadway, Boulder; (303) 449-0874. Grocery and deli on the Hill. Still wrappin' sandwiches after all these years.

Pasta Jay's, 1001 Pearl Street, Boulder; (303) 444-5800. Once the upstart restaurateur of the Front Range, Jay is now an institution.

Narayan's, 921 Pearl Street, Boulder; (303) 447-2816. Boulder has lots of great little restaurants serving up the exotic tastes of the Far East. This is one of the best.

Gold Hill Inn, 401 Main Street, Gold Hill; (303) 443-6461. Six-course dinner for twenty-nine bucks, not including libations of course.

Gold Hill Store, 531 Main Street, Gold Hill; (303) 443-7724. Breakfast and lunch, cold drinks and coffee, sundry sundries.

Maps

Delorme: Colorado Atlas & Gazetteer: Pages 29 D-7, 30 D-1.

24 Left Hand Canyon Challenge

With beautiful scenery, long climbs, and face-peeling descents, this hilly half century has everything you're looking for, and lots of it. Left Hand Canyon is one of the classic hill climbs on the Front Range. The descent on Sugarloaf Road serves up a late plot twist, just to keep things interesting.

Start: Eben G. Fine Park on the west edge of Boulder, at the mouth of Boulder Canyon. If you're driving in from out of town, this is a good place to start because there is usually enough parking here, and this is where the ride will spit you out at the end.

Length: 48.5-mile loop.

Terrain: Classic Front Range. One very long, moderate canyon climb that gets progressively steeper toward the top. Gentle rollers on the Peak-to-Peak Highway. What has gone up, then, must come down.

Traffic and hazards: Well-traveled roads. Shoulders and road surfaces are generally adequate. Motorists are used to seeing lots of cyclists on this route. Dirt alert: Note that the top of Sugarloaf Road is fairly rough dirt for a few miles. Even if you hate dirt, don't let this stop you from trying this ride—just continue into Nederland and descend to Boulder on Highway 119 instead. The descent on Sugarloaf Road—after its surface turns back to smooth pavement—is very steep and fast. Altitude and mountain weather comprise some of the serious hazards here. Bring enough gear.

Getting there: From Denver drive or take the bus northwest up U.S. Highway 36 to Boulder. Take the Baseline Road exit and head west to Broadway. Take a right and go north on Broadway, past the University of Colorado campus, up and over the "Hill," then go left (west) on Arapahoe Avenue just past the Wild Oats grocery store. Follow Arapahoe west until it dead-ends at Eben G. Fine Park, where there should be some parking available. Mileage cues begin at the bridge on the northwest side of the park, where the path exits north over Boulder Creek and then goes under Canyon Boulevard.

The Ride

Start this great loop in the shady cove of Eben G. Fine Park, at the mouth of Boulder Canyon, and head north into the beautiful Mapleton Hill neighborhood. Make your way along the foothills through the pleasant residential areas of west Boulder, using the time-honored conduit of 4th Street, a wide, quiet street that is probably the best north–south bike corridor in the entire town. Just watch the stop-signed intersections up there around mile 1.5. These aren't four-ways, so beware of cars plowing through. 4th deposits you onto the Wonderland Hill Avenue route, which curls around a bit and leads eventually to a rendezvous with Broadway, the main drag. By using 4th and Wonderland Hill, you have delayed this meeting for as long as possible.

Pedaling north on Broadway, behold the splendor of north Boulder. Every town needs a north Boulder: Hell, even Disneyland has a back lot. While it was

From the Peak-to-Peak Highway

once a dusty strip populated with meth addicts, authentic hobos, and barefoot stepchildren playing in the dirt, the other side of the tracks and the River Styx is now being steadily transformed.[1] New retail centers and high-density, affordable housing units have appeared. And now there is even a wide bike lane along both sides of busy North Broadway, an obvious improvement over the old situation from a cyclist's standpoint. It's a cleaner, brighter, much more yuppie-friendly world up in north Boulder these days.

The city of Boulder ends abruptly at mile 4.3, at US 36. North out of Boulder, US 36 becomes the boundary between mountain and plain. The easternmost foothills shoot up on your left, deforested and ranging in color from gold to deep green, depending on the season. To your right is the edge of America's breadbasket, its productivity made possible only by garnishing water from the mountains on your left.

About halfway to Lyons, after a few moderate rollers, is the obvious turnoff to Left Hand Canyon. Make the turn westward, following in the tire tracks of countless

---

[1] I can say what I want about north Boulder, because I used to live there when I cleaned toilets to pay my half of the rent on the trailer.

world-class racers who have used Left Hand for training over the decades. There is no substitute for a 15-mile climb. The first few miles are virtually flat as the blacktop creeps toward the mouth of the canyon. After passing the intersection with Old Stage Road at mile 11.5, the road points upward. Enjoy a long, steady climb on a good surface. Steep pitches are an occasional feature at first, taking over completely by the top. By mile 25 most riders will be suffering mightily and will be comforted by the sight of the Peak-to-Peak Highway looming over Ward, the town on the hill. If this canyon doesn't get the better of you by the end, you might be a world-class cyclist.

The canyon is named for Chief Left Hand (aka Niwot), an Arapahoe chief who adopted a persistently conciliatory approach to dealing with the invasion of gold seekers and settlers who swarmed onto the Front Range after 1858. Niwot and other "peace chiefs" understood the whites' overwhelming numerical superiority and the futility of fighting them. They hoped for some sort of coexistence. On the other side were Indians who preferred to go out in a blaze of glory, like the Sioux and the "Dog Soldiers" of the Cheyenne. The Colorado gold rush brought a state of warfare between these young warriors and the whites who swarmed in and claimed every canyon, stream, and tree on the Front Range. In 1864 Governor John Evans responded by ordering all "peaceful" Indians to report to the military forts, and then implored white civilians to shoot on sight any Indians who remained aloof. This was his final solution: to force the nomadic hunters into a "civilized" lifestyle of farming, and to kill all those who resisted.

Black Kettle, Left Hand, and other leaders brought their ethnically mixed bands to Fort Lyon (not at present-day Lyons, but in south-central Colorado) for food and protection, and found little of either. These acquiescent Indians, who had given up their land and their way of life, had become almost entirely dependent on the U.S. government for sustenance. The increasingly desperate refugees were sent by the fort's commander to camp near Sand Creek (near the Kansas border). They were promised peace, if not food.

It was well known at that time that the Indians who were camped on Sand Creek were not looking for any trouble, and that those who preferred to fight were living near the Smoky Hill River in present-day Kansas. So, when a certain Colonel Chivington turned a force of 700 volunteer cavalrymen out of Fort Lyon toward the Sand Creek camp in November, the move was met with some dismay. But Chivington would not be denied an opportunity to christen the "Bloodless Third" Cavalry. In what was certainly a low point in American history, his soldiers descended on the encampment, over which was flying a white flag as well as the Stars and Stripes. They slaughtered women and babies and reportedly raped and mutilated some of the bodies in an all-day rampage. Satisfied, Chivington rushed back to Denver, where he expected a hero's welcome. A string of more than one hundred scalps was displayed in the Denver Theater, and the *Rocky Mountain News*

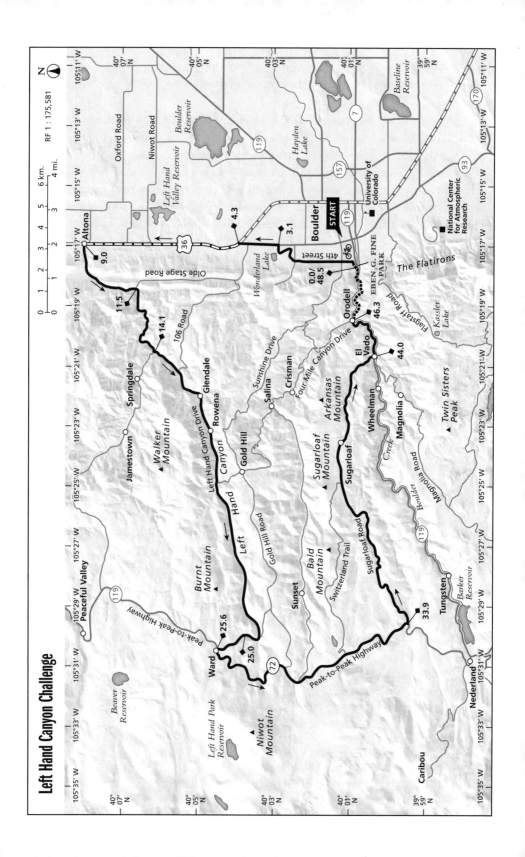

Left Hand Canyon Challenge

RF 1 : 175,581

N

proclaimed: "Bully for the Colorado Boys!" As the horrific details emerged, the Sand Creek Massacre was officially condemned, and Chivington was exiled to obscurity.[2]

Chief Left Hand was wounded in the massacre at Sand Creek and later died of his wounds. The deed was done 150 miles and almost 150 years away from here. But here we are, climbing the canyon that bears the name of the murdered peace chief and pondering how the West was won. In the end the peaceful bands and the militants met the same fate, at the end of a gun. The peace chiefs were then flattened into streets and roads for Front Range residents who rarely pause to consider the unhappy stories behind the names—Neva Road, Little Raven Street, Left Hand Canyon. Hate to be so blunt, but that's pretty much the size of it.

Although there is some additional semi-serious climbing to conquer on the Peak-to-Peak Highway, once you climb out of Ward and make the turn onto the Peak-to-Peak, there is a definite sense of being on top of things. Enjoy intense views while rolling swiftly on what is usually one of the smoothest asphaltic concrete structures you're likely to come across. They did a good job on the Peak-to-Peak Highway. And the shoulders are quite generous. This is the Shangri-la of road cycling right here. To the east are glimpses of the plains far below, and to the west, the high mountains of the Indian Peaks Wilderness. Some folks may feel the need for additional air pressure—in the lungs, not the tires—as the highway rolls along at a respectable 9,000-plus feet above sea level.

Right before the highway falls off into Nederland, bust a left onto Sugarloaf Road (County Road 122), just for kicks. Taking a left here comes with certain problems that might not be cherished or appreciated by everybody. First of all, the road surface is rough gravel with some significant washboarding and will remain so for over 3 miles. (That's about twenty minutes' worth of rough road.) Second, there is climbing involved, which becomes apparent soon after you make the turn. And some pretty tough stuff, too. So, if you're feeling queasy about riding the Loaf, simply continue on the Peak-to-Peak into Nederland and descend Boulder Canyon on Highway 119. It's quite a straightforward solution to the Sugarloaf problem. Note, however, that Highway 119 also has its problematic features. It has much more traffic, for instance. Personally, I prefer Sugarloaf despite the dirt and climbing.

If you've never descended Sugarloaf, it's definitely worth a try. The real face peeling begins not long after the summit of the steep paved climb. It's easy for a normal-sized individual on a road bike to reach 50 mph on this corkscrew of a road—just let go of your brake levers for a few seconds. Much higher speeds might be possible with favorable wind conditions. If only they would close the road to other traffic,

---

[2]Elliott West, *The Contested Plains* (Lawrence: University Press of Kansas, 1998), pp. 287–308. The sordid details of the massacre come from sworn testimony of participants and survivors at the official inquiry, as related by Robert Perkin, "Sand Creek," in Carl Ubbelohde, ed., *A Colorado Reader* (Boulder, Colo.: Pruett Press, 1964), pp. 126–142.

we could really figure some things out; until then, cyclists are urged to descend at more conservative speeds.

If you had a second to look around while descending, which you probably don't, you would notice the surrounding area was charred in a significant wildland fire event. More than 2,000 acres and forty homes around Sugarloaf Mountain burned in the summer of 1989. Heavy smoke plummeted into Boulder and people went about their daily business while breathing through wet bandannas.

The grade of Sugarloaf Road softens into the normal range after about a mile of face peeling, but it stays pretty steep and turny all the way down to its endpoint at Highway 119 and Boulder Creek. The 2.3-mile section of Highway 119 brings noticeably higher traffic intensity. Descend conservatively—here the danger (which can not in good conscience be called remote) is that two or more factors will coincide and contribute to some ugly incident. Lines of speeding cars passing close in the curves do not usually present a problem for a steady rider. Add gravel, debris, or a crumbling roadway that might force a rider into the traveling lane at the wrong time. . . . Ride in such a way that the sudden appearance of complications would not cause disaster. Also along this stretch is a short tunnel that causes some nervousness, as it narrows the roadway a bit, but it's not a huge ordeal. Most riders prefer to hop off the road and onto the multiuse path at mile 46.3 (directly across from the entrance to Four Mile Canyon). The path is surfaced with gravel and features occasional sharp rocks, ruts, and various pinch-flat causers, but is generally tame enough for your road machine.

Hopefully you'll arrive back at the park with a big smile on your face after an adventurous ride. Now that's how you put a road bike through its paces.

Miles and Directions

0.0 Start from Eben G. Fine Park, headed north across Boulder Creek and under Canyon Boulevard on the bike path. Specifically, the mileage cues for this ride start at the big boulder in front of the bridge. (Note: If you find yourself following Boulder Creek, you're on the wrong bike path.)

0.2 The path spills out onto Pearl Street. Continue eastward momentarily.

0.4 Turn left onto 4th Street at the roundabout.

0.5 Turn left onto Spruce Street, then take an immediate right back onto 4th Street, headed north. There's a short, sharp hill here.

2.0 4th Street ends here; continue straight ahead on the bike path for 1 block.

2.1 Carefully turn right onto Linden Hill Road, then take an immediate left onto Wonderland Hill Avenue. (Linden Hill also features a good short but tough climb—save it for another day.) Wonderland Hill will climb a tiny bit and curve around to the east before heading back north. Follow Wonderland Hill Avenue past any intersecting streets until it ends.

2.9 Wonderland Hill Avenue ends here. Take a right onto a short section of bike path that connects to Quince Street eastbound.

3.1 Take a left onto Broadway.

4.3 Turn left onto US 36.

9.0 Turn left onto Left Hand Canyon Road.

11.5 Continue past the intersection with Olde Stage Road on the left.

14.1 Stay left at the fork. (The right fork leads to Jamestown.)

25.0 Now you're climbing a big wall upon which sits the town of Ward.

25.6 Take a left onto the Peak-to-Peak Highway (Highway 72) southbound.

33.9 Turn left onto Sugarloaf Road (County Road 122). **Option:** Continue straight and descend to Nederland, then turn eastbound on Highway 119 into Boulder Canyon. This option cuts out almost all the remaining climbing while adding just a few miles; it also adds a great deal of traffic.

44.0 Sugarloaf Road ends at Highway 119 in Boulder Canyon. Take a left.

46.3 Leave Highway 119 for the multiuse path on the right. Continue down-canyon.

48.5 Arrive back at Eben G. Fine Park.

Ride Information

Restaurants

Mustard's Last Stand, 1719 Broadway, Boulder; (303) 444-5841. Quality fast-food burgers, Chicago-style dogs, veggie burgers, to go or consume on site. Where Boulder Creek flows under Broadway.

Wild Oats Grocery and Deli. Two useful locations in Boulder: 1651 Broadway, (303) 442-0082; 2584 Baseline Road, (303) 499-7636. Big sandwiches, salad bar, refrigerated liquids, bathroom. This place is undeniably useful.

La Iguana Taqueria, 1301 Broadway, Boulder; (303) 938-8888. Heaping portions of Fresh-Mex on the Hill.

Jalino's, 1647 Arapahoe Avenue, Boulder; (303) 443-6300. Excellent pizza and sandwiches.

Bova's Pantry, 1325 Broadway, Boulder; (303) 449-0874. Grocery and deli on the Hill. Still wrappin' sandwiches after all these years.

Pasta Jay's, 1001 Pearl Street, Boulder; (303) 444-5800. Once the upstart restaurateur of the Front Range, Jay is now an institution.

Narayan's, 921 Pearl Street, Boulder; (303) 447-2816. Boulder has lots of great little restaurants serving up the exotic tastes of the Far East. This is one of the best.

Neapolitan's, One West 1st Street, Nederland. Primo Italian in the casual atmosphere of Ned.

Maps

Delorme: Colorado Atlas & Gazetteer: Pages 29 D-6, 7; 30 D-1; 39 A-6, 7.

25 Poorman Cruise

Climbing a large portion of Sunshine Canyon before descending sharply on the dirt-surfaced Poorman Road, this is a short ride with some real bite and an elevation gain of about 1,000 feet.

Start: Eben G. Fine Park, Boulder.
Length: 8.8-mile loop.
Terrain: The salient features of this loop include a legitimately tough climb up Sunshine Canyon, then a steep descent on dirt Poorman Road.

Traffic and hazards: Poorman Road is a generally well-maintained dirt surface, but it is quite steep. Sunshine invites motorists to speed dangerously. The final leg is on the Boulder Creek multiuse path in Boulder Canyon, which demands your rapt attention.

Getting there: This short loop is easily accessed by bicycle from anywhere in town, as Sunshine Canyon is simply the continuation of centrally located Mapleton Avenue. If you're driving in from out of town, however, Eben G. Fine Park is a good place to park and stage a start/finish. Eben G. Fine Park is located on the west edge of Boulder, at the mouth of Boulder Canyon. To get there from central Boulder, simply get on Arapahoe Avenue and head west until you run into the park. From Denver drive or take the bus northwest up U.S. Highway 36 to Boulder. Take the Baseline Road exit and head west to Broadway. Take a right and go north on Broadway, past the University of Colorado campus, up and over the "Hill," then go left (west) on Arapahoe Avenue just past the Wild Oats grocery store. Follow Arapahoe west until it runs into Eben G. Fine Park, where there should be some parking available.

The Ride

There is no possible way to connect Four Mile Canyon and Sunshine Canyon—two of the finest road cycling routes in the known universe—using paved roads exclusively. On the other hand, there are a few ways to link them with dirt roads. One way is to climb all the way to the town of Gold Hill. That loop involves more than 10 miles of continuous climbing, some of it bizarrely steep. The Sunshine–Four Mile loop described here is mellow by comparison, using the Poorman Road connector to drop into Four Mile Canyon. Less than 10 miles long in its entirety, this makes a near perfect loop for Boulder-based riders who want a real ride but don't have a lot of time. It's quick, but extremely fun.

In the grand scheme of things, this loop is moderate in difficulty. Sunshine Canyon, however, is no joke. The climbing begins very gently, curling around, rather than over, the lumpy foothill called Mount Sanitas. The gentleness is temporary. Soon you must contend with occasional pitches of serious mountainside, belying the term "canyon." The final approach to the turnoff at Poorman Road is straight and fairly steep. The turnoff comes after less than 3 miles of climbing—not long, but long enough to spank you good.

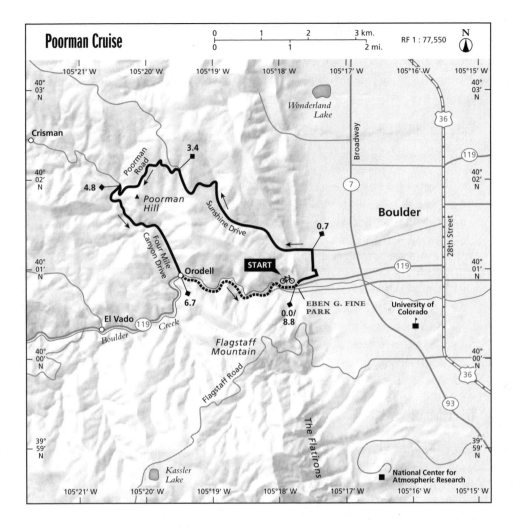

0   1   2   3 km.   RF 1 : 77,550   N

0   1   2 mi.

105°21′ W   105°20′ W   105°19′ W   105°18′ W   105°17′ W   105°16′ W   105°15′ W

40°
03′
N

Wonderland
Lake

36

Crisman

Poorman
Road

3.4

119

40°
02′
N

4.8

Poorman
Hill

Sunshine Drive

Boulder

0.7

28th Street

Broadway

7

40°
01′
N

Four Mile
Canyon Drive

Orodell

START

119

6.7

EBEN G. FINE
PARK

University of
Colorado

El Vado   119

Boulder   Creek

0.0/
8.8

40°
00′
N

Flagstaff
Mountain

36

Flagstaff Road

93

39°
59′
N

The Flatirons

Kassler
Lake

National Center for
Atmospheric Research

105°21′ W   105°20′ W   105°19′ W   105°18′ W   105°17′ W   105°16′ W   105°15′ W

Poorman Road goes around a few curves, then free-falls for a mile to Four Mile Canyon Drive. You'll likely see loads of folks on mountain bikes soldiering up the steep climb, as Poorman Road is a favorite destination for Boulder's less ambitious mountain bikers just looking for a taste of dirt. Attempting the clockwise version of this loop (up Four Mile and Poorman Road, down Sunshine) would probably be inadvisable for riders on road bikes, especially those without triple cranksets, due to the heavy incline of Poorman Road. Descending Poorman is generally not a problem, although it can be thrilling if you want it to be.

Four Mile is surprisingly moderate and tame for a mountain road. You would come to a more complete understanding of Four Mile Canyon and its gentle

◀ *Turning onto Poorman Road*

demeanor if you ever climbed it, which I strongly suggest you do. You descend Four Mile at ho-hum speeds from Poorman to Highway 119, where the sound of the white water of Boulder Creek is drowned out by the sound of traffic. A careful coast down the multiuse path (MUP) completes this abbreviated three-canyon tour of the foothills west of Boulder.

Miles and Directions

0.0 Start from Eben G. Fine Park, riding north on the bicycle-pedestrian path that exits the park by crossing over Boulder Creek on a bridge and under Canyon Boulevard. Reset your odometer at the south end of the bridge.

0.2 The path spills out onto Pearl Street. Continue eastward momentarily.

0.4 Turn left onto 4th Street at the roundabout.

0.5 Turn left onto Spruce Street, then take an immediate right back onto 4th Street headed north. There's a short, sharp hill here. (Actually, this is the steepest part of the whole ride!)

0.7 Turn left on Mapleton Avenue, which becomes Sunshine Drive.

0.9 Pass the Mount Sanitas trailhead and parking area.

3.4 After passing several other residential dirt roads, turn left onto Poorman Road.

4.8 Turn left on Four Mile Canyon Drive (County Road 118).

6.7 Cross Highway 119 and descend Boulder Canyon on the gravel-surfaced MUP.

8.8 The path enters Eben G. Fine Park from the west.

Ride Information

Restaurants

Mustard's Last Stand, 1719 Broadway, Boulder; (303) 444-5841. Quality fast-food burgers, Chicago-style dogs, veggie burgers, to go or consume on site. Where Boulder Creek flows under Broadway.

Wild Oats Grocery and Deli. Two useful locations in Boulder: 1651 Broadway, (303) 442-0082; 2584 Baseline Road, (303) 499-7636. Big sandwiches, salad bar, refrigerated liquids, bathroom. This place is undeniably useful.

La Iguana Taqueria, 1301 Broadway, Boulder; (303) 938-8888. Heaping portions of Fresh-Mex on the Hill.

Jalino's, 1647 Arapahoe Avenue, Boulder; (303) 443-6300. Excellent pizza and sandwiches.

Bova's Pantry, 1325 Broadway, Boulder; (303) 449-0874. Grocery and deli on the Hill. Still wrappin' sandwiches after all these years.

Pasta Jay's, 1001 Pearl Street, Boulder; (303) 444-5800. Once the upstart restaurateur of the Front Range, Jay is now an institution.

Narayan's, 921 Pearl Street, Boulder; (303) 447-2816. Boulder has lots of great little restaurants serving up the exotic tastes of the Far East. This is one of the best.

Maps

Delorme: Colorado Atlas & Gazetteer: Pages 29 D-7, 30 D-1.

26 Morgul-Bismark Cruise

This short loop rambles through the rolling hills south of Boulder on a race course steeped in tradition.

Start: The intersection of McCaslin Boulevard and Marshall Road, just off U.S. Highway 36 in Superior.
Length: 13.3-mile loop.
Terrain: While not in the mountains or even in the foothills, this area is much hillier than the relative flatlands northeast of Boulder.
Traffic and hazards: This entire loop is on very busy rural/suburban roads and highways, but shoulders have been expanded all the way around after decades of very heavy and regular use by recreational cyclists. Marshall Road is a bit skinnier than the rest of the route. Highway 93's shoulder is inconsistent, and segments seemed to be under construction at the time of this writing. Overall, traffic on Morgul-Bismark should not present a problem to a careful rider.

Getting there: From Denver take US 36 to the Superior exit. Go south on McCaslin Boulevard very briefly and park in the vast sea of parking around the grocery store and other big-box stores, near the intersection of McCaslin and Marshall Road/Highway 170. This used to be a rather lonely crossroads. You could also start this loop at the intersection of McCaslin and Highway 128 (which is near the start/finish of the race course) or the intersection of Highways 128 and 93, where there is a small parking area. From Boulder it's a small matter to ride a bike to and from the loop.

The Ride

Morgul-Bismark. Where the heck did that name come from? you ask. Not one of the roads around shares these names, nor is there any natural feature or town nearby with either of these names. You might assume "Morgul-Bismark" had something to do with the native people who once populated this area or is perhaps a misspelled reference to Otto von Bismarck. Actually, the course is named after the dog and cat of the first dude to promote a race on this loop. Do you feel somewhat ripped off?

The Morgul-Bismark loop is an inviting and obvious loop on the map. In addition to providing a fun ride, it has been used as a not-so-fun racing circuit for decades, most famously in the Red Zinger/Coors Classic stage race (now defunct). The Morgul gained more widespread notoriety after it was featured in *American Flyers,* the fourth-best bicycle racing movie of all time, starring Kevin Costner and Rae Dawn Chong.[1] In real life Morgul-Bismark figured prominently in the careers of many great racers, including local heroes Davis Phinney and Alexi Grewal, a young Greg Lemond on his way to Tour de France glory, and the Soviet amateur cycling team, when there was such a thing. European stars like Bernard Hinault and Moreno

---

[1] 3. *Deux Seconds;* 2. *The Triplets of Bellville;* 1. *Breaking Away.* (*American Flyers* is fourth best out of four total bicycle racing movies.)

Argentin raced their guts out on this course. The Morgul-Bismark course molds champions, then breaks them.

Actually, it's not that hard. The difficulty of the racing here is derived not so much from the terrain but from the intensity of the competition, and from bonus environmental hardships like wind and heat around the treeless circuit. Strangely, it's the terrain—with its three steep but smallish climbs, no more than a few hundred feet high—that hogs most of the attention. The little climbs have even been named. Starting from Superior and rolling south on McCaslin Boulevard (that name alone strikes fear in the hearts of Front Range Freds—*McCaslin, oooh*), the first hill you run into is the Hump. It is just that. You roll over it and on you go. Next up is the Wall. Traditionally, the race start/finish line is placed at the top of this hill, so race fans can watch the brutality unfold right in front of their eyes. After climbing it you may agree that the name is overly dramatic. Sure, it's a hill all right, but this hill is just a slightly more severe version of the typical steep rollers that are found all over the area east of Boulder. Look to the west as you climb—that's where the real walls are. The Wall just ain't that bad. But try doing it four or five or six times at race speed, against a stiff wind, and you might start hallucinating.

The two overhyped climbs are behind you within about twenty minutes from the start. There is another one of these harsh rollers lying in wait at about mile 4.5— the Feed Hill, which many Morgul vets claim is actually the toughest of the three. There are more dips and climbs after the route turns north on Highway 93. This is not a flat loop, but it's certainly not a pure climber's loop. The final leg of the Morgul-Bismark course, east on Marshall Road, is primarily a long descent.

On the south side of the loop, Highway 128/West 120th Avenue traces what used to be the northern boundary of the Rocky Flats Plant. After producing plutonium triggers for nuclear warheads (along with the associated waste products) for forty years, Rocky Flats was raided by the FBI in 1989, and a special grand jury was impaneled to investigate possible illegal dumping of radioactive waste and falsification of waste storage records at the site. The investigation focused primarily on plant managers from Rockwell Corporation and EG&G, which had been under contract from the Department of Energy to operate the facility. Interestingly, the grand jury heard loads of toxic evidence—about illegal dumping of radioactive matter into local drinking water supplies, for example—and decided to indict eight individuals, but U.S. Attorney Mike Norton granted a sweet plea deal to Rockwell and shut the investigation down before it was completed. The snubbed jurors wrote a report about their findings anyway, in which they labeled Rocky Flats "an ongoing criminal enterprise." Judge Sherman Finesilver ordered the report sealed. Since then an official, censored version of the grand jury report was released in 1993, and much of the uncensored report was leaked to magazines and newspapers, but grand

◀ *The treeless hills of the Morgul-Bismark Loop, with the Flatirons in the distance*

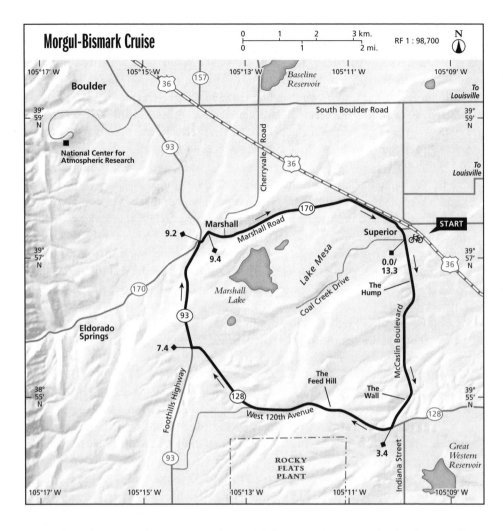

Morgul-Bismark Cruise

0   1   2   3 km.
0   1   2 mi.
RF 1 : 98,700

N

Boulder

105°17' W   105°15' W   105°13' W   105°11' W   105°09' W

Baseline Reservoir

South Boulder Road

39° 59' N   39° 59' N

National Center for Atmospheric Research

To Louisville

To Louisville

Cherryvale Road

Marshall Road

Marshall

9.2

9.4

Superior

START

39° 57' N   39° 57' N

Lake Mesa

0.0/ 13.3

The Hump

Marshall Lake

Coal Creek Drive

93

170

Eldorado Springs

7.4

McCaslin Boulevard

Foothills Highway

The Feed Hill

The Wall

38° 55' N   39° 55' N

128

West 120th Avenue

128

93

3.4

Indiana Street

Great Western Reservoir

ROCKY FLATS PLANT

105°17' W   105°15' W   105°13' W   105°11' W   105°09' W

jury members are still in various stages of fighting, or ignoring, the legal gag order to this day.[2]

Things have only gotten smellier. FBI agent Jon Lipsky, who led the original raid on Rocky Flats, appeared at a news conference in Colorado in August of 2004. Standing with the foreman of the grand jury and a former whistle-blower, Lipsky said: "I am an FBI agent. My superiors have ordered me to lie about an investigation I headed in 1989. We were investigating the U.S. Department of Energy, but the U.S. Justice Department covered up the truth. I have refused to follow the orders to lie

---

[2]As of November 2004. Despite the seal and gag order, the jury's very disconcerting report is still available on the Internet at many sites, for instance, www.staynehoff.net/rocky-flats-grand-jury-report.htm.

about what really happened during that criminal investigation of Rocky Flats."[3] Lipsky and others wanted to bring the issue before the public again, because questions remain (to put it mildly) as to whether or not the cleanup of Rocky Flats was completed properly, or even half-ass properly, and plans are currently moving forward to make the site into a wildlife refuge and recreation area.

As long as such questions remain unanswered, some cyclists will continue to ride past Rocky Flats while breathing through their noses and wondering if they should be wearing lead shorts.

Miles and Directions

0.0 Start riding south on McCaslin Boulevard from the intersection of McCaslin and Marshall Road in Superior.

3.4 Take a right on Highway 128/West 120th Avenue.

7.4 Turn right on Highway 93 (aka the Foothills Highway).

9.2 At the traffic light take a right on Marshall Road.

9.4 Stay right on Marshall Road.

13.3 Return to the massive parking lot.

Ride Information

Restaurants

Tulien's, 808 Main Street, Louisville; (303) 665–6868. Chinese and Vietnamese food, vegetarian-friendly.
Pasquini's Pizzeria, 816 Main Street, Louisville; (303) 673-9400.

Maps

Delorme: Colorado Atlas & Gazetteer: Page 40 A-1.

---

[3] Patricia Calhoun, "True Lies: The FBI Agent Who Raided Rocky Flats Finally Sounds Off," *Westword,* 18 August 2004.

27 Lyons-Estes Park Challenge

South Saint Vrain Canyon might be the finest of all the classic canyon climbs on the Front Range, and there are lots of 'em. Ascend relatively moderate grades to the sublime Peak-to-Peak Highway, skirt the edge of Rocky Mountain National Park, and roll into the town of Estes Park. End the ride with a rewarding canyon descent.

Start: The town of Lyons, where two canyons, two rivers, and two mountain highways converge.

Length: 52.4-mile loop.

Terrain: One long, gradual climb, and some additional significant climbs on the Peak-to-Peak Highway, as well as on exit from Estes Park. Enjoy a long, gradual descent back down to Lyons. Nothing too steep, but a tough loop nonetheless.

Traffic and hazards: Most of this route uses good-quality roads with nice, wide lanes and rideable shoulders. One notable exception: U.S. Highway 36 just east of Estes Park lacks a good shoulder, but it is not a deal breaker. This road section is not critically narrow and the shoulder reappears after a few short miles. Traffic on US 36, the preferred tourist route between Estes/Rocky Mountain National Park and the Denver metroplex, is moderate to heavy, and the road surface is deteriorating in spots. Bike shops are scarce, so haul the necessary equipment.

Getting there: From Boulder go north on US 36 to Lyons. From Denver it is probably easiest to drive Interstate 25 north to US 36 as if you were going to Boulder; then follow US 36 through Boulder and north to Lyons. That's almost an hour's drive from central Denver. The loop begins in Lyons at the intersection of US 36 and Highway 7. Parking in Lyons is a potential problem that might require a bit of creativity. One possibility is the trailhead parking area on the south side of the main drag in Lyons (US 36)—look for it as you come into town from the east. Another good spot to leave a car is the wide gravel turnoff on Highway 7, a half mile up from the intersection with US 36. I have dropped a vehicle here several times and it's never been a problem. If you start here, however, remember to do the math on the mileage cues, which start in Lyons a half mile down the hill.

The Ride

Fifteen miles is plenty long enough for a single climb. After about 10 miles it's like, hey, come on climb, let's get this damn thing over with. But the climb turns a cold shoulder to your sorry pleas. Then the hallucinations kick in, usually around mile 14. For me it's always a giant chicken in Euro team kit, running across the road.

No, South Saint Vrain won't let you off the hook for quite a while. But the climb remains markedly civilized, with its smooth surface and less-than-severe grades. It's a good road for hauling panniers and spinning the little ring, if you're into that. It is not a good road if you're looking to avoid any confrontation with gravity. Between Lyons and Wind River Pass lie about 4,000 feet of vertical gain.

Mount Meeker looms over the Peak-to-Peak Highway

After about mile 14 sun-baked Highway 7 shows signs of wanting to level off. This part of the highway, beyond the intersection with Highway 72, is known as the Peak-to-Peak Highway[1] and is characterized by big rollers on smooth road through subalpine forests. It is an *excellent* cycling road.

At the top of this loop, skirting the relatively pristine Rocky Mountain National Park, take a look back over your left shoulder at the jagged mass of Longs Peak. It's rare for a Front Ranger to ever catch a solid glimpse of this big mountain, which, from the viewpoint of the flatlander, is well hidden behind the pyramidal Mount Meeker. It's safe to say that about a million or more Front Range residents spend their whole lives thinking that Mount Meeker is Longs Peak. In fact, all of Longs that is visible from the plains is one little crescent of silver rock that pokes up from behind Meeker. Meeker is a swell mountain, but the hidden Longs is all chaos, cliffs, and chasms. The Supreme Being had to hide that sucker behind a familiar geometric shape.

---

[1] The so-called Peak-to-Peak Highway is generally considered to span the entire distance between Estes Park and Central City to the south. This span actually includes portions of three different state highways: Highway 7, Highway 72, and Highway 119.

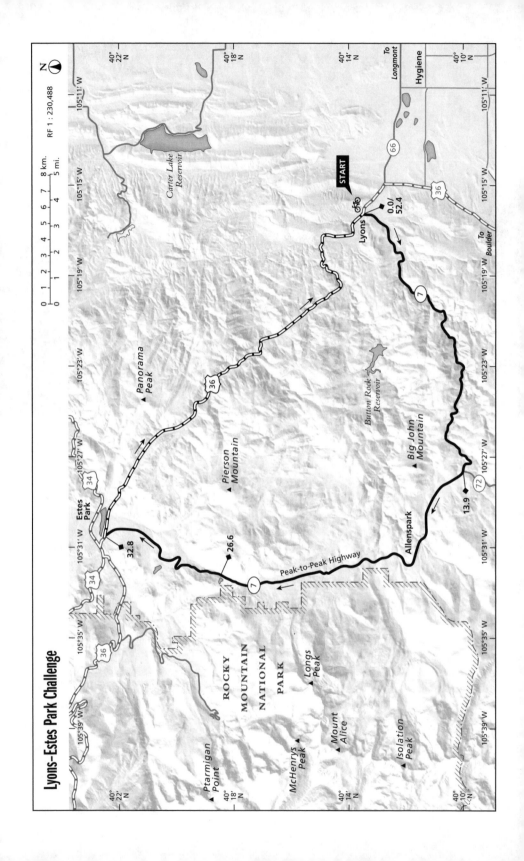

Lyons–Estes Park Challenge

Longs is named for Major Stephen Long, who led expeditions into the area in the early nineteenth century. Like his fellow famous explorer, Zebulon Pike, he went searching for the sources of various rivers, couldn't find them, and never really got close to the mountain that bears his name. Long and Pike gazed on their respective peaks from afar, shuddered, and declared them unconquerable.[2] Since then, of course, both Longs and Pikes Peaks have been climbed by tens of thousands of humans in various states of disrepair. At least Longs Peak doesn't have a road to the top.

Summiting the chasmic Longs Peak is a significant undertaking that generally requires peak baggers to be on the trail well before dawn. Consider, however, the Longs Peak speed record, set by a high school cross-country prodigy named Mike Sullivan more than thirty years ago: one hour, eighteen minutes, and thirty seconds. While the record still stands, modern-day endurance freaks have upped the ante with the Longs Peak Triathlon. In this rite of passage, the sacrificial athlete pedals from Boulder to the trailhead off Highway 7, runs to the base of the Diamond Wall (a massive rock face on the mountain's east side), then climbs the sheer cliff. An unassisted participant would lug ropes and climbing gear the whole way, or else free-climb the Diamond.[3] Either way, it's freaky. There are not many people in the world who could succeed at this, but most of them probably live in Boulder.

Pedaling past Longs, Lily Lake soon appears on the left. This is a really nice place to stop and decompress for a bit—just walk your bike on the trail around the lake, because the rangers get really agitated if you attempt to ride off-road in America's national parks, boy.

You might prefer to postpone your break for just a few minutes, as the town of Estes Park is just a few downhill miles beyond Lily Lake. Estes Park is a tourist town—it sure doesn't have to try to be anything else up against these mountains. If you're looking for an ice cream and an I ♥ COLORADO T-shirt, you've certainly come to the right place. Overlooking the town on the northwest side is the famous Stanley Hotel, upon which the evil hotel in Stephen King's *The Shining* is (loosely) based. That is not how the proprietors wish to have it remembered.[4] Gallivanting in Estes is not a requirement for this ride. The route described in the mileage cues barely touches the town. If you want to cruise Main Street (er, Elkhorn Avenue), see the Stanley, and all that noise, you'll have to tack on a mile or two extra.

Rolling out of Estes on US 36, you'll find the least hospitable section of road on the route. The shoulder that you enjoyed on Highway 7 is conspicuous in its absence and partial absence here, but the road remains a satisfactory conduit. And if you're real tired at this point, you won't be too excited to see a big hill or two up ahead, between you and the canyon that will take you home. The painful truth is that Estes

---

[2] Carl Ubbelohde, Maxine Benson, and Duane Smith, *A Colorado History* (Boulder, Colo.: Pruett Press, 1972), pp. 25–28.
[3] Dougald MacDonald, *Longs Peak* (Englewood, Colo.: Westcliffe, 2004), pp. 28–29.
[4] *Redrum!*

lies in a valley. A few moderately tough pitches test your late-game resolve before the road dumps you into the canyon of the Little Thompson, and it's downhill all the way from there. Keep an eye out for crumbling pavement and gravel on the edge of the slab as you descend at car speed down the canyon.

This route is easily modified and connectable with other loops in the area, thanks to the wonderful Peak-to-Peak Highway, which links all the great canyons. A very popular and ambitious variation on this ride rolls out of Boulder to Lyons, up South Saint Vrain to the Peak-to-Peak (in this case, the intersection of Highway 7 and Highway 72), then south to Left Hand or Nederland (or even Rollinsville) and back to Boulder. Descending to Loveland rather than Lyons is another good option for canyon swappers. Trail Ridge Road is right there as well, west out of Estes Park, for an awesome day ride or for beginning an epic tour.

Miles and Directions

0.0   Start from the intersection of Highway 7 and US 36 in Lyons and pedal south up Highway 7.

13.9   Pass by the junction with Highway 72 after a tough stretch of climbing.

26.6   Pass Lily Lake on the left. This is a nice place to stop that also happens to be near the high point of the ride. From here the road descends into Estes Park.

32.8   Turn right (east) onto US 36 at an obvious junction. (Note: This will take you quickly out of Estes. If you want to enjoy the town or get a bite to eat, take a left here.)

52.4   Arrive back in Lyons at the intersection of US 36 and Highway 7.

Ride Information

Information

Estes Park Chamber Resort Association; (800) 378-3708; www.estesparkresort.com.
Lyons Chamber of Commerce, P.O. Box 426, Lyons, CO 80540; (877) 596-6726 or (303) 823-5215; www.lyons-colorado.com.

Events/Attractions

Rocky Mountain National Park; (970) 586-1206; www.nps.gov/romo/index.htm. A road biker's dream. The entrance fee for cyclists is $5.00 per person.
Stanley Hotel, 333 Wonderview Avenue, Estes Park; (800) 976-1377 or (970) 586-3371; info@stanleyhotel.com.

Restaurants

Andrea's Homestead Cafe, 216 East Main Street, Lyons; (303) 823-5000. Breakfast, lunch, and dinner in Lyons since '77.
Barking Dog Cafe, 447 Main Street, Lyons; (303) 823-9600. Coffees, smoothees, baglees, sandwichees . . .
Ed's Cantina, 362 East Elkhorn Avenue, Estes Park; (970) 586-2919. Comida de Mexico.
Mountain Home Cafe, 457 East Wonderview Drive, Estes Park; (970) 586-1965. Tasty, can't-go-wrong carbo-loading, i.e., pancakes.

Maps

Delorme: Colorado Atlas & Gazetteer: Pages 29 A-6, B-7; 30 C-1.

Fort Collins

This so-called Fort Collins isn't much of a fort. There are no gates or watchtowers, no sentries on duty. Basically, you just roll right into town without a shot fired.

Fort Collins was once a functioning military fort, back in the day, erected to shield settlers and gold rushers from angry Cheyenne and Arapahoe warriors. It was named for the commander of another such fort farther north. What Fort Collins is now is a unique, relatively peaceful, but occasionally riotous college town. At its heart is the thriving campus of Colorado State University, which used to be an A&M school. A town with deep rural roots, Fort Collins is still infused with a strong streak of redneck. This is where the Weld County farm kids come to cruise on a Saturday night, and where their parents come for a night on the town.

Half Boulder and half Greeley, this unique little city is the easiest of all the Front Range cities when it comes to cycling through town. Not only is it the flattest city in the chain, but it is blessed with an incredible and unmatched volume of wide curb lanes. Riders can cruise Fort Collins's busiest streets without ever having to contend with motorists for lane space. In addition, the Fort has two really decent bike paths that follow rivers through town, passing under all the major streets.

Outside the city limits road riders will find several enticing route possibilities. To the west Rist Canyon, Stove Prairie Road, the roads around Horsetooth Reservoir and Carter Lake, and the roads around Masonville are among the best that Colorado has to offer. In every other direction it's a boundless arena for flatland riding.

If you live further south, don't put off a trip to Fort Collins for some first-class riding, and if you live in the Fort, consider yourself lucky.

28 Boulder-Fort Collins Challenge

This is just one of many possible routes between these two fine, bicycle-loving college towns. This route, however, is among the most interesting, passing to the west of a line of hogbacks around Masonville and swooping into Fort Collins from above.

Start: The intersection of Broadway and U.S. Highway 36 at the north end of Boulder.
Length: 52.1-mile point-to-point.
Terrain: Rolling hills, false flats, and a few short, sharp climbs as the route approaches Fort Collins via Horsetooth Reservoir.

Traffic and hazards: These roads have moderately heavy traffic, except for the roads around Masonville, which are relatively quiet. Eighty-third Street has almost no shoulder, and it gets busy around rush hour.

Getting there: The mileage cues begin at the intersection of US 36 and Broadway in north Boulder. To get there from central Boulder, use 19th Street or Folsom Avenue/26th Street to travel north to US 36. From west Boulder take 4th Street as far as it goes, then continue north on Wonderland Hill Avenue and cut east to Broadway at Quince Street.

The Ride

A trip between Boulder and Fort Collins can be quite straightforward and austere. If time happened to be your only concern, you would just get on the Diagonal to Longmont, then jump on U.S. Highway 287 for a straight shot all the way to the Fort on a wide, gravel-strewn shoulder with semis whipping past your ear. Fast, but boring. If you're looking for a fun and interesting ride, however, try this backdoor route to Fort Collins via Masonville. While this route is much more entertaining, and much quieter, it has many small and a few good-sized hills, so it's also much more difficult.

Open the back door to Fort Collins by rolling north out of Boulder on US 36 (the Foothills Highway). How you choose to reach US 36 depends on personal preference and the location of your starting point within Boulder. Folsom Avenue/26th Street, 19th Street, and 4th Street are all good northbound routes from central Boulder.

Options abound for the next phase of this ride. Almost arbitrarily I have chosen Hygiene Road. Nelson Road is also very good. The basic idea is to get east 4 miles—a slight descent the whole way—to 75th Street and take it north through the town of Hygiene and across Highway 66. North of Highway 66 a forced right turn takes you east to 83rd Street, which looks very much like 75th. One and a half miles on 83rd brings you to a small twist and drop into the valley of the Little Thompson, breaking the monotony of these straight roads. Soon you are due east of Carter Lake, although you can't see it. The reservoir is actually hanging over your head.

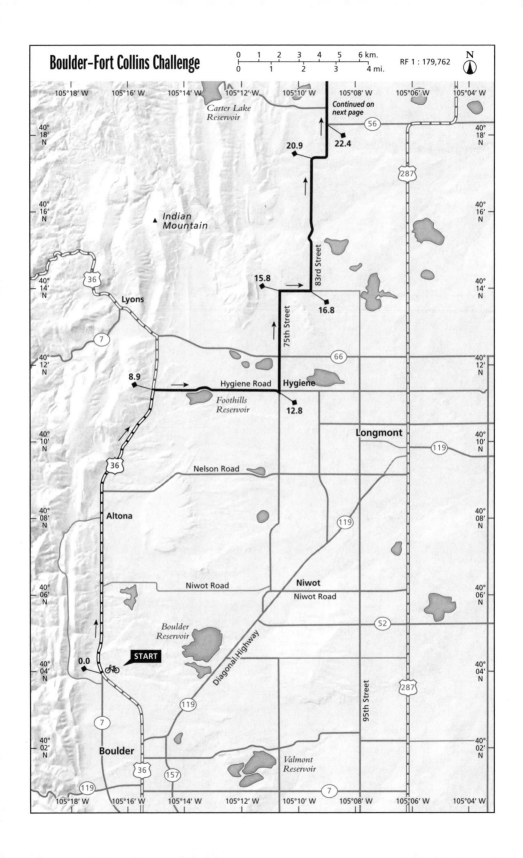

Boulder-Fort Collins Challenge

RF 1 : 179,762

N

Carter Lake Reservoir

56

Continued on next page

22.4

20.9

287

Indian Mountain

36

Lyons

7

15.8

16.8

83rd Street

75th Street

66

8.9

Hygiene Road   Hygiene

Foothills Reservoir

12.8

Longmont

119

Nelson Road

36

Altona

119

Niwot Road

Niwot Road   Niwot

119

52

Boulder Reservoir

Diagonal Highway

95th Street

287

0.0

START

119

7

Boulder

36   157

119

Valmont Reservoir

7

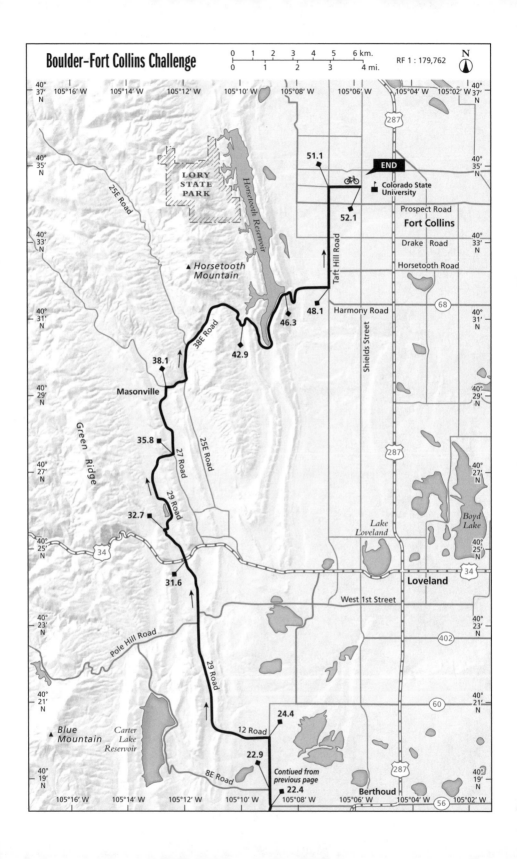

Boulder–Fort Collins Challenge

RF 1 : 179,762

0 1 2 3 4 5 6 km.
0 1 2 3 4 mi.

N

40° 37' N

105°16' W 105°14' W 105°12' W 105°10' W 105°08' W 105°06' W 105°04' W 105°02' W

287

51.1

END

🚲 ■ Colorado State
University

LORY
STATE
PARK

Horsetooth Reservoir

52.1

Prospect Road

Fort Collins

40° 35' N

25E Road

Drake | Road

40° 33' N

Horsetooth Road

▲ Horsetooth
Mountain

Taft Hill Road

48.1 Harmony Road

68

40° 31' N

38E Road

46.3

42.9

Shields Street

38.1

Masonville

40° 29' N

35.8 ■

27 Road

25E Road

287

40° 27' N

Lake
Loveland

Boyd
Lake

32.7 ■

29 Road

40° 25' N

34

31.6 ■

Loveland 34

West 1st Street

Green   Ridge

40° 23' N

Pole Hill Road

402

29 Road

40° 21' N

60

▲ Blue
Mountain

Carter
Lake
Reservoir

24.4 ■

12 Road

22.9 ■

287

8E Road

Contiued from
previous page 22.4 ■

Berthoud

56

40° 19' N

105°16' W 105°14' W 105°12' W 105°10' W 105°08' W 105°06' W 105°04' W 105°02' W

Horsetooth Reservoir

After mile 24 watch for the turnoff onto Road 12. Here is where a less ambitious rider might continue straight north on a more sedate—some would say more logical—route into west Loveland. Road 12 (turning into Road 29) is a challenge, but it rewards all those who ride it. Crossing U.S. Highway 34, Road 29 (the pavement formerly known as Road 12) shoots you right into a quaint little residential area hidden away near the Big Thompson River. The road surface here is about as wide as a good-sized bike path. Road 29 curls into a small ravine, then makes a sharp right across the river.

The road beyond the Big Thompson has been widened, surfaced, and rerouted, a warning sign of impending development in this lonely area behind the hogbacks. As of today the road is still extremely quiet. Really, the roads to the east of Roads 29, 27, and 25E are considered to be the backdoor routes to Fort Collins. Road 29 is the back door to the back door, and feels like it. That's a compliment.

After climbing past a small reservoir, join Road 27 near Masonville. The roads around Masonville, partly due to guidebooks like this one, have become very popular with Front Range cyclists. The scenery is pleasant, the roads are smooth enough, and the terrain rolls pleasantly. Better yet, while more cyclists discover this area every day, the motor traffic remains noticeably lighter than on the roads to the east, which are laid out in a flat grid.

North from Masonville the road (now 38E) approaches the southern tip of Horsetooth Reservoir and goes over some serious little hills. More than 40 miles in, this is the toughest part of the ride. You might seem far from your goal at this point, but fear not—really you are right on top of Fort Collins.

If this is your first visit to the Fort, you will find much to like about it, starting with the bicycle-friendly streets. Almost every major street in town has a stripe denoting bicycle-only space on the right side—wide curb lanes everywhere. In addition, there are two long multiuse paths following rivers on diagonal vectors across this small city. The result is that Fort Collins is a very easy place to get around on a bicycle.[1]

Miles and Directions

- **0.0** Start riding north on US 36 from its intersection with Broadway.
- **8.9** Turn right on Hygiene Road.
- **12.8** Take a left on 75th Street.
- **13.8** Cross Highway 66.
- **15.8** The road takes a ninety-degree right.
- **16.8** Turn left on 83rd Street.
- **20.9** The road jogs east a half mile before continuing north.
- **22.4** Pass the intersection with Highway 56.
- **24.4** Take a left on Road 12. Here's where the route starts to get interesting.
- **31.6** Cross US 34. Continue on Road 29, which is just a thin little strip of asphalt at this point.
- **32.7** Take a sharp right over a bridge. Begin a little climb.
- **35.8** Take a left on Road 27 at the T intersection.
- **38.1** At the Masonville crossroads take a right toward Fort Collins.
- **42.9** Begin a short climb. (Heh—"short.")
- **48.1** Take a left on Taft Hill Road. (You are essentially in Fort Collins at this point and can use any number of routes to get where you want to go.)
- **48.6** Cross West Horsetooth Road.
- **49.6** Cross West Drake Road. (Note: The Spring Creek multiuse trail crosses Taft Hill Road here and has a trailhead just a few blocks east on West Drake Road. The Spring Creek path is a fully separated path that cuts at a diagonal across Fort Collins to the northeast.)

---

[1] It is not a cyclist's paradise, however. In the winter of 2003, several cyclists were victims of drive-by baseball bat attacks, struck in the back while riding in Fort Collins. Police eventually rounded up three high school kids who were responsible for the assaults, which the kids called "bicycle boxing." Personally, I have not noticed any greater frequency of negative incidents in Fort Collins compared to other Front Range cities.

50.6 Cross West Prospect Road.

51.1 Take a right on West Elizabeth Street. (Watch for the bike shop on the right side of the road if you need it.)

52.1 Arrive in central Fort Collins at the intersection of Elizabeth and Shields Streets, right across the street from the Colorado State University campus. Rioting is not mandatory, but it may help you fit in.

Ride Information

Restaurants

Mustard's Last Stand, 1719 Broadway, Boulder; (303) 444-5841. Quality fast-food burgers, Chicago-style dogs, veggie burgers, to go or consume on site. Where Boulder Creek flows under Broadway.

Wild Oats Grocery and Deli. Two useful locations in Boulder: 1651 Broadway, (303) 442-0082; 2584 Baseline Road, (303) 499-7636. Big sandwiches, salad bar, refrigerated liquids, bathroom. This place is undeniably useful.

La Iguana Taqueria, 1301 Broadway, Boulder; (303) 938-8888. Heaping portions of Fresh-Mex on the Hill.

Jalino's, 1647 Arapahoe Avenue, Boulder; (303) 443-6300. Excellent pizza and sandwiches.

Bova's Pantry, 1325 Broadway, Boulder; (303) 449-0874. Grocery and deli on the Hill. Still wrappin' sandwiches after all these years.

Pasta Jay's, 1001 Pearl Street, Boulder; (303) 444-5800. Once the upstart restaurateur of the Front Range, Jay is now an institution.

Narayan's, 921 Pearl Street, Boulder; (303) 447-2816. Boulder has lots of great little restaurants serving up the exotic tastes of the Far East. This is one of the best.

Big City Burrito, 510 South College Avenue, Fort Collins; (970) 482-3303. These burritos are large and tend to be quite good. Made to order.

Coopersmith's Pub and Brewing, 5 Old Town Square, Fort Collins; (970) 498-0483. An older specimen of the ubiquitous Front Range "brewpub."

Bisetti's, 120 South College Avenue, Fort Collins; (970) 493-0086. Nice Italian place near downtown Fort Collins. Price is moderate and up.

Accommodations

Hotel Boulderado, 2115 13th Street, Boulder; (800) 433-4344; www.boulderado.com. Boulder's classy landmark hotel.

Armstrong Hotel, 259 South College Avenue, Fort Collins; (970) 484-3883; www.the armstronghotel.com. The old hotel downtown has been renovated—going for a hip noir kind of thing—which is a bummer for those of us who used to stay there long ago. Prices have been renovated as well, into the mid-high range.

Maps

Delorme: Colorado Atlas & Gazetteer: Pages 20, 30.

29 Fort Collins Bike Path Ramble

Tour Fort Collins's two major bicycle-pedestrian paths on this mellow ramble. Combined with an easy road section, the two paths form a big triangle-shaped loop around the town.

Start: The intersection of the Poudre Trail and Timberline Road in eastern Fort Collins. (This is just one of many possible starting points along this loop. Others include the Poudre Trail trailhead on North Taft Hill Road and the Spring Creek Trail trailhead on Drake Road.)
Length: 16.2-mile loop.
Terrain: Quite flat.

Traffic and hazards: Typical bicycle path hazards: dogs, children, joggers, skaters, and semi-alert bike riders like yourself. The section of this loop along North Taft Hill Road is easy to deal with, mainly due to its wide curb lane and segregated bike space. This is one of the easiest rides in the book, traffic-wise.

Getting there: From downtown Fort Collins head east on Mulberry Street/Highway 14 to Timberline Road. Take a right (south) on Timberline and find the dirt parking area where the Poudre Trail passes under the road. From Denver drive north on Interstate 25 to Fort Collins exit 269 and head west on Mulberry Street/Highway 14 for 2 miles to Timberline Road. Go south on Timberline 0.3 mile and park at the small dirt parking area where the Poudre Trail passes under the road.

The Ride

After riding almost the entire lengths of Fort Collins's two prized multiuse trails, you might agree that this town has the nicest bicycle facilities on the entire Front Range. With both major waterways through town accompanied by fully separated paths that flow with the rivers under major roads, this town is maximizing its possibilities in that regard. At the time of this writing, the paths of Fort Collins were continuing to be reworked, repaved, and improved. In addition, the Fort's major streets are almost all engineered with bicycles in mind, which means cyclists on these roads rarely come into conflict with motorists for lane space.[1] You'll experience both types of facilities on this easy 16.2-mile loop.

Obviously, with paths that flow all the way through town, there will be many possible points of entry. You'll start from the Poudre Trail's intersection with Timberline Road, a good place to begin if you're out east or coming from outside of town. If you're down on the south side, you might want to start at the Spring Creek Trail's trailhead on Drake Road (near the intersection of Drake and Taft Hill Road in southwest Fort Collins); those on the north side might want to launch from the Poudre Trail trailhead on Taft Hill Road, about 0.7 mile north of Vine Drive. It's all good.

---

[1] An exception is College Avenue, the main north-south drag, which is completely off-limits to bikes. No great loss there.

The Poudre Trail

Heading southeast by the Poudre, you immediately roll into an undeveloped area of ponds and open fields. Not long after is the turnoff to the Spring Creek Trail, which takes you back into town. If you would like to continue with this semirural action, go left at the fork here and keep following the Poudre. This excellent—although somewhat useless—section of trail winds through a wooded area, past a series of water treatment facilities, and dead-ends at a place called the Environmental Learning Center. The ELC, run by Colorado State University's College of Natural Resources, sits on 212 acres of prairie and wetlands and includes raptor cages, a self-guided nature walk, and various other opportunities for hands-on learning. The ELC is open to the public and is a great place to haul your toddlers. This side trip adds about 3 miles total to the loop.

Back on the Spring Creek Trail and headed southwest, the surface is inconsistent. Which is to say the surface is poor at times, with badly cracked and poorly repaired asphalt. This path meanders through a series of parks in the Fort's suburban south side. At mile 2.0 cruise into Edora Park and pass the truly heartwarming sight of little kids tearing it up on a real BMX track. Even though it is meandering, sometimes poorly surfaced, and scattered with frivolous users, the Spring Creek Trail is a very useful tool for serious transportation in spite of itself, as it allows cyclists to

Fort Collins Bike Path Ramble

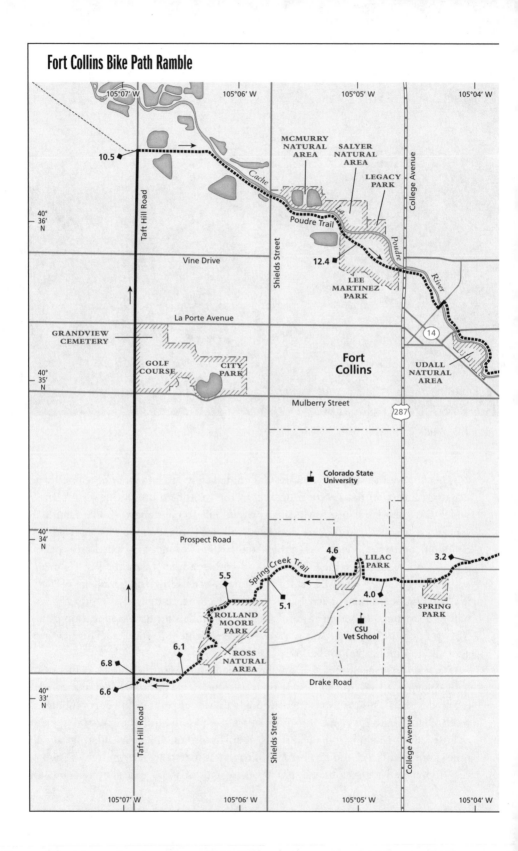

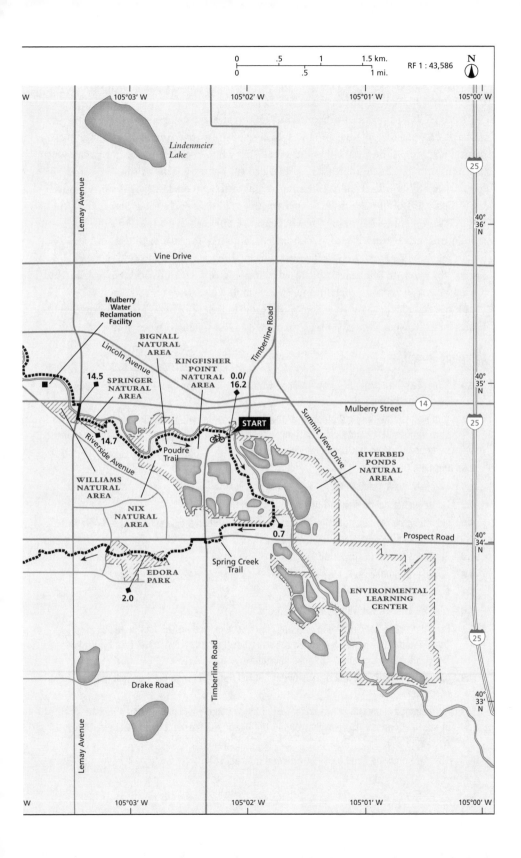

RF 1 : 43,586

0   .5   1   1.5 km.
0   .5   1 mi.

105°03' W
105°02' W
105°01' W
105°00' W

40° 36' N
40° 35' N
40° 34' N
40° 33' N

Lindenmeier Lake

Lemay Avenue

Vine Drive

Mulberry Water Reclamation Facility

Lincoln Avenue

BIGNALL NATURAL AREA

KINGFISHER POINT NATURAL AREA

0.0/ 16.2

14.5

SPRINGER NATURAL AREA

Mulberry Street

(14)

25

14.7

Riverside Avenue

Poudre Trail

START

Summit View Drive

RIVERBED PONDS NATURAL AREA

WILLIAMS NATURAL AREA

NIX NATURAL AREA

0.7

Prospect Road

Spring Creek Trail

EDORA PARK

2.0

ENVIRONMENTAL LEARNING CENTER

Timberline Road

25

Drake Road

Lemay Avenue

Timberline Road

105°03' W
105°02' W
105°01' W
105°00' W

avoid stopping at intersections. Four-plus miles more of gentle meandering brings you all the way back across Fort Collins to Taft Hill Road, where you jump off the trail and head north on the street.

Taft Hill Road provides a boring but rather pleasant cycling route, even though traffic is heavy. This positive situation is derived from the simple fact that there is plenty of space on the right side of the road. Taft Hill cuts straight north across town, unceremoniously. Just under 4 miles on Taft Hill brings you from one trail crossing to another, the Poudre Trail. You'll take a right and head back east and a little south. Note that the Poudre also rolls west from this trailhead to Laporte and is the gateway to some great rides west of town. Like the Spring Creek, the Poudre Trail east is inconsistently surfaced and occasionally annoying in its bumpiness and lack of repair, but is being improved every year. The path traces the north side of town, following the river on a southeast diagonal past ponds and cottonwood stands. Like the Spring Creek, it passes under the major crossings.

Fort Collins is so easy to navigate by bicycle that it's a wonder anybody drives here. Harsh winters, you say? Heck, that's why God invented wool and fenders.

Miles and Directions

0.0 Start from the Poudre Trail's intersection with Timberline Road, and start riding southeast on the Poudre Trail.

0.7 Turn right on the Spring Creek Trail. **Side-trip:** Continue on the wide concrete path to the Environmental Learning Center, 1.5 miles further on. The winding path is fast and fun, but unfortunately does not continue beyond the ELC.

2.0 Pass the BMX track.

2.4 Carefully cross Welch Drive.

3.2 Go through a cul-de-sac and under Stover Street.

4.0 Go through a tunnel under the railroad tracks. If you need a bike shop, turn left here for the distant shopping area.

4.6 Stay right as a spur shoots off to the left.

4.9 Stay left at another fork.

5.1 Pass under Shields Street.

5.5 Pass an intersection with Stuart Street trails.

6.1 Pass the Drake Road trailhead and pass under Drake. **Option:** Get off the trail at the Drake Road trailhead (also an alternate start/finish for this loop). Travel west on Drake to Taft Hill Road. This is about 0.1 mile shorter.

6.6 After the Spring Creek Trail passes under Taft Hill Road, get onto the sidewalk and head north on Taft Hill.

6.8 At the intersection with Drake Road, take a place in the bike lane on the right-hand side of Taft Hill Road northbound. Stay on Taft Hill Road past Prospect Road, Mulberry Street, and Vine Drive.

10.5 Turn right onto the Poudre Trail at a signed trailhead.

12.1 Stay right as a spur branches off on the left.

12.4 Stay right at an intersection with the Hickory Street Trail.

14.5 The path becomes a "sidepath" and turns right on Lemay Avenue.

14.7 A sharp right turn takes you back around and under Lemay Avenue.

16.2 Arrive back at the start/finish on Timberline Road.

Ride Information

Events/Attractions

Environmental Learning Center, Fort Collins; (970) 491-1661; www.cnr.colostate.edu/elc/.
The Fort Collins BMX Track, Edora Park, 1420 East Stuart Street, Fort Collins; (970) 208-1355. Races on Thursday and Saturday.

Restaurants

Big City Burrito, 510 South College Avenue, Fort Collins; (970) 482-3303. These burritos are large and tend to be quite good. Made to order.
Coopersmith's Pub and Brewing, 5 Old Town Square, Fort Collins; (970) 498-0483. An older specimen of the ubiquitous Front Range "brewpub."

Bisetti's, 120 South College Avenue, Fort Collins; (970) 493-0086. Nice Italian place near downtown Fort Collins. Price is moderate and up.

Accommodation

Armstrong Hotel, 259 South College Avenue, Fort Collins; (970) 484-3883; www.the armstronghotel.com. The old hotel downtown has been renovated—going for a hip noir kind of thing—which is a bummer for those of us who used to stay there long ago. Prices have been renovated as well, into the mid-high range.

Maps

Delorme: Colorado Atlas & Gazetteer: Page 20.

30 Rist Canyon Challenge

This trip involves a long but moderate climb up Rist Canyon—one of the finest road climbs on the Front Range—followed by a very fast descent into Poudre Canyon. The final phase of the ride is a very long, slight descent back to Fort Collins on Highway 14, which occasionally has heavy traffic.

Start: The Poudre Trail trailhead on North Taft Hill Road, just north of Fort Collins.
Length: 43.2-mile lariat.
Terrain: Mountainous. Rist Canyon is moderate overall, but long, and steeper at the top.

Traffic and hazards: Rist Canyon is generally quiet, although the road could be wider. The descent on Stove Prairie Road is tricky. Traffic is heavier in Poudre Canyon, and the shoulder is thin to nonexistent. Confident riders only for this one.

Getting there: This challenging loop is easily accessed by bicycle from anywhere in town, but the Poudre Trail trailhead parking area on North Taft Hill Road is as good a place to drop a vehicle as any if you need to do that. To find the trailhead drive west from College Avenue on any of Fort Collins's major roads 2 miles to Taft Hill Road. Go north on Taft Hill all the way through town. Three quarters of a mile north of Vine Drive, turn right into the trailhead parking area. From out of town take Interstate 25 to the Highway 14 exit (Mulberry Street), then go west through town to Taft Hill Road and north to the trailhead.

The Ride

Rist Canyon is one of the most hospitable and enjoyable climbs around, distinguishing itself from its Front Range canyon cousins through its generally moderate grade. Rist does get steep occasionally—and for one longer section near its summit the grade stays over 10 percent—but seems merciful enough to veterans of the Front Range gravity wars. At about 10 miles this climb is quite a bit shorter than many of the area classics. The total elevation gain is about 2,200 feet.

After topping out and then bopping along the hilltops for a while, Rist Canyon Road falls into a precipitous descent, a real hair-ripping fall to Stove Prairie. This is typical for roads that cross the first range of mountains (Deer Creek, Golden Gate, Coal Creek, Sugarloaf, and U.S. Highway 36 to Estes Park, to name a few). The descent continues after the turn on Stove Prairie Road. With tight turns twisting down this heavily forested hillside, Stove Prairie Road is a green blur. There is one tiny little climb in the middle of it.

The final leg on Highway 14, descending 16 miles of Poudre Canyon, is anything but a blur. Even though it's downhill the whole way, Poudre Canyon is flat enough that any stiff headwind can stop you cold. This is a long section of seated pedaling—a situation that often leads to a condition commonly known as sore ass syndrome. Stay light on the bike and shift position often to relieve pressure on the

The Poudre Trail, which crosses the river west of Fort Collins

nether regions. Tourist traffic is often quite heavy in Poudre Canyon, and the shoulder is not all that cooperative. Highway 14 is a full degree more hectic than Stove Prairie Road, but still a fine road for a confident rider.

Rist Canyon is destined to become a favorite of anyone who tries it. It is quite possible, however, that you might find it even better to turn left on Stove Prairie instead of right and descend to Masonville on that excellent, rolling, back-of-beyond section of road. Traffic is more calm than in Poudre Canyon, although the Masonville route leaves you with plenty of back-side climbing around Horsetooth. Doing that loop clockwise, climbing Stove Prairie from the south, is also an awesome ride. Unfortunately, you can't climb both Rist Canyon and Masonville to Stove Prairie in the same ride, unless you get absolutely nuts on it. I dare ya'.

Miles and Directions

0.0 Start from the Poudre Trail trailhead on North Taft Hill Road and ride northwest along the trail.

1.6 The path travels over a lengthy wood trestle bridge.

2.5 The path spills out onto roadway. Head west on Highway 14 through Laporte.

Rist Canyon Challenge

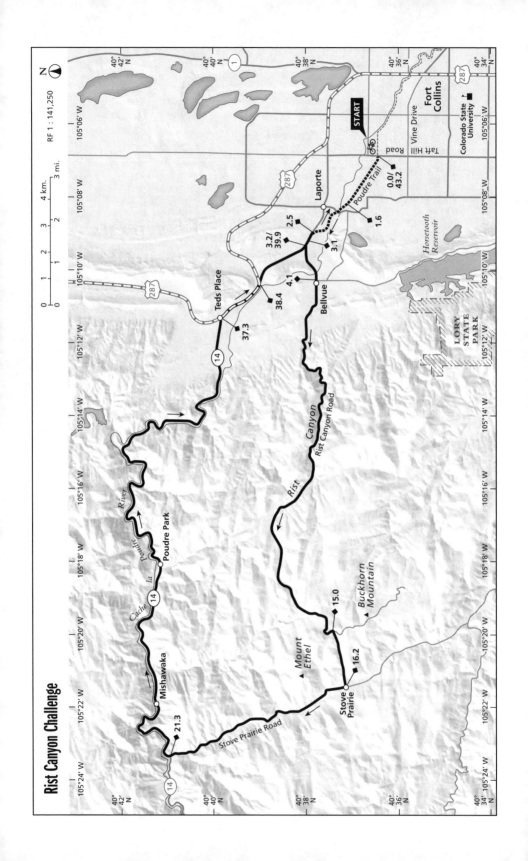

3.1 Even though the sign here might seem like it's pointing you to Bellvue, don't turn on Galway Drive. Keep going straight.

3.2 Turn left on Rist Canyon Road (52E).

4.1 Pass the intersection with Road 23 at Bellvue.

15.0 Top out and start a fast descent to Stove Prairie.

16.2 Turn right on Stove Prairie Road (Road 27). **Option:** Turn left here and descend to Masonville, a very nice stretch of road in either direction. At Masonville continue east, then north, on Road 38E, and loop back to Fort Collins past the south side of Horsetooth Reservoir.

21.3 Turn right on Highway 14 and follow the Cache la Poudre River back to town.

37.3 Turn right as Highway 14 joins U.S. Highway 287.

38.4 Where US 287 branches left, go right on Road 54G (not 54E).

39.9 Stay left as the road passes the junction with Rist Canyon Road Road (52E).

40.7 Turn right and get back onto the Poudre Trail.

43.2 Arrive back at the trailhead parking area.

Ride Information

Restaurants

Big City Burrito, 510 South College Avenue, Fort Collins; (970) 482-3303. These burritos are large and tend to be quite good. Made to order.

Coopersmith's Pub and Brewing, 5 Old Town Square, Fort Collins; (970) 498-0483. An older specimen of the ubiquitous Front Range "brewpub."

Bisetti's, 120 South College Avenue, Fort Collins; (970) 493-0086. Nice Italian place near downtown Fort Collins. Price is moderate and up.

Accommodation

Armstrong Hotel, 259 South College Avenue, Fort Collins; (970) 484-3883; www.the armstronghotel.com. The old hotel downtown has been renovated—going for a hip noir kind of thing—which is a bummer for those of us who used to stay there long ago. Prices have been renovated as well, into the mid-high range.

Maps

Delorme: Colorado Atlas & Gazetteer: Pages 20 D-1, 19 C-7.

31 Horsetooth Cruise

This short loop out of Fort Collins packs a lot of punch. Cruise out of town via Laporte, then hold onto your socks as Road 23 takes you on a roller-coaster tour of scenic Horsetooth Reservoir.

Start: The Poudre Trail trailhead on North Taft Hill Road, just north of Fort Collins.
Length: 15.6-mile loop.
Terrain: Road 23 up to and along Horsetooth Reservoir has many steep ups and downs.
Traffic and hazards: Road 23 has some high-speed curves that demand your focused attention. Traffic is moderate on the high-speed two-lane highways outside of Fort Collins. The roads in town generally feature a segregated space for cyclists—Overland Trail is a good example, with a bike lane the whole length.

Getting there: This short loop is easily accessed by bicycle from anywhere in town, but the Poudre Trail trailhead parking area on North Taft Hill Road is as good a place to drop a vehicle as any if you need to do that. To find the trailhead drive west from College Avenue on any of Fort Collins's major roads 2 miles to Taft Hill Road. Go north on Taft Hill all the way through town. Three quarters of a mile north of Vine Drive, turn right into the trailhead parking area. From out of town take Interstate 25 to the Highway 14 exit (Mulberry Street), then go west through town to Taft Hill Road and north to the trailhead.

The Ride

The history of the development of the Front Range has depended on one thing above all others: water. Within a few years after the gold rushers swarmed in, farmers were cutting ditches to divert water from the Cache la Poudre and other Front Range rivers. Still, in drought years the canals ran dry and farming was nearly impossible. By the 1930s the Front Range needed water for power generation and many other reasons besides agriculture. There was not enough water flowing down onto the plains to support the growth in population and industry. Rather than curbing development here to match available resources, Front Rangers gazed longingly at the water in the mountains and on the Western Slope, and designed a grand scheme to abscond with as much as they could get. The resulting Colorado–Big Thompson Water Project siphoned water from lakes in the high country and pumped it through, under, and sometimes over mountains to new reservoirs and canals on the Front Range—transforming this near desert into the land of 10,000 lakes. Well, make that 1,000 lakes. Horsetooth Reservoir, with which you'll get up close and personal on this ride, is among the most spectacular products of this auda-

Horsetooth Reservoir ▶

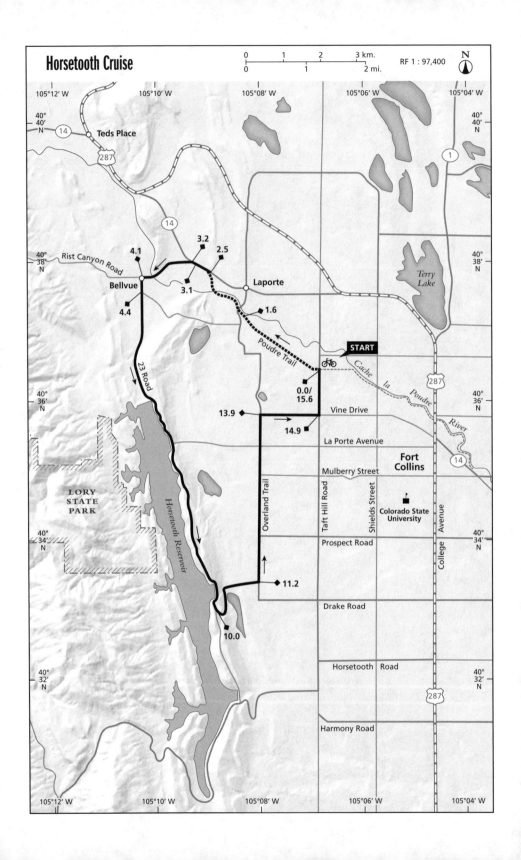

Horsetooth Cruise

0 1 2 3 km.
0 1 2 mi.

RF 1 : 97,400

N

105°12' W   105°10' W   105°08' W   105°06' W   105°04' W

14 Teds Place
287

14

Rist Canyon Road
40° 38' N

40° 40' N

4.1
3.2
2.5
3.1
Bellvue
4.4
Laporte

1.6

Poudre Trail

START

Cache   la   Poudre

0.0/ 15.6

13.9   Vine Drive
14.9

La Porte Avenue

River

Fort Collins

Mulberry Street

23 Road

Horsetooth Reservoir

LORY STATE PARK

Overland Trail

Taft Hill Road

Shields Street

Colorado State University

College Avenue

Prospect Road

11.2

Drake Road

10.0

Horsetooth   Road

Harmony Road

Terry Lake

40° 38' N

40° 36' N

40° 34' N

40° 32' N

287

14

1

cious project. Others include Carter Lake and Pinewood Lake.

A good way to begin this loop is to travel on a diagonal from Taft Hill Road to Laporte using the Poudre bicycle-pedestrian trail. The Poudre Trail can be a useful tool for nonmotorized transportation, and here it just happens to be perfectly placed for your needs. From Laporte ride the short trip to Bellvue (you'll know it when you see it) and hang a left on Road 23. Road 23 is another one of these great Front Range roads that is snuggled into a forgotten valley between the first spine of ridges and the actual mountains. The only thing is, now this valley is partially dammed up and filled with water, so little Road 23 has to find a way up and around.

If you think Road 23 is just going to roll over and play dead, think again. This road pops up to dam-top level in one no-nonsense ramp. This is a rather rude introduction to Horsetooth Reservoir. The road dances along the ridge for a short time, then drops abruptly. The sight of this man-made lake is impressive—you might want to put the ride on hiatus for a bit just to take in the view. Another steep climb, another steep drop, and you're escaping the Horsetooth water storage zone and rolling down fast toward the Fort. It makes you wonder—if there is ever a big earthquake or something, Fort Collins is going to get wet. The route back into town goes right past Hughes Stadium, scene of some rather respectable American-style football in recent years. The exodus is hard to stop once it starts, so if you want to sit and eat somewhere, or stare at the water, the best place is right after the road tops the dam on the north side.

This quick ride is a great mix of gravity-induced challenge, thrills, and scenery.

Miles and Directions

0.0   Start from the Poudre Trail trailhead on North Taft Hill Road and ride northwest along the trail.

1.6   The path travels over a lengthy wood trestle bridge.

2.5   The path spills out onto roadway. Head west on Highway 14 through Laporte.

3.1   Even though the sign here appears to point you to Bellvue, *don't* turn on Galway Drive. Keep going straight.

3.2   Turn left on Rist Canyon Road Road (52E).

4.1   Turn left on Road 23.

4.4   Pass an intersection with Road 50E.

10.0   Turn left on Road 42C. **Option:** Continue straight here, and eventually turn left on Road 38E and then on Taft Hill Road, elongating the loop back into town by about 3.3 miles.

11.2   Turn left on Overland Trail (now headed north).

13.9   Turn right on Vine Drive.

14.9   Turn left on Taft Hill Road.

15.6   Return to the trailhead.

Ride Information

Restaurants

Big City Burrito, 510 South College Avenue, Fort Collins; (970) 482-3303. These burritos are large and tend to be quite good. Made to order.

Coopersmith's Pub and Brewing, 5 Old Town Square, Fort Collins; (970) 498-0483. An older specimen of the ubiquitous Front Range "brewpub."

Bisetti's, 120 South College Avenue, Fort Collins; (970) 493-0086. Nice Italian place near downtown Fort Collins. Price is moderate and up.

Accommodation

Armstrong Hotel, 259 South College Avenue, Fort Collins; (970) 484-3883; www.the armstronghotel.com. The old hotel downtown has been renovated—going for a hip noir kind of thing—which is a bummer for those of us who used to stay there long ago. Prices have been renovated as well, into the mid-high range.

Maps

Delorme: Colorado Atlas & Gazetteer: Page 20 D-2.

32 Carter Lake-Rattlesnake Challenge

Starting from Loveland, this strenuous route tours some prime gently rolling terrain around Masonville before pointing upward at a brutal angle. Riders are invited (but not required) to test their strength on the road to Pinewood Lake, one of the toughest climbs around, before looping back to Loveland via the excellent road that traces the east shoreline of Carter Lake.

Start: The intersection of Wilson Avenue and Eisenhower Boulevard/U.S. Highway 34 in Loveland. (Note: Park at the trailhead for the Big Thompson Trail, about 0.3 mile south of Eisenhower Boulevard on Wilson Avenue. You won't actually use this trail, but it's a good place to drop a vehicle for a road ride.)

Length: 45.3-mile loop.

Terrain: This ride features one very difficult (optional) climb to Pinewood Lake. There is an additional, much shorter climb to Carter Lake. The rest of the ride is on flat or gently rolling land.

Traffic and hazards: Most of these roads are generally moderate in traffic intensity. The brief sections on US 34 have wide shoulders. On the secondary roads wide shoulders are scarce, but drivers expect to see bikes on these popular cycling roads. The descent from Pinewood Lake is steep and somewhat technical, hazardous if you ride beyond your abilities.

Getting there: Take U.S. Highway 287 to Loveland. US 287 becomes Lincoln Avenue northbound through Loveland, and Cleveland Avenue southbound. Go west on Eisenhower Boulevard/US 34 for almost 2 miles, then turn south on Wilson Avenue. Park at the bottom of the hill in the dirt parking area provided at the Big Thompson Trail (a paved multiuse path) trailhead. The mileage cues begin at the intersection of Wilson and Eisenhower.

Cloudless skies over Carter Lake

The Ride

Loveland is a natural starting point for this three-part loop that links some of the classic road sections in the vicinity of Masonville and Carter Lake.

Any ride out of Loveland should take in the excellent roads around nearby Masonville, because they're great roads to ride and so readily available. This route takes you first to Masonville via Glade Road (Road 25E) and then back around on Road 27. This is one of the nicest little side loops anywhere, a ride in itself. Finishing this first phase of the ride, a 15-mile country jaunt, you're just getting started.

Head south past US 34 on Road 29, dealing with some heavy road damage, and make the right turn toward Carter Lake. The climbing begins rather gently, following rolling hills for 2 miles to the Carter Lake turnoff below Flatiron Reservoir. At this intersection you have a choice: Continue straight, and up, and attempt one of the toughest climbs around, or cut the ride short by hanging a left and moving on to the Carter Lake portion.

The 1,300-foot climb to Pinewood Lake and Rattlesnake Park is somewhat obscene. Looking at it from the bottom, it looks like a screen shot from *Lord of the Rings.* Nobody in their right mind would go up there. *And then there's you.*

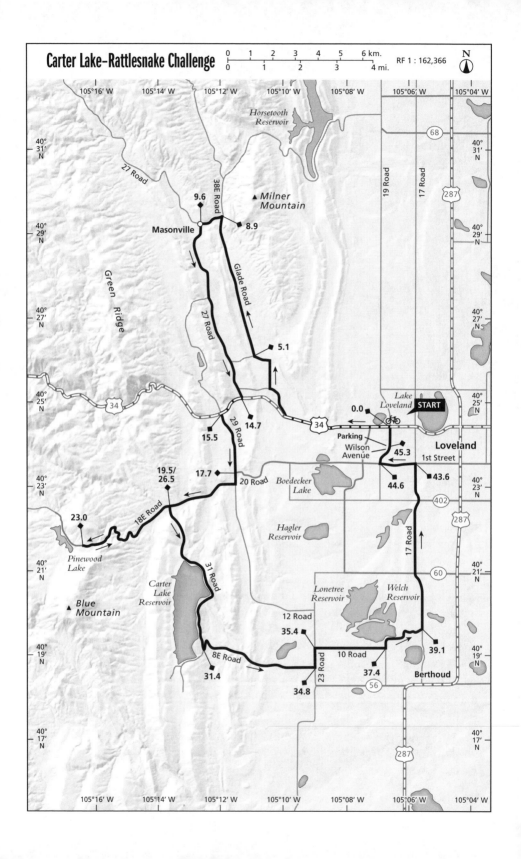

Carter Lake–Rattlesnake Challenge

RF 1 : 162,366

N

Climbing the steep, stark, golden hills, Pole Hill Road with its flashing guardrail immediately recalls Lookout Mountain. But "Rattlesnake" (as it is known to some locals) is much more difficult than Lookout. In fact, it dishes out more pain than almost any other paved climb in Colorado. It really is up there with Magnolia and the second tier of Golden Gate in intensity. However, it is a bit shorter, at around 3.5 miles.

Why do we climb such a hill, for no apparent reason, when we could just turn left and pretend it's not there? Why not let this sleeping rattlesnake lie? Because we are bicyclists on the Front Range, and this is what we do. Because, having learned of this hill's existence, we cannot get it out of our minds. It will mock us until the day we face that sucker head-on. Because it's there.[1] Because it's there, and we are here. Why not give it a shot—since this climb forms an out-and-back spur on this route, if you can't make the summit you can just turn around, and it won't ruin the loop.

Pinewood Lake and Rattlesnake Park are actually quite a bit lower than the summit of the climb, over the back side. I'll leave it up to you whether or not you want to descend to the lake and climb back out. I can't bring myself to do it, personally. Gazing on it from afar will just have to do. Actually, Pinewood Lake has been nearly drained in recent years due to Colorado's ongoing drought, so it's not the prettiest reservoir you ever saw—more like a big mud spot.

Descending Rattlesnake, take a right on Road 31 and roll south toward Carter Lake to begin the third distinct phase of this ride. Immediately you face more climbing, but nothing like what you just saw. The climb to Carter Lake is a well-known, sought-after workout for Front Rangers. Compared to Rattlesnake, however, it has no bite. Road 31 rises above water level and follows the eastern shore of this great-looking reservoir, which like so many others in this area was created in the 1930s as part of the Colorado–Big Thompson Water Project. After about 3 miles of pleasant lakeside cruising, point yourself downward and flow like water toward Loveland. The last 10 miles of this loop make for a nice cool-down on flat terrain.

If you're really feeling your oats, launch a Pinewood/Carter epic from Fort Collins or, even better, from Boulder.

Miles and Directions

0.0 Start riding west on Eisenhower Boulevard/US 34 from Wilson Avenue.

2.2 Veer right onto the thin little residential road without a road sign.

2.7 Turn right onto Glade Road.

3.9 After twisting and turning a bit, turn right and stay on Glade Road.

---

[1]The famous statement "Because it's there" was the answer given by mountaineer George Leigh Mallory in 1923 when asked, Why climb Everest? Mallory attempted to climb Everest the following year and never returned. His frozen corpse was discovered seventy-five years later by another climbing party.

5.1 Take yet another right onto Glade Road, which here is a straight two-lane highway with a 50 mph speed limit.

8.9 Turn left on Road 38E. (Turning right would take you to Fort Collins, eventually.)

9.6 Take a left on Road 27 at Masonville. (Come back here sometime and ride up Stove Prairie Road to Rist Canyon or Poudre Canyon.)

14.7 Turn right onto US 34 briefly.

15.5 Turn left on Road 29. Watch for a bit of road damage.

17.1 Pass the intersection with Road 20.

17.5 Turn right on Road 18E.

19.5 Pass the junction with the Carter Lake road (Road 31) and begin a very difficult climb on Pole Hill Road. **Option:** If you're not feelin' it, simply turn left here and cut out the Pinewood Lake climb, knocking 7 miles off the route.

23.0 Turn around at the top of the climb. Pinewood Lake and Rattlesnake Park are down below you at this point. It is very difficult not to turn around here, as opposed to descending off the back side.

26.5 Back at the junction with Road 31, turn right toward Carter Lake.

31.4 Turn left on Road 8E.

34.8 Turn left on Road 23.

35.4 Take a right on Road 10. **Option:** There are multiple options for returning to Loveland from this point, all are pretty equal in mileage. Road 10 turns to dirt after a while, but it's nice and quiet compared to some of the other roads around.

37.4 Turn left on Road 19, then make a quick ninety-degree right turn.

39.1 Turn left on Road 17.

43.6 Turn left on 1st Street.

44.6 Turn right on Wilson Avenue.

45.3 Arrive back at the parking area. (The intersection with Eisenhower Boulevard is about 0.3 mile north of here.)

Ride Information

Restaurants

Adelita's Fine Mexican Food, 414 East 6th Street, Loveland; (970) 669-9577.

Cabin Country Natural Foods, 248 East 4th Street, Loveland; (970) 669-9280. Grocery. Closed Sundays.

Annapurna, 1360 East Eisenhower Boulevard, Loveland; (970) 461-1056. Indian.

Maps

Delorme: Colorado Atlas & Gazetteer: Page 30 A-1-2, B-1, 2.

Rides at a Glance

(Listed in order of distance)

Rambles

4.8 miles	NCAR Ramble, ride 18
10.4 miles	Tour de Downtown Ramble, ride 15
14.9 miles	Palmer Park Ramble, ride 4
16.2 miles	Fort Collins Bike Path Ramble, ride 29
22.5 miles	Washington Park–Highline Canal Ramble, ride 17
24.7 miles	Boulder Creek–Gunbarrel Ramble, ride 20
33.7 miles	Cherry Creek Reservoir Ramble, ride 16

Cruises

7.8 miles	Broadmoor Cruise, ride 2
8.8 miles	Poorman Cruise, ride 25
11.7 miles	Woodmen Cruise, ride 5
12.2 miles	Denver–Golden Cruise, ride 13
13.3 miles	Morgul-Bismark Cruise, ride 26
15.1 miles	Lookout Mountain Cruise, ride 14
15.6 miles	Horsetooth Cruise, ride 31
22.4 miles	West Colorado Springs Cruise, ride 3
30.1 miles	Boulder–Hygiene Cruise, ride 19
34.9 miles	Morrison MUP Cruise, ride 9
48.2 miles	Bear Creek–Morrison Half-Century Cruise, ride 8
54.4 miles	Big South Suburban Bike Path Cruise, ride 7

Challenges

13.1 miles	North Cheyenne Canyon Challenge, ride 1
21.4 miles	Four Mile Canyon–Gold Hill Challenge, ride 23
33.0 miles	Magnolia Road–Nederland Challenge, ride 22
33.4 miles	South Deer Creek Canyon Challenge, ride 11
33.8 miles	Flagstaff–Coal Creek Challenge, ride 21
43.0 miles	Deer Creek Canyon–Evergreen Challenge, ride 10
43.2 miles	Rist Canyon Challenge, ride 30
45.3 miles	Carter Lake–Rattlesnake Challenge, ride 32
48.5 miles	Left Hand Canyon Challenge, ride 24
52.1 miles	Boulder–Fort Collins Challenge, ride 28
52.4 miles	Lyons–Estes Park Challenge, ride 27

Classics

52.5 miles	Golden Gate–Coal Creek Classic, ride 12
75.4 miles	Denver–Colorado Springs Classic, ride 6

About the Author

Robert Hurst is a fifth-generation Front Ranger who was born in Colorado Springs, lived for eight years in Boulder, and currently resides in Denver. After racking up more than 3,000 days as a bike messenger, he wrote *The Art of Urban Cycling: Lessons from the Street*. Robert is also the author of *Mountain Biking Colorado's San Juan Mountains: Durango and Telluride*.

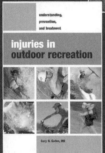
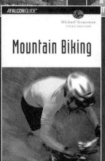